D1408430

©2001 artistpro.com, LLC

Library of Congress Catalog Card Number: 00-100534

Art Director: Stephen Ramirez
Cover: Stephen Ramirez
Book Design and Layout: Linda Gough
Cover photo: Susana Millman
Publisher: Mike Lawson;
Editorial Director: Patrick Runkle; Editor: Mary Cosola; Editorial Assistant; Sally Englfried
Associate Editor: Jessica Westcott

EMBooks is an imprint of artistpro.com, LLC
236 Georgia Street, Suite 100
Vallejo, CA 94590
707-554-1935

Also from EMBooks
The Independent Working Musician
Making the Ultimate Demo, 2nd Ed.
Anatomy of a Home Studio
The EM Guide to the Roland VS-880

Also from MixBooks
The AudioPro Home Recording Course, Volumes I, II, and III
I Hate the Man Who Runs This Bar!
How to Make Money Scoring Soundtracks and Jingles
The Art of Mixing: A Visual Guide to Recording, Engineering, and Production
500 Songwriting Ideas (For Brave and Passionate People)
Music Publishing: The Real Road to Music Business Success, Rev. and Exp. 5th Ed.
How to Run a Recording Session
Mix Reference Disc, Deluxe Ed.
The Songwriters Guide to Collaboration, Rev. and Exp. 2nd Ed.
Critical Listening and Auditory Perception
Modular Digital Multitracks: The Power User's Guide, Rev. Ed.
The Dictionary of Music Business Terms
Professional Microphone Techniques
Sound for Picture, 2nd Ed.
Music Producers, 2nd Ed.
Live Sound Reinforcement

Printed in Auburn Hills, MI
ISBN 0-87288-744-8

Making Music
with Your Computer

Second Edition

by Brent Edstrom

236 Georgia Street, Suite 100
Vallejo, CA 94590

Contents

Preface
Acknowledgements
About the Author

To Jennifer and Evan.
For your love and support.

Preface

I have long been fascinated by the concept of using computers to make music. Though I have always enjoyed the special communication that exists when performing live with other musicians, I have found that the use of computers to create music provides a unique and often deeply satisfying form of musical expression. The modern-day computer musician is at once a composer, orchestrator, arranger, synthesist, engineer, and chameleon of styles. Not only does MIDI and computer technology provide amazing possibilities for the creation of nontraditional music, I have found that the process of imitative sequencing of traditional instruments has helped me to better understand the unique capabilities of these instruments.

As a professor of MIDI and synthesis, I have had the opportunity to review many outstanding publications on the topic of music and computers. When researching texts for class it became apparent that, though many fine books cover the technical issues of computers and MIDI, precious few books cover the topic of using technology to create music. It is my goal that *Making Music with Your Computer* will provide a helpful resource for students and professionals who want to learn more about the musical aspects of MIDI and computer technology.

Brent Edstrom

Acknowledgements

Thanks to Mike Lawson and the fine folks at MixBooks and artistpro.com. I appreciate the opportunity to bring *Making Music with Your Computer, Revised Edition,* to fruition.

I am grateful to Dr. Mario Gaetano and Dr. Mark Holliday for generously giving of their time to read and comment on portions of the manuscript. Thanks to Dr. Bruce Frazier, Dr. Shannon Thompson, and Dr. John West for listening to portions of the audio CD.

Special thanks to Dr. Will Peebles for going way beyond the call of friendship in reading and commenting on several hundred pages of text. I am grateful for your keen insights and frank criticism.

I would also like to acknowledge my primary teachers: Dr. Gregory Yasinitsky, Dr. Loran Olsen, and Bill Dobbins. Your patience and dedication to teaching had a profound impact on my musical development.

Finally, I would like to thank the wonderful students at Western Carolina University, Whitworth College, and Spokane Falls Community College.

About the Author

Brent Edstrom received a Master of Music degree in Jazz Studies and Contemporary Media from the Eastman School of Music in 1991. He studied classical piano performance at Washington State University. Edstrom has performed with many jazz and popular artists. Performance credits include Bob Berg, Bob Mintzer, Clark Terry, Lee Konitz, George Robert, Frank Gambale, Chuck Isreals, Jon Faddis, Ernie Watts, Peter Erskine, Bobby Shew, and Buddy Baker.

Edstrom has been active as an electronic music specialist. He has worked in conjunction with studios in the Pacific Northwest and Northeast to produce a variety of jingles, industrials, films, and dance videos. In addition to teaching and performing, Brent Edstrom has worked as a freelance editor, transcriber, and arranger for Hal Leonard Publishing Corporation. He has produced many transcriptions and arrangements for Hal Leonard including: *The Kenny Barron Collection, Narada Piano Sampler, Jelly's Last Jam, Wynonna Judd Folio,* and *The Art Tatum Collection*—fifteen note-for-note transcriptions of America's ultimate jazz virtuoso. Edstrom recently completed a second book of transcriptions of the music of Art Tatum.

The author currently lives in North Carolina where he maintains an active composition and performance schedule. Mr. Edstrom is assistant professor of MIDI/synthesis, jazz studies and theory at Western Carolina University.

PART ONE: MIDI MUSICIANSHIP

1. Sequencing Bass and Drums

2. Practical Music Theory

3. Chord and Scale Relationships

4. Contemporary Keyboard Techniques

5. Music Composition

6. Real-World Arranging

7. Electronic Orchestration

Sequencing Bass and Drums

Unless you have been living in a cave for the past few decades, you have probably noticed that much of today's popular music revolves around bass and drums. It could be said that they are the building blocks for pop music. For many MIDI musicians, establishing a good groove is the first step in creating a new composition. Because of the importance of bass and drums in pop music, we will devote this chapter to exploring this concept.

SEQUENCING DRUM PARTS

One of the best ways to learn about sequencing drum parts is to watch a live drummer in action. The primary goal of a drummer is to provide the rhythmic feel or *groove*, but when you listen closely to a good drummer you find that there is much more to it than simple timekeeping. Good drummers often delineate the form of the music, they provide interesting textures and fills, they create excitement behind a soloist, and they may lead or react to the ensemble dynamically.

You may elect to use either a traditional or nontraditional approach to sequencing drum tracks. In a traditional approach, the goal is to mimic what a "real" drummer would do. In nontraditional drum sequencing, MIDI technology is used to create drum parts that are not necessarily playable by a live drummer. Which approach is the best? It all depends on what you are trying to accomplish with your sequence.

I once had the pleasure of playing a few concerts with Ralph Humphries from the Frank Zappa band. He spoke on the subject of sequencing drums, and I was surprised to learn that he does not always attempt to sequence "realistic" drum grooves. The example he used involved keeping an eighth-note hi-hat part going through a drum fill. Although this would not be possible using traditional drumming technique, it is easy to do with a sequenced drum part. His observation was that if a live drummer *could* play time on the hi-hat during a fill, he probably would (this from a drummer). Since then, I have worried much less about creating drum sequences that sound like the real thing. Just keep the aesthetics of the tune in mind as you sequence and you will find an approach that works for you.

TRADITIONAL DRUM SEQUENCING

When creating drum parts it is helpful to consider the traditional function of percussion instruments in a drum kit. A basic kit includes a bass drum (kick), snare, hi-hat cymbals, ride cymbal, one or more crash cymbals, and one or more toms. Most drummers also use a variety of other percussion instruments such as woodblock, cowbell, tambourine, shaker, guiro, bell, or clave.

The instruments in a traditional drum kit can generally be divided into two groups: instruments that divide or subdivide the beat and those that provide the unique accent or weight that defines the groove. The following chart shows common usage of the primary percussion instruments listed above. It is important to remember that this is just one of many ways of using these sounds—many wonderful drum grooves have been recorded or sequenced using the instruments in nontraditional ways.

Figure 1.1 Traditional usage of a drum kit

Instrument	Common Function
Hi-hat	Division or subdivision of beat (eighth or sixteenth-note subdivision is most common). A drummer will also open and close the hi-hat using a foot pedal. It is common to close the hi-hat on beats two and four in 4/4 time.
Ride cymbal	Same function as hi-hat cymbals.
Snare drum	Often used on the backbeat (beats two and four in common time). Also used in conjunction with crash or toms for fills as well as for general rhythmic accompaniment (comping).
Bass drum	Used in conjunction with the snare to delineate the "weight" of a groove. Most drummers add a little kick to add low-end to a cymbal crash.
Crash cymbal	Often used as part of a fill to "set up" a figure elsewhere in the ensemble or to mark the form.
Toms	Usually used for fills but may also be used for backbeat or subdivision of the pulse.

When creating a traditional drum sequence, many MIDI musicians will start with the hi-hat cymbals. There are four common ways to play the hi-hat cymbals: stick on closed hi-hat, stick on half open, stick on full open, and the sound of the hi-hat being closed using a foot pedal. By using this combination of sounds in consort with well placed accents, a virtually limitless combination of interesting pulses may be achieved.

The following examples demonstrate a few of the common hi-hat patterns. Note that, in the examples in this book, the bass drum is represented on the bottom space of the percussion clef, snare on the third space, and cymbals above the staff.

Figure 1.2 Basic rock

Figure 1.3 Basic funk

Figure 1.4 Basic swing (snare "comps" freely)

Note that in the previous examples an "x" denotes a closed hi-hat and the triangle indicates an open hi-hat.

In situations where you must mimic a real drum set, pay close attention to the relationship between open and closed hi-hat. An open hi-hat must eventually close, and the sound that the hi-hat makes as it closes is an important part of many traditional grooves. In a swing tune, for example, it is common for the drummer to close the hi-hat on beats two and four for most of the tune. Again, you can learn much by observing live drummers. One of my favorite tricks is to use sticks on half-open hi-hat in a simple quarter note rhythm. Although it is simple to play, this technique provides a particularly rocking sloppiness that can be very effective.

Although you still hear many hi-hat oriented drum grooves, many of the traditional eighth- and sixteenth-note patterns have become clichéd. This is especially true of many sequenced versions of these grooves. Most synthesized drum kits are simply not up to the task of reproducing the wide variety of nuance that a good drummer can get from his or her hi-hat cymbals.

A common variation on the traditional hi-hat approach involves using auxiliary percussion or even nontraditional percussive sounds to provide basic subdivisions of the beat. Shakers, maraca, tambourine, brushes on hi-hat or snare, or any number of sampled sounds can be used in a similar fashion to create some truly interesting grooves.

RIDE CYMBAL

The ride cymbal is typically used to provide rhythmic divisions or subdivisions of the beat similar to the function of the hi-hat. Many drummers will include more than one ride cymbal in their gig bags: Chinese and inverted ride cymbals are just two examples. Although there are many examples of songs that use the ride cymbal during an introduction or first verse, ride cymbals are most often saved for an exciting part of the tune such as a last chorus, interlude, or bridge. When used in this manner, the ride cymbal can provide a refreshing change to the sometimes monotonous hi-hat cymbals.

Most drummers are able to get a wide variety of sounds out of a single ride cymbal. The placement of the stick and the force used to strike the cymbal determine the specific sound or color that is achieved. In MIDI terms, just two sounds are usually available: "ringing" or "bell" ride cymbal sounds. The ringing ride comes from striking the ride cymbal near the edge of the cymbal. The more percussive bell sound is achieved by striking the ride on the bell of the cymbal (the hump in the center of some ride cymbals). The following example illustrates the use of the bell sound in a typical rock groove:

Figure 1.5 Rock groove: bell ride, kick, and snare drum

KICK AND SNARE

The kick or bass drum is almost always used in conjunction with the snare drum for most popular music grooves. A fun experiment involves looping an eighth or sixteenth note hi-hat pattern. By simply experimenting with different kick and snare patterns, an astounding variety of grooves may be achieved. Drummers often talk in terms of "weight" when describing a groove. Though the term is vague, you can get a sense of this concept by varying the position and frequency of kick and snare attacks. A groove that uses a snare only on beat four will provide a "lighter" weight than a groove that includes snare hits on beats two and four.

The bass or kick drum is most often used near the first and third beats in common time. I use the term "near" because, depending on the style of music, the kick may be offset by an eighth or sixteenth note to imply an underlying subdivision of beats. The snare is usually placed near or directly on the backbeat—beats two and four in common time. The following examples demonstrate a few of the many common kick and snare patterns.

Figure 1.6 Common bass drum and snare patterns (rock)

Note that all of the examples above are variations of a basic rock groove with snare on beats two and four. Experiment with different hi-hat and ride patterns—the possibilities are limitless.

Tip: It is sometimes difficult to play an active hi-hat or snare part using only one finger or alternating fingers on a MIDI keyboard. Because most synthesizers (and some software such as Emagic's Logic sequencer) will allow you to assign specific sounds to specific keys, a good way to overcome this problem is to assign a snare or hi-hat sound to two or more adjacent keys. For most players it is easier to use two or three fingers on adjacent keys than trying to use alternating finger technique on a single note on the keyboard. With a little practice you will find that you can even achieve natural sounding drum rolls and repetitive fills. If your synthesizer supports the feature, try detuning each of the snare sounds slightly for an even more realistic effect. (The pitch of a snare will change depending on where it is struck and the velocity with which the stick strikes the head of the drum.)

DRUM FILLS

Drummers often use fills as a way of marking the form, setting up a rhythmic figure, or adding an extra element of excitement behind a solo. Creating realistic fills requires special attention on the part of a MIDI musician—it is easy to get carried away when programming drum fills. With that said, let's look at some concepts that can help when trying to sequence drum fills.

One of the most difficult concepts to master when sequencing fills involves the function of each drum in a fill. Unlike the function of the hi-hat, ride, kick, and snare in a traditional groove, the function of these instruments is less clear in a fill. Although it is common to hear fills performed on just the snare or toms, most drummers will use a combination of percussive instruments during a fill (a fact that many MIDI musicians ignore). A fun way to experiment with this type of fill is to record a traditional fill using the toms or snare. Use your sequencer to transpose some of the notes to another sound such as a tom or hi-hat. The example that follows is possibly the most clichéd of all MIDI drum fills, the descending tom fill.

Figure 1.7 Basic sixteenth note tom fill

By transposing some of the notes to other instruments in the drum kit, a more natural drum fill is achieved. Experiment as in the following example. Many interesting variations are possible using the transposition method.

Figure 1.8 Variation of descending tom fill

Tip: Step time entry can be a helpful tool when sequencing drum fills at a fast tempo. Enter a sequence of sixteenth or thirty-second notes with a variety of percussive instruments: snare, toms, kick, etc. This can be an interesting way to come up with new fills that would be difficult to play using traditional keyboard entry techniques.

Another detail that can be difficult to master is determining when to place a fill in a sequence. If I could make a general observation, most of us MIDI musicians use way too many drum fills. The old adage of "less is more" certainly applies here. In talking and playing with many great drummers I have come to realize that the best drummers tend to be very subtle with regard to fills. Good drummers tend to make very slight changes at the end of a phrase and save the "big stuff" for when it is really needed—perhaps once or twice in an entire song (if even that much!). One way to get a handle on when to use a fill is to wait until a sequence is nearly complete before adding any fills. You can establish basic grooves and variation grooves to use while sequencing and then listen, with the ears of a drummer, to places that a fill could be effective. Once you have determined where fills need to be inserted, it is easy to cut out the under-lying drum groove and insert appropriate fills in these places. Sometimes I will even retake the entire drum track when a sequence has taken shape. This allows me to respond and interact with the other sequenced tracks in the way that a real drummer might approach the song in live performance.

Tip: A good way to practice your "fill chops" is to play a groove for four or eight bars. In the last bar (or even the last beat or two) of the phrase, perform a simple snare or tom fill. The goal here is to make the fill a natural extension of the groove. Again, grandiose fills are not what is usually needed—simply adding some subtle variations to the original groove will usually do the trick.

When I listen to popular music, I often like to focus on the drums and imagine how I would sequence the drum tracks. As a general rule I tend to fall into the trap that most synthesists do: it is hard to avoid the temptation to make the drum tracks overly complicated. The next time you have the opportunity to listen to a live drummer, pay close attention to amount of rhythmic activity going on. You will generally find that the best drummers are fairly restrained; they tend to play only what is needed to establish the groove. Anything more tends to get in the way. A good rule of thumb for us nondrummers is to use restraint; it is always easy to add extra drum parts later in the sequencing process. Of course, some styles of music depend on "thick" drum parts as is the case with "techno" or "hip-hop."

NONTRADITIONAL DRUM SEQUENCING

Drum substitution. It is interesting to note that, in the early days of drum machines, the goal was to achieve the most realistic drum sounds possible. Unfortunately, these early machines were horribly inept at reproducing drum sounds. In the nineties, we came full circle, and these early drum machines became attractive because of how undrumlike they sound. These fake-sounding drum sounds are used quite often in techno, hip-hop, and rap genres. I like to use the term *drum substitution* to describe this approach. With drum substitution, a variety of sounds can be substituted for instruments in the traditional drum set. One way to experiment with drum substitution is to think of the quality or timbre of the original instrument and substitute another percussive sound with a similar timbre. Hi-hat cymbals, for example, are characterized by a mid-to-high frequency range and brilliant tone. The sound of a bell, shaker, lid of a pan, or even a toy cymbal could be suitable substitutes for the hi-hat. Similarly, the sound of a slamming door, gun shot, car horn, or other percussive sound might be candidates to substitute for the snare. If you own a sampler, you can come up with all sorts of interesting substitutes.

Linear drumming. A relatively new approach to drumming involves thinking of the drumset as a linear series of instruments. To create a "*linear*" groove, two or more percussive instruments may work together to create a pulse that would have traditionally been established using only one instrument. A common example involves hi-hat subdivision. Instead of using only the hi-hat to produce a series of sixteenth notes, use a combination of hi-hat, shaker, tambourine, or other similar instruments to establish the subdivision:

Figure 1.9 Basic hi-hat subdivision and linear variation

The overall goal of providing a sixteenth note pulse is met, but the variety of sounds used to produce this pulse is much more interesting. Note that the drum transposition fill presented earlier in this chapter is also an example of a linear approach to drum sequencing.

To quantize or not to quantize. Students often ask me if they should avoid drum quantization[1]. The question is not an easy one to answer. On the one hand, slight imperfections of time can be very important in establishing a realistic groove. On the other hand, too many rhythmic inaccuracies can undermine an otherwise good drum track. For most of us, the answer lies somewhere in the middle. It may be advantageous to quantize some component of the drums such as hi-hat or kick and snare and keep some subtle rhythmic inaccuracies in another part. However, if you have good time and are attempting to create "natural" sounding drum tracks, the nonquantizing approach is best. For some styles of music such as techno, quantizing of rhythms is the very essence of the genre: techno wouldn't be techno without the heavily quantized and computerized sound.

Groove quantization. Most professional sequencers now include groove quantization options that provide a more realistic result than simple numeric quantization. With groove quantization, timing (and velocity) data is extracted from digitized audio recordings. This "groove information" is then used to adjust or quantize rhythms for a more natural result. Some programs even let you record and extract timing data from an audio track. Cool.

Techno and dance grooves. If you are interested in sequencing techno drum grooves or other modern drum styles, the following tips may be helpful. As I mentioned previously, techno or dance music is usually heavily quantized. Most of these recordings also rely on looping of either digitized drum grooves or loops of MIDI drum riffs. Although these styles still use traditional drum functions such as snare on backbeat and hi-hat for rhythmic subdivision, the sounds are usually not traditional and the orchestration is often thick. I have found good results by layering sounds from two or more drum kits. (Listen to the *Techno Toys* example on the demonstration CD for an example of this technique.) You may also want to purchase commercially available prerecorded loops; many techno musicians maintain a huge palette of such loops. We will look at a variety of traditional and nontraditional grooves at the end of this chapter.

Tip: Try the following as a way to develop new and interesting drum grooves. Sequence a four- or eight-bar techno groove. Then extract the hi-hat, kick, and snare to different tracks. Make a copy of each of the loops and paste these clips to new tracks. Assign the new tracks to a different drum kit and channel and experiment with a variety of transpositions. I have discovered many fascinating variations using this trick.

Sequencing bass tracks. The bass has two important functions in popular music: to establish the harmonic progression and provide appropriate rhythmic activity. This rhythmic activity will usually complement or even double rhythms occurring in the drumset. Though less common, the bass may also be used as a melodic instrument.

There are a number of traditional bass sounds provided on most synthesizers: plucked electric, picked electric, slap, fretless electric, and acoustic bass. The plucked and picked electric bass sounds are typically used for pop, rock, and country styles. Slap bass is often heard on pop recordings or in funk music. Fretless electric is most often used for pop, jazz, or Latin styles. The acoustic bass is used almost exclusively for jazz, Latin, and some styles of country (no offense to the Stray Cats). Synthesized bass sounds can also be effective for many styles such as techno or pop.

When selecting a bass sound you may want to consider nontraditional sounds as well. If a patch has a full and slightly percussive low end it may work well as a bass instrument. Some patches I have used include the harp, electric piano, and a variety of synthetic voices.

The bass provides the foundation tones for a given harmonic progression, usually the root and fifth. As with the drums, it is generally a good idea to work with a clear and simple bass line. If the bass line is overly complex, it may get in the way of other tracks as you add instruments to a sequence. However, in some styles of music, bass lines are more intricate than others, funk music being one such example. Although it is not a steadfast rule, the bass will usually play the root of a chord whenever there is a change in the harmonic progression. In the following bossa nova example, the bass revolves around the root and fifth with the root clearly stated on every chord change.

Figure 1.10 Bossa nova bass

Of course, the bass is not limited to only playing roots and fifths of chords. A common variation involves the use of chromatic or diatonic passing tones. In the next example, note how chromatic approach tones are used to approach both the I and IV chords in a simple rock style.

Figure 1.11 Chromatic approach tones

Another common bass trick is to use an upper neighbor tone. Experiment with tones either a half or whole step above the root or fifth.

Figure 1.12 Upper neighbor tones

In some styles of music the bass may be very complex. Note that though the bass line in the next example is fairly intricate, the harmony is still clearly presented by a preponderance of roots.

Figure 1.13 Funk bass line

To this point we have looked at bass lines that rely heavily on the root and fifth of chords in a progression. For some styles, such as rockabilly or blues, all the notes of a triad might be used.

Figure 1.14 Rockabilly blues bass line (using a triad)

The bass may also function as a harmonic pedal, a single note that remains under a variety of chords.

Figure 1.15 Bass pedal tone (C F/C G/C etc.)

Octaves can be very effective in a bass line. In the 1970s, this sound was common in the much maligned disco craze. I also hear it used in techno and other styles.

Figure 1.16 Octave bass line

For swing music, the bass typically plays a series of quarter notes with an occasional eighth or triplet figure inserted for variety. Note the use of chromatic approach tones in the following example.

Figure 1.17 Swing bass

In popular music, the drums and bass maintain an important relationship. It is always a good idea to listen closely to your drum tracks when sequencing a bass line. In many situations, the bass and kick drum will have a sympathetic relationship. The bass line may double some or all of the rhythmic figures in the kick drum.

Figure 1.18 Relationship of bass guitar and kick drum

Another approach is to use the bass in contrast to the drums. Notice how, in the next example, the bass falls into the "cracks" of the drum track.

Figure 1.19 Bass vs. drums

Although it would be impossible to list examples of every style of bass and drum groove, the following examples should get you started in exploring a variety of styles. Notice the relationship between the bass and drum parts in the following figures. In nearly every instance bass and drums complement each other. Clearly, the best way to expand your vocabulary of bass and drum tracks is to listen to lots of music.

Figure 1.20 Rock 1

Figure 1.21 Rock 2

Figure 1.22 Country

Figure 1.23 Country waltz

Making Music with Your Computer

Figure 1.24 Pop ballad

Figure 1.25 Bossa nova

Figure 1.26 Funk

Figure 1.27 Swing

Figure 1.28 Hip-hop

As you experiment with sequencing bass and drum grooves, remember that many successful grooves are the result of nontraditional techniques. One of the great things about MIDI is the ease with which you can experiment. The examples listed above will get you started with some of the more common grooves, but take the time to cut and splice, slice and dice—a world of grooves awaits your discovery!

[1]Quantizing involves using software or hardware sequencers to analyze rhythmic values and "fix" rhythmic inaccuracies.

CHAPTER 2

Practical Music Theory

What is a chapter on practical music theory doing in a book on computers and MIDI? Learning to use MIDI technology is only a small part of the equation of becoming an accomplished MIDI musician. To be competitive in the music industry you must learn how to communicate with other musicians. After all, very few professional projects such as jingles, industrials, or films are done exclusively with MIDI technology. In nearly every case, MIDI performers and composers will work closely with other musicians. Being able to communicate your ideas to other musicians via a simple chart is an absolute must in the current marketplace. Understand that the bottom line for any commercial music project is money: an inefficient musician (a musician who cannot communicate his or her ideas to other musicians) is simply not marketable. If you plan to work as a session player, you must also develop reading skills. Though it is important to learn to read notes and rhythms, keyboardists and guitarists will usually be called upon to read chord charts.

Theory can also help you to be more proficient as a composer and performer. Though an understanding of intervals, popular chord symbols, and chord and scale relationships will not necessarily help you to write the next hit song, theory can be a great time saver. You can easily find a solution to a composing roadblock with a basic understanding of popular music theory.

Finally, though there is much more to popular music theory than chords and scales, understand that chords are the building blocks for much of the music we hear today. If you understand the common choices, it will help you to find solutions, both common and not-so-common, when you are composing or improvising.

Before we dig into the finer details of chords and chord-scale relationships, let's start by establishing some groundwork.

Intervals. Intervals describe the distance between two notes. They are the building blocks for chords. Although there are many types of intervals, there are really only two categories: those that derive from the *imperfect* group and those that derive from the *perfect* group.

If we compare each note of a major scale to the root of the scale, you will see that the resulting intervals are either "major" or "perfect." Of course, it would make more sense to describe all intervals in the same way, but this is part of the historical legacy that is very much a part of music. Learn the terminology; it is an important part of the way we communicate as professional musicians.

In the following example, you will see that in a major scale all of the resulting intervals are either major or perfect when compared to the root or *tonic* of the scale. Remember that the "major" group of intervals includes seconds, thirds, sixths, sevenths, ninths, tenths, and thirteenths. The "perfect" group of intervals includes the unison, fourth, fifth, octave, eleventh, and twelfth.

Figure 2.1 Intervals of a major scale

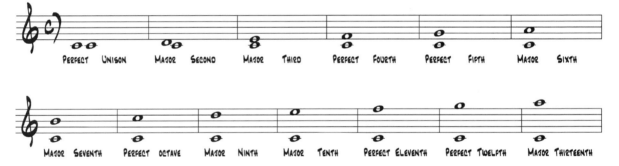

To properly describe an interval, you must determine the generic interval (i.e., a fourth, fifth, sixth, etc.) and the qualifier (perfect fourth, major sixth, and so on). The first step is easy. To find the generic interval between an A and the D above, count the letters from A to D starting with A as number one. You will see that the interval from A to D is a fourth.

Figure 2.2 Perfect fourth interval

Determining the interval qualifier is a bit more tricky. Compare the "major" and "perfect" interval groups in the next example.

Figure 2.3 Comparison of interval groups

As you can see, there is some overlap between intervals. A minor third will sound the same as an augmented second. How do you determine what to call the interval? Remember always to start with the generic description: the interval between C to D sharp is an augmented second because the distance from C to D is some kind of second. Similarly, the interval from C to E is a type of third (major third); C to E flat is a minor third. Remember that the letter names of the notes always determine the generic interval.

Tip: Although notes may look equidistant on the staff, it may be helpful to visualize a keyboard when determining intervals. For example, the interval from the note A to B is a major second while the interval from B to C is a minor second (note that there is no black key between B and C).

Figure 2.4 Augmented second vs. minor third

The best advice I can give you to help you to visualize intervals and chords is to *memorize all major triads*. A major triad is made up of an interval of a major third and a perfect fifth. All chords and intervals can be easily found if you know the major triads in all keys. There are only twelve major triads (not counting enharmonic equivalents) so we are not talking about a huge commitment here. If you don't already know them, study and play the following triads until you know them cold.

Figure 2.5 Major triads

Whole steps and half steps. The terms whole and half step are often used to describe an interval or scale. The term *half step* (semitone) describes any adjacent keys on the piano: E-F, A-B flat, B-C, and G-A flat are all half steps. A *whole step* is made up of two half steps: E-F sharp, A-B, B-C sharp, and G-A are all whole steps.

Figure 2.6 Half steps and whole steps

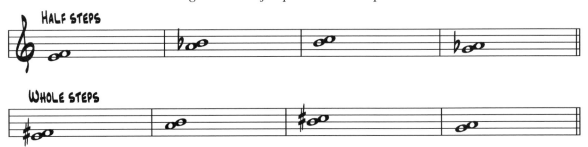

Tips on finding intervals. As I mentioned previously, intervals are easy to find if you know all of the major triads. I think you will find the following table helpful in finding or describing intervals. Study these concepts until you know them well. I always cringe when I hear musicians describe nonexistent intervals such as a "major fifth" or "perfect third."

Figure 2.7 Common intervals and relationship to major triad

Interval	Relationship of Top Note to Major Triad
major second	up a whole step from the root of a triad
minor third	half step below a major third
perfect fourth	whole step below perfect fifth
major sixth	whole step above a perfect fifth
minor seventh	whole step below an octave
major seventh	half step below an octave
major ninth	major second plus one octave
major tenth	major third plus one octave
perfect eleventh	perfect fourth plus one octave
major thirteenth	major sixth plus one octave

For practice, let's find the interval of a perfect fourth above E flat. Visualize an E flat major triad: the perfect fifth is a B flat. The note A flat is a whole step below this note. A flat is a perfect fourth above E flat. Add an octave to that same A flat and it becomes a perfect eleventh. Isn't that easy?

Figure 2.8 Finding a perfect fourth above E flat

Triads. Triads are chords that contain three notes. There are four types of triads: major, minor, augmented, and diminished. Other specialty chords such as suspended chords will be handled later in the chapter. Note that the only difference between major and minor triads is the third. An augmented triad consists of a major third and an augmented fifth factor. A diminished triad consists of a minor third and diminished fifth.

Figure 2.9 The four triads

A word about chord nomenclature: there are many ways to describe triads (a few of the variations are listed above). Avoid the temptation to use uppercase and lowercase *M* to describe major and minor triads or seventh chords. I have been burned more than once trying to decipher a hastily written manuscript— it is much better to use *maj* and *min*. Of course the distinction between *M* and *m* will be clear if you use a computer to prepare manuscripts. Note that a chord without any qualifier is always understood to be major.

Augmented and diminished chords are interesting in that they are symmetrical: the augmented triad consists entirely of intervals of a major third (C-E, E-G sharp). The diminished triad consists entirely of minor third intervals (C-E flat, E flat-G flat).

Figure 2.10 Augmented and diminished triads are symmetrical

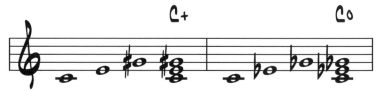

Inversions. Any chord, triad or otherwise, can be inverted. To invert a chord, move the lowest note of the chord up an octave (or the highest note down an octave). There are three possible positions for a triad: root position, first inversion, and second inversion.

Figure 2.11 Inversions of a triad

In popular chord notation the inversion is not usually specified. It is up to the player to select an inversion that is appropriate for the given musical context. If a note other than the root is prominent in the bass, it is sometimes helpful to notate the chord as a *polychord*. In the next example the third factor of an A major chord (the note C sharp) is used in the bass.

Figure 2.12 Triad with the third in the bass

Note that my use of the term polychord is not entirely accurate. In traditional music theory, the term polychord denotes one complete chord structure placed over another complete chord structure. In popular music it is always understood that the denominator of such a structure refers to a single note, not an entire chord. If you really intend to indicate a true polychord, it is best to specify this by writing a complete description of each chord (e.g., A major/C major or C/E7).

Common seventh chords. Seventh chords contain a triad and an interval of a seventh. There are four common types of seventh chords: major seventh, minor seventh, major-minor seventh, and minor-major seventh. Study the following example closely. These chords are the basis for more complex chords that include extensions and alterations. The diminished seventh, a special type of seventh chord, will be covered later in this chapter.

Figure 2.13 The four common seventh chords

Confusion abounds regarding proper notation and spelling of seventh chords. A short diversion is probably in order. In traditional (classical) theory, both the third and seventh factors are used when describing a seventh chord: a major seventh chord would be described as *major-major seven* (a major triad and major seventh). Similarly, a minor seventh chord would be described as *minor-minor seven* (minor triad and minor seventh). In popular music we use a shorthand to describe these chords: major-major seventh is shortened to *major seventh*, minor-minor seventh is shortened to *minor seventh*. If no qualifier is used, the seventh chord is understood to be a major-minor seventh. A D7 chord would consist of a D major triad with a minor seventh interval (the note C).

If you know all of the major and minor triads, it is very easy to construct seventh chords in any key. To construct any type of seventh chord, find the triad that the chord is built on and add the appropriate type of seventh. (Remember that an interval of a seventh can easily be found in relation to an octave: a major seventh is a half-step shy of an octave, a minor seventh interval is a whole step shy of an octave.) The following table will help.

Figure 2.14 Constructing seventh chords

Seventh Chord		Chord Elements
maj 7	(Cmaj7)	major triad, major seventh
min 7	(Cmin7)	minor triad, minor seventh
7	(C7)	major triad, minor seventh
min (maj 7)	Cmin(maj7)	minor triad, major seventh

It is important to understand that when using popular music chord symbols, key signatures are never an issue when spelling these chords. A C7 chord will always be spelled as C-E-G-B flat, no matter what the current key signature is.

Extensions. Notes higher than a seventh that are added to a chord are called extensions. There are three possible extensions: major ninth, perfect eleventh, and major thirteenth. (As you will soon see, extensions are sometimes altered as is the case with a minor ninth or augmented eleventh.) I am often asked why a chord such as a Cmaj13 is not described as a C6. The answer is that a thirteenth chord implies that all other chord factors could be included in the voicing: 1-3-5-7-9-(11)-13. A simple major 6 chord would only contain 1-3-5-6. In other words, the greater the value of the extension, the more potential notes could be included in the chord. There are a few exceptions to this rule that we will get to in a moment. It is also important to note that, when reading popular chord symbols, no specific ordering of notes is implied: the thirteenth of the chord may be "voiced" a major sixth above the root.

Figure 2.15 Major 6 vs. major 13 chords

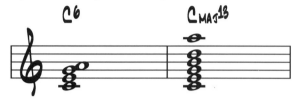

Another common question regarding extensions involves determining what type of seventh to use in the chord. There is a very simple solution to this question: *replace the number of the extension with the number seven to determine what type of seventh chord to use.* For example, a C13 chord is based on a C7 (major-minor seventh). A Cmin9 chord is built upon a Cmin7 chord (minor-minor seventh). A Cmin11 is a Cmin7 chord with a major ninth and perfect eleventh added. The important thing to remember is that, unless specified, *extensions are never altered:* ninths and thirteenths are always major, elevenths are always "perfect" regardless of the type of chord or key signature.

Figure 2.16 Extensions of seventh chords

Alterations. Once you understand the concept of constructing triads, seventh chords, and extensions, the concept of alterations is easy. The technical definition for an altered chord is a chord structure where one or more of the chord factors has been altered. In popular music, the most common form of altered chords is altered dominant chords where the fifth has been raised or lowered. The following example illustrates alterations of a C7 chord.

Figure 2.17 Alterations of a C7 chord

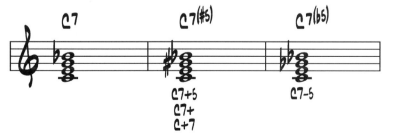

Alterations of the ninth are also common. For example:

Figure 2.18 Examples of altered ninth factors

Roman numerals. Roman numerals are used to describe the relationship of a chord to a given key. In the key of G major the I chord is G, the IV chord is C, and the V chord is D. Roman numerals are often used by musicians to describe a progression of chords. They are particularly helpful when transposing a song to a new key (i.e., a ii-V-I in G will have the same relationship as a ii-V-I in D). Note that lowercase roman numerals are generally used for minor chords, uppercase for major chords. The next example lists diatonic triads in the key of G major.

Figure 2.19 Diatonic triads in G (Roman numerals denote function in the key)

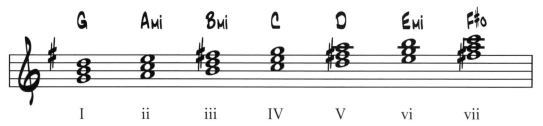

Chord groups. I find it particularly helpful to think of chords in terms of groups of related chords. Each of the chords in the following groups are interchangeable. A Cmin9 will work in most of the places a Cmin7 would work. A Cmaj13 is usually interchangeable with a Cmaj9 chord. Of course, it is important to consider the context of the music: a complex jazz chord probably won't be appropriate in a simple triad-oriented country tune. (Some country songs do use complex chords though!)

You will find that the concept of chord groups is great for finding solutions. If you are composing a song and know that the chord you are looking for has a major quality, all you need to do is to look at the tonic major group to see what the common options would be. Not every harmonic choice can be based on chord groups, but it is a great place to start. After all, music is a well-defined language. The better you understand the common elements of the language, the better you will be at expressing yourself.

Each of the following groups of chords represents harmonic choices that are roughly interchangeable. The chords progress from simple on the left to complex on the right. Take time to experiment with each of the structures. Keep an ear open to how these sounds might be used in a composition or performance. One word of advice: each of the chords in these examples is presented in close position with the root in the bass—not usually the "hippest" of voicings. We will look at ways of creating good voicings from these structures in Chapter 4, "Contemporary Keyboard Techniques."

TONIC MAJOR

The tonic major chord group represents common variations of a major chord. The sixth, ninth, and thirteenth are common extensions added to this structure. Note that a perfect eleventh *is not* a good note to add. The technical reason: the resulting minor-ninth interval between the third of the chord and the eleventh sounds dissonant in this context. An augmented eleventh is sometimes used, most often as the last chord of a jazz song. If a major-major chord functions as IV in a given key, it is also common to add an augmented eleventh.

Figure 2.20 Tonic major chord group

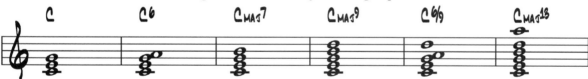

TONIC MINOR

The only difference in the spelling of tonic major and tonic minor chords involves the third. Tonic minor chords are based on a minor triad. This group of chords is very dark. These chords often function as tonic chords in a minor blues or other tune containing a minor tonal center. This group of chords can also be helpful when scoring for film. The final chord of the *Perry Mason* theme is a striking example of this chord structure (minor major ninth).

Figure 2.21 Tonic minor chord group

SUPERTONIC MINOR

This is one of the more helpful chord groups. The description of *supertonic* implies that these chords might function as ii chords in a given key. This is often the case, but you will also find this chord at work as a tonic, mediant, or submediant chord. The ninth and perfect eleventh may be added to the basic seventh chord structure. A thirteenth may also be used, though this extension is less common. This chord group is often found in pop music as well as jazz and other styles.

Figure 2.22 Supertonic minor chord group

A common variation of the supertonic chord group involves lowering the fifth by a half step. This variation is often used as a ii chord in a minor key, though the effect of the chord can be helpful in many other situations. These chords are often described as *half-diminished chords*. The triad is diminished but the seventh is a minor seventh, not a diminished seventh, hence the term half-diminished.

Figure 2.23 Half-diminished chords

"BLUES" DOMINANT

I use the term "blues" to describe these chords, as they are often found in blues progressions. The term dominant may be a bit misleading though. The term *dominant* technically refers to a specific harmonic function—a dominant chord functions as V in a given key. Popular musicians tend to misuse this term to describe any major-minor seventh chord regardless of the key. You will find these chords in nearly every style of music from Debussy to Tower of Power. These chords do sometimes function as actual dominant chords.

Figure 2.24 Blues dominant chord group

ALTERED DOMINANT

We have already seen an example of altered dominant chords earlier in the chapter. These chords almost always function as a V chord in a given key. Common choices involve alterations of fifths and/or ninths. These chords are complex and must not be used haphazardly. Altered dominant chords are helpful in that they provide a heightened sense of movement to a tonic chord. You will find examples of these chords, all styles of popular music. Many classical composers also used altered dominant chords to great effect.

Figure 2.25 Altered dominant chord group

Though you will hear many musicians refer to these chords as *lydian dominant* chords, they almost never function as an actual dominant chord (V in a key). The term *lydian* refers to the lydian mode, which we will discuss in the next chapter. In this case, lydian is synonymous with an augmented fourth or augmented eleventh. These chords can resolve almost anywhere except down by a perfect fifth (i.e., they don't usually function as dominant seventh chords).

Figure 2.26 Lydian dominant chord group

DIMINISHED

Diminished chords are used less frequently in popular music, as they tend to sound dated in many situations. One common use for these chords is between ii and iii in a major key (either ascending or descending motion).

Figure 2.27 Diminished chords

To make a diminished chord sound more modern, try substituting a tone that is one whole step above any of the tones in the chord. For example:

Figure 2.28 Additions to a diminished chord

The term *sus* has evolved from traditional classical theory. Traditionally, the term *suspension* was used to describe a dissonant interval that resolves to a consonant interval. The next example demonstrates this concept.

Figure 2.29 4-3 Suspension

In popular music nomenclature we use the term *sus* to describe a chord that contains either a perfect fourth or major second *instead* of a third. For example:

Figure 2.30 Suspended chord group

Suspended chords are a mainstay of popular music. Because a third factor is not present, the chords have a vague quality that is suitable for many styles of music. Note that it is sometimes common to notate suspended chords as polychords, especially if they function as ii/V in a given key.

Figure 2.31 Suspended chords as polychords

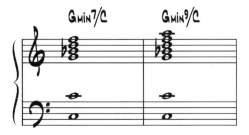

We have covered much ground in this chapter. Although the concept of intervals and the great variety of standard chords may seem a bit daunting at first, you will see that an understanding of chords and harmony is a valuable asset during the composition and sequencing process. In Chapter 5, "Music Composition," we will look at other important theoretical concepts such as formal structures and melodic devices. I would encourage you to familiarize yourself with the harmonic concepts presented here. I have found them to be very useful.

To conclude this chapter, I would like to mention that, though many wonderful compositions have been written that rely on traditional chord vocabulary, many successful compositions use nontraditional techniques. Whatever style of music you enjoy sequencing, I think you will find these concepts to be a helpful foundation. Just remember to let your ears be involved.

Chord and Scale Relationships

Jazz musicians have long understood the need for a way to categorize and relate linear sounds (scales) to vertical structures (chords). Though many musicians still play by ear, knowledge of common chord and scale relationships can be a great time saver. As you sensitize your ears to the common relationship of chords and scales, your ability to hear and assimilate new vocabulary will be greatly enhanced. Although a knowledge of chord and scale relationships will not necessarily help you to improvise or compose a great melody for a given set of changes, scales provide a useful palette of sounds that musicians can use as a starting point for further exploration.

It should be stressed that chord and scale relationships are not an end-all; a tremendous amount of music (both popular and classical) has been written that does not follow traditional scale relationships. It is important to understand that the common scale relationships are simply a categorization of common or "stock" sounds that are found in popular music. As you begin to explore these concepts you should remember that, though scales can provide a shortcut to common vocabulary, scales can also be limiting. To better illustrate this point I will show you a trick. A teacher once told me, "You can use *any* note over *any* chord. As long as the note makes melodic sense it will work." In the following example, every possible chromatic tone is used over an F9 chord. I think you will agree that the lick works well.

Figure 3.1 All twelve tones used over an F9 chord

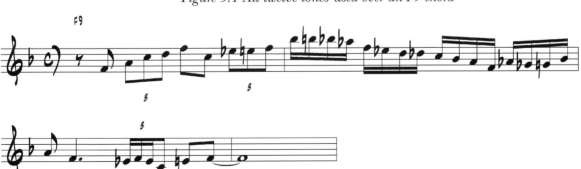

Even though there are many "wrong" notes (i.e., notes that would not be considered appropriate for this chord), the wrong notes are melodically sound; they function as embellishments or passing tones for consonant tones. Play through the example and keep in mind as you work with scale relationships that the scales presented in this chapter are simply a starting point. They represent some of the common relationships of scales and chords. On the one hand, scales can be liberating because they will help your ear to hear advanced relationships between linear and vertical structures. On the other hand, scales will be limiting if you confine yourself to using only the most common chord and scale relationships.

PREPARATION

If you have not yet developed fluency with all of the major scales, you will want to take the time to learn these scales. As we progress through the chapter, I will show you how nearly every scale presented in this chapter can be derived from a simple major scale. Even advanced chords such as a half-diminished chord or altered dominant can be handled with this technique.

If you are serious about developing your computer musician chops, major scales are a wonderful place to start. Keep in mind that there are only twelve possible major scales. Even if you only master two scales per week you will greatly improve your keyboarding skills in less than two months! You may also want to consider purchasing a resource such as Hannon's *The Virtuoso Pianist in 60 Exercises,* available from Alfred Publishing.

The following example lists the common fingerings used for each of the major scales.

Figure 3.2 Fingerings for the major scales

Major Key		Right and Left Hand Fingerings
C	r.h.	1,2,3,1,2,3,4 (1)
	l.h.	5,4,3,2,1,3,2 (1,4)
F	r.h.	1,2,3,4,1,2,3 (1)
	l.h.	5,4,3,2,1,3,2 (1,4)
Bb	r.h.	2,1,2,3,1,2,3,4 (1)
	l.h.	3,2,1,4,3,2,1 (3)
Eb	r.h.	2,1,2,3,4,1,2,3 (1)
	l.h.	3,2,1,4,3,2,1 (3)
Ab	r.h.	2,3,1,2,3,1 (2,3,4)
	l.h.	3,2,1,4,3,2,1 (3)
Db	r.h.	2,3,1,2,3,4,1 (2,3)
	l.h.	3,2,1,4,3,2,1 (3)
Gb	r.h.	2,3,4,1,2,3,1 (2)
	l.h.	4,3,2,1,3,2,1 (4)
B	r.h.	1,2,3,1,2,3,4 (1)
	l.h.	4,3,2,1,4,3,2 (1,3)
E	r.h.	1,2,3,1,2,3,4 (1)
	l.h.	5,4,3,2,1,3,2 (1,4)
A	r.h.	1,2,3,1,2,3,4 (1)
	l.h.	5,4,3,2,1,3,2 (1,4)
D	r.h.	1,2,3,1,2,3,4 (1)
	l.h.	5,4,3,2,1,3,2 (1,4)
G	r.h.	1,2,3,1,2,3,4 (1)
	l.h.	5,4,3,2,1,3,2 (1,4)

It is helpful to note that all of the scales consist of three- and four-note groupings. If you can recognize the three- and four-note groupings, you will find that the scales will be easier to master. For example, the fingering for a scale such as D flat major can be visualized as a variation of C major. Think of this scale as starting with the thumb of the right hand starting on C. With this approach it is evident that D flat uses the same grouping of three notes and four notes found in a simple C major scale.

Figure 3.3 Visualizing D flat with the thumb starting on C (same pattern as C major).

One way to visualize scales is to remember that they represent a linear or scalar version of a chord. Consider a Dmin7 chord. As we learned in the previous chapter, it is common to add extensions such as a ninth, eleventh, and thirteenth to this chord. As you will learn, a dorian scale is a common scale that works well over a minor-seventh chord. Note how, in the next example, the dorian scale simply consists of all the possible chord tones for a minor-thirteenth chord. Again, scale relationships provide a helpful means of categorizing chord and scale relationships.

Figure 3.4 Dmin13 chord and relationship to D-dorian scale

Before we delve into the intricacies of common chord and scale relationships, let's take a moment to learn about modes. The so-called *church modes* are used to describe various tonalities that derive from the major scale. One of the confusing things about modes is that, for each major scale, there are seven possible modes. It is important to remember that modes represent a specific tonality within a major scale. Even though C major and D dorian share all of the same notes, we use the term D dorian to describe a minor tonality found within the C-major scale. How then is it possible to tell the difference between a C major scale and a D dorian mode? In D dorian, the tonic is D. We would also expect to find a preponderance of notes from the tonic triad: D-F-A in this case. Even though these two scales share the same notes, a D dorian melody or progression will sound minor. A C major melody or progression will tend to emphasize C as the tonic note. Play through the following example to get a sense of the difference between a C major and D dorian melody:

Figure 3.5 C major vs. D dorian melody

The following list illustrates the terms used to describe the various modes of a C major scale. Keep in mind that these relationships will work for *any* major scale. In other words, because we know that D dorian was the second mode of C major, any other dorian mode can be easily found by starting on the second note of a given major scale.

Figure 3.6 Modes of C major (ionian, dorian, phrygian, lydian, mixolydian, aeolian, locrian).

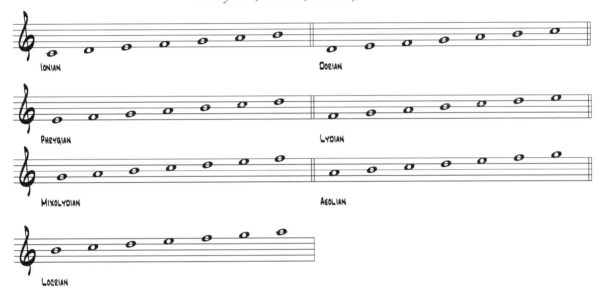

Modes can be of great help as a composition tool. Each of the modes reflects a specific mood or vibe. I have often asked a group of students to write down three or four terms to describe the quality of sound of the modes. In nearly every case, the students use similar terms to describe the various modes. The point here is that modes can be a great shortcut to a specific musical effect. If you want an uplifting quality of sound, the lydian mode might be a good starting place. In contrast, the phrygian mode evokes a sense of tension, darkness, and mystery.

Here are two tips that you might find helpful as you explore the concept of modes. Several years ago I had the pleasure of performing several concerts with Frank Gambale from the Chick Corea Electric Band. Gambale discussed the concept of modes and suggested the following exercise:

1. Select a major key.
2. Pick one of the modes from the key you have selected.
3. Place the root of the mode in the left hand.
4. Use the IV and V chords (from the key, not the mode) in your right hand.
5. Improvise using these concepts.

As simple as this suggestion is, you will find that you can easily get a sense of how each of the modes work by implementing Gambale's suggestion. The following examples demonstrate how to use this concept for F dorian and G phrygian modes found in the key of E flat. Just remember that, to use this suggestion, you must first find the IV and V chords from the relevant major scale.

Figure 3.7 IV and V tip (exploring F dorian and G phrygian modes)

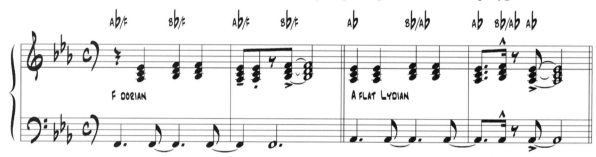

Another suggestion you might find helpful is to compose melodies that clearly imply a specific mode. Select a major key and pick a mode from the key. Create a melody and see if you can clearly imply the underlying mode. A good way to check your work is to play the melody for a friend. After you perform the melody, ask the friend to sing the tonic note (i.e., the note that would sound like home or give a sense of finality to the melody). If the melody is clear in its presentation of a mode, the tonic note will be very clear. If the tonic is not clear, see if you can change the melody to better imply the mode. A modal melody will tend to have the following characteristics:

• Preponderance of tonic notes and notes from the tonic triad.
• The melody will emphasize color tones (i.e., the notes that give the mode its unique character); a lydian melody will use #4 while a major-scale melody will use natural-4.
• A modal melody will not stray (i.e., the melody will be most successful if the approach is clearly modal, not wandering in quality).

The first three scales we will look at all derive from a major scale. These modes are all found diatonically in a major scale and can be described using the modal terminology: ionian, dorian, and mixolydian. Take the time to carefully explore each of the chord and scale relationships presented in this section. I find it helpful to think in terms of static tones and moving tones. A static tone is a note that does not sound as if it needs to move (i.e., first, third, or fifth degrees of a major scale). A moving tone is one that implies motion or tension. The fourth degree of a major scale is one such note. Try to develop a second sense regarding static and moving tones; most great melodies use a combination of moving and static tones. A melody that primarily uses moving tones will tend to sound haphazard. A melody that only uses static tones may sound "rambly."

Major scale. One of the more obvious chord-scale relationships is the major scale. This scale is used over any chords that derive from a major triad or major seventh chord.

Figure 3.8 Major scale for major chords (C6, Cmaj7, Cmaj9, C69, etc.)

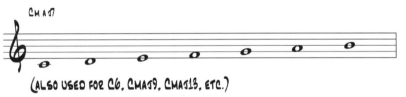

Dorian scale. The dorian mode is most often used for chords from the supertonic chord group. A D dorian (C major) would be a good scale choice for a Dmin7 chord. Although I use the term D dorian to describe this scale, you may find it easier to think of using a major scale down one whole step for a minor seventh chord. Remember that chord and scale relationships simply imply a palette of useful notes; there is no specific starting note or ordering implied by the chord and scale relationships.

Figure 3.9 Dorian scale for minor seventh chords (Dmin7, Dmin9, Dmin11)

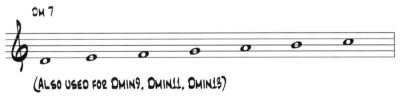

Mixolydian scale. The mixolydian mode is typically used for the dominant seventh or "blues dominant" chord group. As with the major scale and dorian scale examples, the mixolydian scale represents a linear version of a dominant seventh chord (i.e., the mixolydian scale contains all of the notes of a dominant 13 chord).

Figure 3.10 Mixolydian scale for dominant seventh chords (G7, G9, G13)

The astute reader will note that each of the chords and scales listed in this section derives from C major. If the harmonic progression derives from a specific key, it may be easier to think of using a single major scale for all of the chords in a progression. The following diatonic progression illustrates this approach.

Figure 3.11 C major scale for a I vi ii V progression (Cmaj7-Amin7-Dmin7-G7)

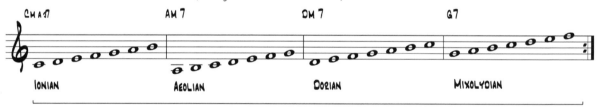

Note that in this example I used an A aeolian scale (C major) instead of A dorian (G major). The reasons for this are fairly obvious: each of these chords is found in the key of C major. In this situation it makes more sense to select notes that are also in C major. Though an A dorian would not be an incorrect choice, the F sharp found in the A dorian scale would certainly take us out of the key for a moment, which is probably not the best solution for a diatonic progression of chords. How can you tell when to use a diatonic scale or use a scale that is not in the key? Your ears and the musical context will always provide the best solution. As I mentioned before, the common chord and scale relationships provide only a starting point; you should always feel free to make alterations that make more sense for the given musical context.

If you have ever taken a traditional theory course, you may have learned that a melodic minor scale uses different notes in the ascending and descending versions.

Figure 3.12 Traditional melodic minor scale

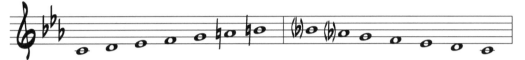

This rather strange scale is the result of developments in tonal music. It was common for composers to use a leading tone when approaching a tonic note in a natural minor scale. In the key of C minor for example, the resulting interval from A flat to B was awkward to sing, so composers often used a raised sixth degree (A natural) for ascending melodic passages. The traditional form of melodic minor scale developed as a result of this tendency to use the raised sixth and seventh scale degrees on an ascending passage and natural minor for a descending passage. Please note that in popular music we almost always use the ascending form of this scale.

An easy way to construct a melodic minor scale is to visualize a major scale with one "wrong" note. The wrong note I refer to is the third degree of the scale. To use this trick, simply play a major scale that includes a minor third instead of a major third. This is an easy way to find the ascending mode of a melodic minor scale.

Figure 3.13 Constructing a melodic minor scale (major scale with a minor third)

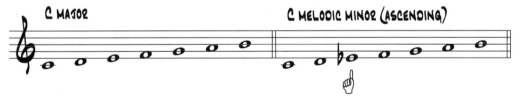

I have found the melodic minor scale to be remarkably helpful. This simple scale can be used to handle four of the more complex chords found in popular music: tonic minor, half-diminished, altered dominant, and lydian dominant.

Tonic minor chords. The melodic minor scale is useful as a palette of notes to use over a tonic minor chord. The major seventh and major sixth intervals found in this scale can sound wonderful when used over a minor blues progression. Please note that the root of this scale is the same as the root of the given chord, as shown below.

Figure 3.14 C melodic minor for C minor(major7) chord (tonic minor chord group)

Half-diminished chords. A melodic minor scale can also be used over a half-diminished chord. (Reminder from Chapter 2: another name for a half-diminished chord is minor7 flat 5). To find the appropriate melodic minor scale for a half-diminished chord, find the third of the chord. The third of the half-diminished chord is the root of the melodic minor scale. See the following example:

Figure 3.15 C melodic minor for Amin7(b5)

Altered dominant. Altered dominant chords are often found in jazz and pop music. A melodic minor scale sounds great when applied to an altered dominant chord. To find the appropriate melodic minor scale for this chord, construct a melodic minor scale a half-step above the root of the chord (e.g., C melodic minor for a B7 altered chord). It is helpful to note that the altered scale includes the primary chord factors of a dominant seventh chord (root, third, and seventh) and all of the altered tones (b5, #5, b9, #9).

Figure 3.16 C melodic minor for a B7alt. chord

Lydian dominant. The melodic minor scale can be a good solution for a lydian dominant chord. A lydian dominant is any dominant seventh chord that includes #4 or #11. A melodic minor scale built on the fifth of any lydian dominant chord provides an elegant solution to this complex chord.

Figure 3.17 C melodic minor for an F7#11 chord

MAJOR SCALE TIPS

At the start of the chapter I suggested that most of the scales in this chapter can be easily constructed by relating the scale to a simple major scale. Let's review what we have learned so far and relate these concepts to a major scale. The three diatonic scale solutions all derive from a major scale; they are modes of a major scale. An easy way to construct each of these scales is to think of the relevant major scale as in the following example:

Figure 3.18.1 Using major scales

Chord Group	Example Chords	Relevant Major Scale
Tonic major	Cmaj7, C6, Cmaj9, etc.	Major scale on root of the chord
Supertonic	Dmin7, Dmin9, etc.	Major scale down one whole step from root of chord
Dominant 7	G7, G9, G13	Major scale up a perfect fourth from root of chord

Figure 3.18.2 Major scales for diatonic chords

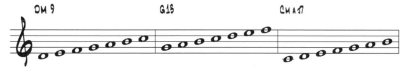

The ascending form of a melodic minor scale is easily constructed by changing the major third of a major scale to a minor third. The melodic minor scale is helpful as a scale solution for four complex chords.

Figure 3.19.1 Using major scales

Chord Group	Example Chords	Relevant Major Scale
Tonic minor	Cmin(maj7), Cmin6, etc.	Melodic minor on root of chord
Half dim.	Cmin7(b5)	Melodic minor built on third of chord
Alt. dom.	B7alt.	Melodic minor scale up half-step
Lydian dom.	F7(#11), F9(#11)	Melodic minor scale built on fifth of chord

Figure 3.19.2 Applications of melodic minor scale

As you can see, major scales can be very helpful. An understanding of the seven chord-scale relationships listed above will provide a palette of notes for most any musical situation from jazz to pop to country and rock. With that said, a few other chord-scale relationships are also helpful.

BLUES SCALE

I will admit this freely: I am not fond of the blues scale. Don't get me wrong, the blues scale is very useful for many musical situations. What I do not enjoy is listening to musicians who use this scale in a haphazard way. I would suggest that, though this scale is often used in a blues context, *very few* mature blues performers rely exclusively on this scale. As you explore the blues scale, be sure to take some time to listen to recordings to develop a sense of how this scale might best be used.

The basic blues scale is constructed as follows:

Figure 3.20 Basic C blues scale

All of the notes of this scale work fairly well over any of the chords in a blues progression. One of the things I have noticed is that many mature blues performers will use other tones in addition to the basic blues scale. In the key of C for example, the notes G, A, C, and D are often used by blues performers. These tones are particularly well suited for riff (repetitive) types of blues motives.

Figure 3.21 Basic C blues scale with other "good" notes

In addition to the basic blues scale and *riff* tones, many blues performers will consider using notes from the underlying harmonic progression. Consider, for example, the tonic chord of a I-IV-V blues. The tonic chord in a C blues is usually a C7 (C9 or C13). The third of this chord is an E natural, a note not found in the basic blues scale. Clearly, chord tones are always available as potential melodic notes, so the E natural could be included in a melody over the I or V chords. You will want to avoid using this note over the IV chord because the clash between this note and the seventh of the IV chord is not pleasant. If you consider adding all of chord tones found in a blues progression as potential melodic notes, it is clear that almost any note from the chromatic scale can be used in a blues melody or improvisation. The following example illustrates this concept. Remember that *any* note will work as long as the note functions in a melodic fashion.

Figure 3.22 Including all chord tones with the basic blues scale (i.e., results in a chromatic scale)

To get a sense of some of the variations that are possible when playing over a blues progression, play through the following excerpt. Note that, though this example relies heavily on the basic blues scale and riff notes, many chord tones and embellishments are also evident. As always, your ear should guide you as to how to best use these concepts. Experiment with these sounds and listen to recordings. This is the best way to develop a convincing vocabulary for any style of music.

Figure 3.23 Excerpt: Twelve-bar blues solo using blues scale, riff tones, chord tones, and embellishments

DIMINISHED SCALES

Diminished scales are useful in two situations: as a resource for diminished chords and when applied to altered dominant chords. The diminished scale gets its name from the fact that it is constructed from two fully diminished chords placed one whole step apart from one another.

Figure 3.24 Diminished scale consists of two diminished chords placed one whole step apart from one another

If you analyze the series of half and whole steps in this scale you find that the scale is symmetrical, it consists of alternating half and whole steps. This scale is sometimes called the *half-whole* scale or *octatonic* scale.

Figure 3.25 Half and whole steps of a diminished scale

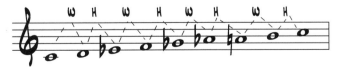

The most obvious application of this scale is for fully diminished chords. To construct the scale, use a series of whole and half steps starting with the root of the given diminished chord.

Figure 3.26 Diminished scale applied to a fully diminished chord

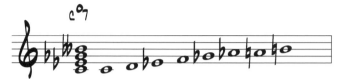

The diminished scale can also be helpful when applied to altered dominant chords. A suitable candidate is a C13(b9) chord. Common practice is to construct a diminished scale based on the root of the chord, but notice that the interval ordering is alternating half and whole steps, not whole and half steps.

Figure 3.27 Whole-half scale applied to a C13(b9) chord

NONTONAL SCALES

Whole tone. There are a number of nontonal scales used primarily in music of the twentieth century. The whole-tone scale was brought into vogue by Claude Debussy in the late nineteenth and early twentieth century. This scale is unique in that it does not include any semitones: it is constructed entirely of whole tones. This scale is useful when applied to an altered dominant chord (e.g., C7#5). The scale may also be used as a melodic or harmonic resource when your goal is to obscure any sense of functional harmony.

Figure 3.28 Whole tone scale

Pentatonic scale. As you know, the word penta describes the number five. A pentatonic scale is a scale that consists of only five pitches. Although any collection of five pitches can qualify as a pentatonic scale, the most common approach is to use 1-2-3-5-6 in a major key. These same tones also work well when applied to a relative minor as in the next example.

Figure 3.29 Pentatonic scale for major key and relative minor (1-2-3-5-6)

The pentatonic scale is particularly well suited for compositions that you intend to have a world music or ethnic quality. The pentatonic scale is found in folk music from many parts of the world including the United States. I found the following excerpt in an old Methodist hymnal.

Figure 3.30 Folk-like melody

Pentatonic scales are also used in many styles of pop music including blues, rock, and rhythm and blues. Many saxophonists and guitarists utilize this scale as in the following example.

Figure 3.31 Pentatonic blues excerpt

If you have made it this far, you are now familiar with most of the common chord and scale relationships. As I have previously stated, don't get in the rut of relying only on scales as you compose and improvise. The chord-scale relationships will help you to find good notes for any harmonic setting, but most great music does not easily fit into well-defined chord-scale paradigms.

You will want to consider many techniques as you begin to apply the common chord-scale relationships. One of the difficulties that you may run into has to do with using scales in a musical context. It is one thing to understand the theory of chord-scale relationships, but it is sometimes difficult to apply these concepts in real time. The following suggestions will help you to explore this useful concept.

THE WINDOW APPROACH

I often find it helpful to limit my choices as I explore a new musical concept such as chord-scale relationships. Pick one or two scales (such as a melodic minor scale) to experiment with. Play the scales and listen to how the scale sounds when applied to a given chord. Use your sequencer to record a one-chord vamp and loop or paste this vamp several times. Begin by improvising using only the first three or four notes of the given scale. Try to pace your improvisation so that the minimal number of notes is not a limitation (i.e., use lots of space and repetition). With this type of approach you will quickly learn how to "handle" and manipulate the first half of any scale. When you are comfortable with the first three or four notes, repeat the exercises but focus on the top three or four notes. When this is entirely comfortable, allow yourself to use any of the notes of the given scale. You will find that you can easily develop the facility to use a scale (even a complex one) in an effective and musical manner.

You may want to expand this technique to include a more complex harmonic progression. In the next example, a minor ii-V-i progression is used as a way of exploring three of the possible applications of the melodic minor scale. Note how this melody uses only the first four notes of each scale.

Figure 3.32 Excerpt: using the first four notes of melodic minor scales for a minor ii-V-i progression

RUNNING EIGHTH NOTES

Another technique that can help you to become more fluent with chord-scale relationships is to use a series of running eighth or sixteenth notes. For this exercise, try to gracefully move from one scale to the next (i.e., continue the moving line and start the next scale with a note that is either a step above or below the ending note of the previous chord). Though this is a difficult technique to master, with a little practice you will find that you can move fluently through almost any harmonic progression.

Figure 3.33 Moving eighth notes (minor ii-V-i progression)

DON'T ALWAYS START ON THE ROOT

We are creatures of habit. Though this is helpful when driving a car, habits can inhibit your ability to use a scale effectively. Most of us tend to start on the root of a given scale. One way you can get more comfortable with using scales is to start them on unusual places such as the third or fifth degree. Practice playing through a progression of chords and start on various notes. Although you will probably find this awkward at first, it is a good way to become familiar and fluent with common chord-scale relationships.

Figure 3.34 Starting on the fifth degree of each scale

Another practice technique involves applying a pattern or shape to a series of scales. Select a series of pitches such as 1-2-3-5-3 for a scale. Apply this same pattern or shape to each relevant scale in a progression of chords. I have found this technique to be a great way to develop new vocabulary that might otherwise be uncomfortable to play (or difficult to hear).

Figure 3.35 Applying a pattern to a progression of chords

SCALE-TONE CHORD CONCEPTS

One of the most helpful practice techniques involving scales is the concept of scale-tone triads or seventh chords. The idea here is to use triads or other chord structures that are diatonic to a given scale. In a major scale, for instance, the scale consists of the following triads.

Figure 3.36 Triads found in a C major scale

Scale-tone chords can be used to enhance a chordal accompaniment, or they can be used in a melodic fashion. Keep in mind that this technique will work for *any* scale.

Figure 3.37.1 Scale-tone triad excerpt (C major scale) melodic example

Figure 3.37.2 Scale-tone triad excerpt (C melodic minor scale)

Figure 3.37.3 Scale-tone triad as a chord embellishment of F7

Scale-tone seventh chords can also be effective in many styles of music. John Coltrane used this technique as the basis for his *sheets of sound* approach to many tunes. Listen to Miles Davis's *Kind of Blue* ("So What" track) for an excellent demonstration of scale-tone seventh chords.

Figure 3.38 Scale-tone seventh chords (D-dorian mode)

THINGS TO TRY AND THINGS TO AVOID

I sound like a broken record, but remember that scales can be wonderfully useful as a shortcut to hearing advanced chord and scale relationships. As you explore this concept, try to get past the academic approach of chord-scale relationships and try to internalize these sounds. If you are able to internalize these relationships, many of the melodies and solos found on popular music recordings will become very accessible to you. Also remember that, although scales are helpful, they can also be limiting. Avoid the temptation to stay within the "appropriate" scale; many other options such as embellishments and passing tones should be available to you as you compose and improvise.

The following examples represent the application of scales to a variety of harmonic progressions in a variety of styles. These excerpts are not meant to be comprehensive. My goal is that they will provide a starting point for further exploration.

Figure 3.39 Jazz harmonic progression

Figure 3.40 Rhythm and blues excerpt (blues scale and pentatonic vocabulary)

Figure 3.41 Pop style solo (various chordscale relationships, pentatonic vocabulary)

Figure 3.42 Modal example (dorian and lydian modes)

Figure 3.43 Application of melodic minor scales

Making Music with Your Computer

Contemporary Keyboard Techniques

Never do I suffer from melancholy,
Incessantly I play the echiquier...

The echiquier was an early keyboard instrument (sometimes called the checker). This quote is attributed to Imbert Chandelier[1], a fifteenth century musician. If Chandelier were with us today, he would see just how prophetic his comments were. The keyboard, in all its variations from the early clavichord and organ to the modern piano and synthesizer, has certainly attained prominence as a key ingredient of many musical genres. The reasons for this are simple: the keyboard has a range that approximates an orchestra, most keyboards are capable of a wide range of dynamics, and the modern synthesizer has an almost unlimited range of timbral possibilities. If you consider the great variety of popular music recordings that include keyboard or piano tracks, it is evident how important this instrument is to the contemporary computer musician. In this chapter we will explore a variety of keyboarding concepts that will allow you to enhance and expand your MIDI sequences. Although our goal is not to turn you into the next Liberace, you will find that a sufficient amount of keyboard facility will be an asset to almost any style of music you wish to create.

The keyboard (piano, organ, synthesized pad, etc.) has two primary functions in popular music: establishing or enhancing the harmonic progression and providing rhythmic activity. Of course the keyboard may also be used as a melodic instrument. In some styles of music, the keyboard may also be used to provide a "pad" or textural component by establishing a sonic setting for music that may or may not include a clear harmonic progression or rhythmic pulse.

Before we delve into the details of keyboarding concepts, it might be helpful to consider some general ideas that relate to texture. Although the term *texture* is vague, I use this term to describe the summative effect of a musical passage: how the elements of rhythm, harmony, voicing, register, dynamic, and timbre work together to create a specific texture. It is important to understand that most successful compositions use a variety of textures to retain the attention of a listener. Although textural changes are not solely the job of a keyboardist, most good keyboardists understand how to implement textural changes in an accompaniment.

As you explore the concepts presented in this chapter, experiment with the following textural tools:

- Tessitura: low "meaty" voicings vs. high "pretty" sounds
- Dynamics
- Complexity (or lack of complexity) of voicings
- Rhythmic activity (or absence of rhythmic activity)
- Timbre (e.g., changing from a piano patch to a synth or organ sound)

Again, listeners will tend to be more interested if your music is not static; one of the best ways to create this sense of variety is through the use of changing textures.

CHORD VOICINGS

One of the most challenging keyboard concepts to master is how to voice chords. By the term voicing, I mean the specific ordering of chord tones on a keyboard (or in an orchestration). If you consider that it is acceptable to double (or even triple) notes of a given chord and that these tones may be placed in any register and in any order or inversion, it is evident that the mathematical permutations of voicing a simple triad are staggering. To get a sense of the many possibilities, play through the following voicings of a simple seventh chord.

Figure 4.1 A few of the many voicings of a C7 chord

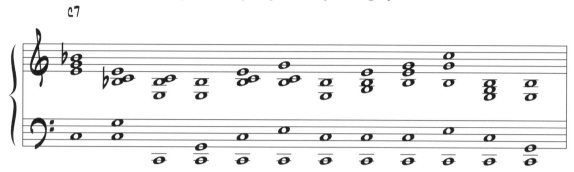

Although the variety of voicings is almost limitless, we can narrow the range of options by applying some general rules. The following tips can be of great help as you explore the concept of chord voicing. Keep in mind that these tips are just that—tips. As you will see later in this chapter, the tips may not be applicable in many situations.

CHORD VOICING TIPS

1. Wide structures work best in a low register.

Figure 4.2.1

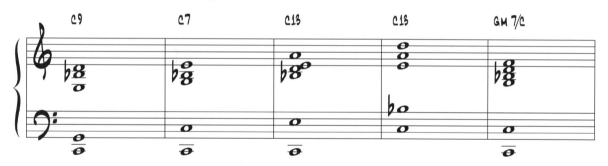

2. Avoid large gaps between the hands (i.e., a sixth or more).

Figure 4.2.2

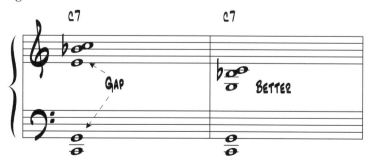

3. Avoid using a half-step between the upper two notes of any chord.

Figure 4.2.3

4. It may be desirable to omit a primary chord factor when voicing complex chords.

Figure 4.2.4

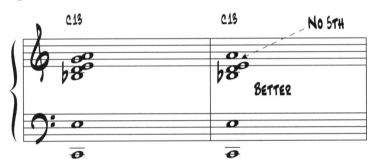

5. Consider voice leading—it is rarely effective to "jump" around in root position. In other words, it is generally desirable to find the smoothest way to move from one chord to the next. Use common tones and tendency tones when possible.

Figure 4.2.5

I have noticed that most keyboardists tend to rely on specific left-hand structures. Although there are no steadfast rules, the following structures may be used as the basis for voicing a wide variety of chords.

Figure 4.3 Common left hand structures

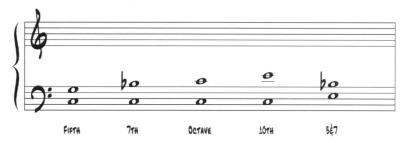

A helpful way to experiment with the structures listed above is as follows:
- Pick a chord that you wish to voice
- Select an appropriate left-hand structure
- Play the melody note in the right hand
- Add other chord tones in the right hand to complete the voicing (keeping in mind chord voicing tips 2, 3, 4, and 5)

With a little experimentation, you will soon find that you can create an appropriate voicing for almost any chord. With a little practice, creating pleasing chord structures "on the fly" will be easy.

Another common voicing scenario involves voicing complex chords, meaning chords that include extensions or alterations. As I mentioned in Voicing Tip #4, it is often helpful to omit specific notes from a chord in order to include color tones such as ninths and thirteenths. The goal here is to create a structure that best conveys the given chord quality while still retaining the texture of the moment (for example, you probably want to avoid using a seven note-voicing in the middle of a four-part texture). Although we will look at the concept of extensions in greater detail in Chapter 6, "Real-World Arranging," the following tips will get you started:

Figure 4.4 Adding extensions (tips for four-note voicings)

1. To add a ninth, omit the root.
2. To add a thirteenth, omit the fifth.
3. To add an augmented eleventh, omit the fifth.
4. To add a perfect eleventh, omit the fifth or the third (if the chord is a half-diminished chord).

The next example can be found in any jazz theory book. I include it here for two reasons: it demonstrates an approach to voicing complex chords using the four-note voicings tips in Figure 4.4, and it illustrates the concept of voice leading. Notice how gracefully the chords flow in this example.

Figure 4.5 ii-V-I Close position (two variations)

An "open position" variation to the previous example is as follows.

Figure 4.6 ii-V-I Open position (two variations)

In the last example you might have noticed that the left hand utilized one of our common left hand structures: the third and seventh chord factors. These so-called *drop-two* structures can be very helpful in situations where you wish to create an "open" sound while still maintaining a complex chord voicing. The term *drop two* comes from lowering the second note (from the top) of a close-position chord one octave as is evident in the next example.

Figure 4.7 Drop-two voicings

Tip: You can easily create a drop-two voicing for any chord using the following chord factors: 3-7-1-5 or 7-3-5-1. If you also consider the tips on adding extension tones, it is easy to use these structures as the basis for any complex chord. Of course these rootless voicings tend to work best in situations where you allocate a bass track to play the root of the chord.

Figure 4.8 Drop-two voicings for a variety of chords

Understanding the theory of good chord voicings is only half the battle. It is also essential to be able to use these structures in context. As you practice, work through the following exercises. In due time you will be a harmonically proficient computer musician! Just remember to practice these etudes in all keys and with both hands. Also note that even if keyboard is not your primary controller, most of these concepts will relate directly to a MIDI guitar or marimba.

Figure 4.9 Primary chord qualities (descending half-steps)

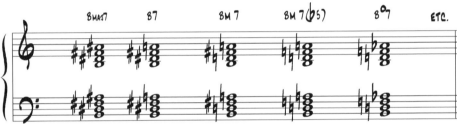

Figure 4.10 Triads and seventh chords in inversion

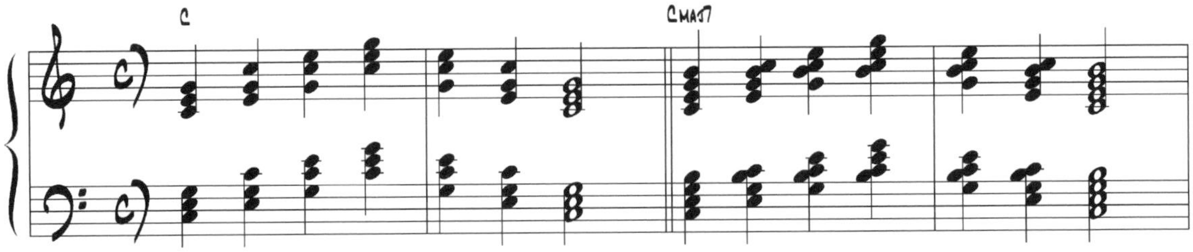

Figure 4.11 Triads around the circle of fifths (utilize common tones)

Figure 4.12 Seventh chords around the circle of fifths

Figure 4.13 ii-V-I close position (all keys)

Figure 4.14 ii-V-I open position (all keys)

4.15 Voice melodies in close or open position (place the melody in the top voice)

Although this list of etudes is by no means comprehensive, these chord exercises will give you a solid foundation for further exploration. Apply these concepts to other tunes and progressions. Be creative. The possibilities are endless!

RHYTHMIC CONCEPTS

As I mentioned earlier in the chapter, harmony is only one aspect of contemporary keyboard technique. To excel as a keyboardist you will also want to develop a variety of rhythmic textures. We will begin our discussion with a look at some common left-hand rhythmic techniques.

Extended Alberti bass. The term *Alberti bass* refers to a common eighteenth century technique in which the left hand is used to arpeggiate the notes of a chord (usually a triad) as an accompaniment to a melody in the right hand. Domenico Alberti (1710-1740) was a composer who frequently employed this technique.

Figure 4.16 Alberti bass Mozart Sonata in C Major K. 545

Although the Alberti bass sounds rather dated, you will still hear this technique used in popular music. I use the term *extended Alberti* to describe a more common variation. Instead of arpeggiating a triad in close position, open up the chord and place it in the bass register (e.g., root-fifth-tenth instead of root-third-fifth).

Figure 4.17 Extended Alberti

I have found this technique to be exceptionally helpful in a variety of styles including jazz ballads, pop, new age, and country. The following example illustrates one possible approach. Notice how the right hand helps to fill in the harmony underneath the melody.

Figure 4.18 Extended Alberti excerpt

Chapter Four

Ostinato. *The New Harvard Dictionary of Music* describes an ostinato as "a short musical pattern that is repeated persistently throughout a performance or composition or a section of one." The concept of an ostinato can be helpful for a variety of styles. Entire compositions have been created that rely on a simple repetitive pattern in the left hand. An added benefit of experimenting with ostinatos is that they can help you to develop independence between the right and left hands.

Figure 4.19 A few of the many left-hand ostinato patterns

Try placing an ostinato under a simple progression of chords (e.g., I-IV-V-I). Repeat the pattern until it is comfortable and then experiment with variations. Again, this concept can be used with a great many musical styles. The following excerpt demonstrates the use of an ostinato in the left hand.

Figure 4.20 Ostinato excerpt

Piano picking. I use the term *piano picking* to describe the keyboardist's version of guitar finger-picking technique. If you have ever watched a guitarist finger pick, you will note that the right hand is used to arpeggiate the notes of a chord. In most cases, the arpeggiation is fairly random (e.g., a low note might be followed by a high note, then a middle tone, and so on). In keyboard terms, think of the instrument as being divided into three sections: low, middle, and high registers. The fifth finger of the left hand handles low tones and the fifth finger of the right hand handles high tones. The fun begins when you allow the first three fingers of the right and left hand to share in the role of arpeggiating or "picking" a chord. Notice how the right and left hand work together in the next example to create a sense of moving sixteenth notes.

Figure 4.21 Piano picking

To really master this technique, you need to develop the ability to vary the rhythms in real-time. The "piano picking" sound is a mainstay for nearly every type of popular music including country, pop, and some styles of rock. We will even see a variation later in this chapter under the anatomy of keyboard styles section (funk clavichord example). As with the ostinato example, I suggest practicing this technique with a single chord or simple harmonic progression until the variations become second nature to you. The following example demonstrates a few of the many variations of this technique.

Figure 4.22 Piano picking variations

SCALE-TONE CONCEPTS

In Chapter 3 we learned about common chord and scale relationships. In addition to using scales as an aid to composition and improvisation, keyboardists will often use scale-tone triads to enhance a passage of music. One of the great benefits of scale-tone triads is that they provide the keyboardist with a way of providing variations to a progression of chords without the necessity of using complex chord structures that might not be appropriate for the given musical context. It would be inappropriate to use ninth and thirteenth chords in a "down and dirty" blues tune. Scale-tone triads provide a way of enhancing the progression while still retaining an appropriate harmonic context. You will find that first and second inversion triads tend to work best.

Figure 4.23 Scale-tone triads over an F7 (two inversions)

Remember that the trick for using scale-tone triads is to find a balance between chord tones and passing tones. Once you have established some arrival points, just make certain that the triads move diatonically within the given scale (i.e., the appropriate scale for the current chord or key center). Notice how I used a few chromatic passing tones in the next example to enhance a typical blues or gospel keyboard lick.

Figure 4.24 Scale-tone triad excerpt

Keep in mind that scale-tone triads can be used for nearly any chord, even altered dominants or diminished chords. If you are like me, you will wonder how you ever got by without using scale-tone triads.

My goal in this section is to present a variety of common keyboard concepts. It goes without saying that an entire book could be written on each of the topics that follow. Please note that my intention is not to provide a comprehensive list of techniques but rather to give some hints that will point you in the right direction for further exploration. Of course one of the best ways to develop a vocabulary of styles is to listen to recordings.

Blues. Blues is a vast topic. Many outstanding books are available that cover the intricacies of this genre and its many permutations such as jazz-blues, rhythm and blues, gospel, and the like. With that said, there are several concepts that can get you started in this style.

Blue notes have always been an essential part of blues vocabulary. A blue note is a note that is slightly out of tune when compared to our Western European system of tuning. The most common blue tones fall between a minor and major third in a given key (usually called a *blue third*) and between #4 and 5 in a key. Blues vocalists, saxophonists, guitarists, and others tend to use blue notes to great effect when performing. One of the limitations of traditional keyboard instruments such as piano, organ, or electric piano is that the keyboardist can't realistically bend notes. The work-around for blues keyboardists is to use grace notes to achieve a similar effect. The following examples demonstrate a few of the many common blues licks used by keyboardists. Note that it is often nice to add a pedal tone (a repetitive note) in the top voice.

Figure 4.25 Blues licks: grace notes and pedal tones

Thirds are also commonly used by blues keyboardists. The following lick comes from Jimmy Smith.

Figure 4.26 Blues lick from "Big Fat Mama," Jimmy Smith

Another common blues concept is the use of repetitive figures. Mature blues performers will often use a repetitive pattern for a chorus (or more) as a way of building tension and excitement in a solo. It is also common to use a *cross rhythm* (a repeating three beats against four phrase) when performing a repetitive pattern. Experiment with the following licks and let one rip for a chorus or more next time you sequence or perform a blues number; they are always crowd pleasers. Note: listen to the lead guitar from the *Rhythm and Blues* recording on the demonstration CD to hear an example of this technique.

Figure 4.27 Common repetitive figures

Trills and tremolos are also used by many blues keyboardists. As with blue notes, a limitation of piano and electric piano is the inability to sustain a note for more than a few beats. The most common way to use a blues trill is to trill between two notes a minor or major third apart, such as 6-1, 3-5, or 5-7, in a given key.

Figure 4.28 Blues trills

One other blues tip that relates specifically to the organ involves using a sustained note in the right hand. My favorite version of this lick is to do an ascending gliss. At the top of the gliss, grab a note (usually the tonic) and hold this note with your fifth finger as you continue to improvise with the other four fingers of the right hand. I will often use this lick for a chorus or more at the end of a solo. When properly executed the audience should be on their feet by the end of the solo!

Figure 4.29 Sustained note (organ lick)

We have only scratched the surface of blues vocabulary, but these tips will get you started on the road to further exploration. The following excerpt incorporates many of the concepts presented in this section.

Figure 4.30 Hammond B3 blues excerpt

Country concepts. As with blues, country keyboard is a vast topic. Country music has evolved over the last decade to the point where there is much crossover between country, blues, and pop genres. If I had to pick one technique that best typifies country keyboard, I would present a concept perfected by Floyd Cramer. In this style, the quintessential country "twang" is achieved by the use of grace notes. In contrast to a blues grace note, the country grace note typically embellishes the third of a chord. A fun way to experiment with this concept is to play a series of major triads (e.g., I-IV-V-I). As you play through the progression, use the note that is one whole step lower than the third of the chord as a grace note. The following example is a typical country piano phrase.

Figure 4.31 Country grace notes

Note that you may wish to include other tones such as the root as a part of the embellishment. As with all of the techniques listed in this section, the Floyd Cramer style can certainly be overused. On the other hand, few other licks so successfully convey the country twang.

Many country keyboardists will incorporate an interval of a sixth in the right hand. This sound can be great to use in a country solo or to support or complement a melody.

Figure 4.32 Sixths in the right hand—country style

Another country device you may wish to explore involves an approach very similar to licks you might hear on mandolin or guitar. This "picking" style is usually applied as an embellishment to a simple triad. In the next example, a chromatic approach is used to embellish the third of a major triad. The repetitive nature of this lick nicely conveys the picking style characteristic of many of the country stringed instruments.

Figure 4.33 Fast country "picking" style

Rock keyboard. Call me a traditionalist, but when I think of rock keyboard my heart is still with the early pioneers such as Keith Emerson and Rick Wakeman. Obviously, some wonderful rock music has since been recorded that utilizes keyboards, but the sixties were certainly a time when keyboards were a key component of many rock bands. In contrast to some of the other styles we have looked at, my comments in this section will relate more to general concepts than specific playing techniques.

The function of a keyboardist in a rock band is varied. In the 1960s and 1970s, groups such as Yes and Emerson, Lake & Palmer utilized keyboards in a variety of ways: melody, comping, textural (i.e., synthetic sounds), and as a solo or improvisational instrument. The arsenal of instruments traditional rock keyboardists utilized included Hammond B3, electric piano, acoustic piano, clavinet, and analog synthesizer.

Today the role of the keyboardist has changed. Most of the rock albums that get airtime utilize keyboard as a textural device (i.e., synthesizer, piano, or organ pads to provide a change of texture behind a solo or at an important section of the tune). In my estimation, the reason for this change has more to do with economics than with aesthetic reasons. The days of 15 or 20 minute "jam" tunes are over. For a band to reasonably expect to get airtime, songs must be presented in a concise format. If you spend some time analyzing rock tunes that are on the air today, you begin to realize that solo sections tend to be concise, and most of the solo work is done with electric guitar. Of course, there are many exceptions where keyboards have maintained a prominent presence (e.g., the piano intro on "Old Time Rock 'n Roll" or the synthesizer motive on the Van Halen tune "Jump").

One of the difficulties rock keyboardists deal with is what to play for a "power chord." Power chords are harmonic structures that guitarists often use in rock music. A power chord usually consists of an interval of a fourth or fifth played on the lower strings of the guitar.

Figure 4.34 Power chord

Unlike traditional tertian (chords built in thirds) structures, a power chord contains no third. The absence of a third results in a chord that is indeterminate—a power chord is neither major or minor. For keyboardists, the goal is to find a voicing and rhythmic pattern that complement the sound of the power chords. A common technique is to use open fifths to provide a background pad or rhythmic figure as in the next example.

Figure 4.35 Keyboard pad over guitar power chords

Although the piano is used infrequently in heavier rock styles, keyboardists will occasionally use a repetitive figure in the upper range of the piano.

Figure 4.36 Repetitive keyboard figure over power chord riff (guitar)

A keyboard sound that is still very much in vogue is the Hammond B3 organ. The B3 is often used for its classic rock sound and can be heard on cuts from Tom Petty, Bruce Springsteen, and others. One of the things I had to learn when first playing the B3 was to avoid approaching this instrument like a piano. Because the organ has no sustain pedal, you must use a legato (connected) style of playing when using an organ patch. Avoid the temptation to use the damper pedal. Though it might be easier to play this way, the damper pedal will negate any stylistic accuracy that might otherwise be achieved.

When you consider the function of the organ, it is evident that the function of the B3 is to "sweeten" the music. Unlike the piano, it is rarely used as a primary part of the groove. In some styles of music such as funk, however, the organ may take a more prominent rhythmic role. The most common technique is to use sustained notes in the mid to upper register. Add a bit of Leslie (rotating speaker sound) at a key point in the phrase; it is a characteristic sound that will add much to a bridge or interlude.

Figure 4.37 Hammond organ accompaniment

Another common technique is to use the Hammond sound to add fills that complement a vocal line or melody. These fills are often reminiscent of the Floyd Cramer grace notes presented earlier in this chapter.

Figure 4.38 Hammond organ fills

Often the piano is used to provide another classic rock sound. The piano is particularly effective when used on rock tunes that have a more traditional harmonic progression (i.e., music that is not based on the power chord sound). An effective way to use the piano in this context is to use octaves in the left hand.

Experiment with tertian structures in the mid register in the right hand. The goal here is to provide a full sound with rhythms that complement the bass, drums, and guitar. The piano picking technique presented previously can be very effective for this style of music.

Figure 4.39 Rock piano (full sounding voicings with "piano picking")

A variety of synthesized sounds are also used by rock keyboardists. Analog sounds such as a square or triangle wave can really cut through a mix of guitars. When used in this context, aggressive synthesized sounds are usually used to complement a primary rhythmic figure of the tune. In some cases the synth will even function as a melodic instrument. As with other rock keyboard sounds, use synthetic sounds judiciously: in most cases you will want to use these sounds to enhance an introduction, bridge or interlude.

Figure 4.40 Aggressive synth patch (rhythmic complement to the bass and drums)

Funk. Though a variety of keyboard instruments are typically used in funk music, I will focus on the clavichord and organ. Keep in mind that many of the concepts that I present in this section will be applicable to other keyboard instruments such as electric piano.

Rhythm is the essence of funk music. When you listen to a great funk recording, such as cuts by Tower of Power or Earth, Wind and Fire, it becomes evident that the groove is a result of many layers of rhythmic activity. A common mistake many players make is to play a keyboard track (or bass or drums) that is overly complicated. My best advice here is for you to remember that, although the overall groove may sound complicated, great funk grooves generally consist of layers of rhythms that are relatively simple and are typically *very* repetitive. As you experiment with repetitive patterns, try repeating the pattern with a slight variation at the end of a phrase or transition into a bridge or interlude.

One of my favorite funk organ techniques is to use both the left and right hand to create a percussive rhythmic riff. The great Chester Thompson from Tower of Power often used this technique on recordings from the 1970s and 1980s. Once again, remember not to get carried away. The most effective funk grooves will tend to be very repetitive.

Figure 4.41 Percussive organ riff

As with many of the other techniques presented in this chapter, it would be easy to devote an entire chapter to the concept of the clavichord. Though the clavichord has been used on many funk and pop recordings, it is interesting to note that the traditional clavichord dates back to the late fifteenth century.

Tip: If you enjoy music history, you may want to check out some of the music of Domenico Scarlatti. Scarlatti was a Baroque composer who wrote a large number of sonatas (more than 500) specifically for the harpsichord, a close relative of the clavichord. Believe it or not, many of these sonatas are actually rather funky. When I play his sonatas I often get the feeling Scarlatti would have loved to jam in a modern-day funk group.

Perhaps the most famous of all of the popular recordings that utilize the clavichord is the Stevie Wonder recording of "Superstition." As with the organ, the clavichord requires a style of playing that is very different from traditional piano technique. The right and left hands will often work together to provide a complex rhythmic pulse. It is helpful to visualize the keyboard as being divided into three or four sections as in the piano picking examples discussed earlier in this chapter. Though it certainly works well to incorporate triads or other chords into this style of playing, many keyboardists will use very sparse voicings (e.g., just roots and fifths). Use the following examples as the basis for some experimentation in this style.

Figure 4.42.1 Clavichord excerpt: chord version

Jazz. In the big band era jazz reigned supreme in American pop culture. Though jazz has never managed to regain its prominence with the general public, the jazz influence is still evident in many areas of popular music. Jazz-derived harmonies are common in many styles of music from pop to funk. Because jazz music is often associated with a sense of sophistication and elegance, producers often elect to use jazz recordings in commercial and film productions.

One of the most important considerations for developing a convincing jazz sound is the use of extended and altered harmony. Mainstream jazz relies on sophisticated chord voicings and harmonic progressions. A general rule of thumb is to add extensions such as ninths and thirteenths when possible. Altered dominants are often used to create a heightened sense of motion at V-I cadences. Good jazz pianists also spend years developing the ability to use good voice leading techniques when playing through a harmonic progression. Obviously, a few paragraphs will not do justice to such a vast topic. Play through the examples and use them as the basis for further exploration of this art form. The following example demonstrates the principles of extended and altered harmony. Note the use of smooth voice leading and inner-voice movement.

Figure 4.43 Jazz: harmonic progression (alterations and extensions)

When playing a melody or improvising a solo, the common jazz piano approach is to use colorful or complex voicings in the left hand while the right hand maintains a horn-style approach. Some tips for developing a jazz-style right hand include using chord tones, chord-scale relationships, and common embellishments such as changing tones, chromatic approach tones, and turns. The next example illustrates a typical jazz style right hand over a ii-V-I-vi progression in the left hand. Note that in this style, the left hand functions very much like a guitar: use rhythms that complement the lines in the right hand.

Figure 4.44 Jazz style solo: right hand horn style with left hand comp

When *comping* (accompanying) in a swing style, I find it helpful to visualize using a balance of on-beat and syncopated figures. Without offbeats the music will not swing. On the other hand, too many syncopations may become chaotic. The following examples demonstrate a few of the common vertical structures and rhythms found in a typical jazz keyboard accompaniment.

Figure 4.45 Jazz comping: vertical structures and rhythmic variations

If your interests lie in the direction of solo jazz piano you may wish to explore some of the techniques associated with this genre. The masters of jazz piano—such as Bill Evans or Chick Corea—have developed a style of playing that transcends the two-handed approach common in some other styles of keyboard music. One way to visualize this technique is to rethink the traditional approach to the keyboard: instead of thinking in terms of left vs. right hand, visualize the keyboard as an orchestra. The left hand typically handles bass notes, the right hand usually covers the melody. Both the left and right hand may share in the function of harmony and rhythm. This "three-handed" approach, though tough to implement, is a mainstay of these masters of jazz piano. If you allow yourself the ability to become flexible with regard to orchestration (i.e., the function of the right and left hands), you will find that this technique will open many doors for you in your approach to jazz keyboard and other styles as well. Note that this technique can be particularly helpful when you sequence string or brass tracks.

Latin. As with funk music, rhythm is the primary ingredient in Latin styles. One of the most helpful keyboard techniques is the *montuno*. A montuno is a repetitive figure, much like an ostinato, that is central to many Latin styles. The following example demonstrates a montuno for a ii-V progression.

Figure 4.47 Montuno example: ii-V progression

It is often helpful to visualize moving notes when constructing a montuno. Look for notes that change from one chord to another as in the previous example or construct a mini-melody into the montuno pattern as in the next example. Though the passage consists entirely of a simple major seventh chord, this montuno utilizes both the sixth and seventh for variety.

Figure 4.48 Montuno for a Cmaj7 chord (using major sixth and major seventh)

Another common Latin keyboard technique involves using both hands to arpeggiate the notes of a chord. Latin keyboardists will often utilize an interval of a sixth in this type of setting. Experiment with rhythmic variations and a variety of ascending and descending motion.

Figure 4.49 Latin keyboard example: arpeggiation in sixths

One other Latin keyboard technique you may wish to explore is to use both hands in tandem to provide a particularly strong rhythmic groove. As with funk, you will probably want to avoid lots of extraneous variations. Keep a pattern going for a while and implement variations at major points of the tune such as a bridge or solo section.

Figure 4.50 Latin comp: two hands in tandem

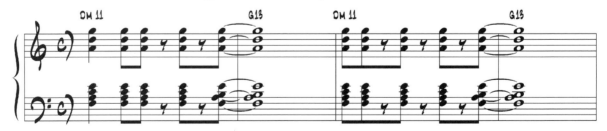

With regard to improvised lines, Latin keyboardists draw much of their vocabulary from jazz music. The horn-style right hand over left hand comp tends to work very well for this style of music.

Figure 4.51 Latin (jazz) solo with left hand comp

Pop and New Age. A chapter on contemporary keyboard techniques would not be complete without a discussion of pop keyboard concepts. We already covered many techniques that are used in pop music such as extended Alberti, piano picking, and common left hand repetitive patterns. Though a pop keyboardist will tend to utilize textural elements that are common in mainstream rock or jazz, a key difference is the approach to harmonic vocabulary. Because we have already looked at many of the playing techniques associated with pop music I will focus on two harmonic elements that are common to this style: suspended harmony and polychords.

Though much pop music revolves around traditional tertian harmony (triads and seventh chords), many pop tunes incorporate suspension chords. *Sus* chords are interesting in that they obscure the boundaries of a traditional harmonic progression. A sus-2 chord, for example, does not contain either a major or minor third. Because suspension chords sound rather ambiguous, they can function in many ways. In the following example, notice how a simple sus-2 chord can be used over a variety of bass notes.

Figure 4.52 Sus-2 chord over a variety of bass notes

Another aspect of some pop tunes that I find attractive is the emphasis placed on the bass line. Many pop songs utilize a bass line that is linear (i.e., the bass functions as a melodic complement to the melody and harmonic progression). In rock and country, it is common for the bass to focus on the tonic of each of the chords in a progression. Though roots are certainly common in pop music, it is also common to hear the bass on another chord tone such as the third or the fifth. As you experiment with this concept, look for linear connections between the primary chords in a chord progression. I have found that a more linear approach can provide wonderful results.

Figure 4.53 Pop progression with linear bass line

One other technique that is common in pop music is the concept of the polychord. Though we talked about polychords in Chapter 2, we will revisit the concept here. As with suspension chords, the goal of polychords in a pop progression is to obscure the harmonic progression. One of the most common progressions found in most styles of music is a I-IV-V-I progression. Though this technique might be considered clichéd, pop musicians will often place this type of progression over a pedal point. The resulting polychords are certainly stylistic for this genre.

Figure 4.54 Polychord progression

In a similar vein, polychords are often used to tone down a more traditional progression such as a V-I cadence. Here, the subdominant (IV) is placed over V in the bass. The IV-V chord is one of the most common structures found in pop music.

Figure 4.55 IV-V polychord

The following example demonstrates many concepts relating to pop music. Some of the elements you may wish to study in this example include the use of suspension and polychords, the linear bass line, and incorporation of the piano picking technique from earlier in this chapter.

Figure 4.56 Pop example (suspension chords, linear bass movement, and piano picking)

Making Music with Your Computer

I hope that this chapter has provided you with some new concepts and vocabulary to explore as you create music with your computer. As I stated in the beginning of the chapter, the styles and concepts presented here are by no means comprehensive, but they will provide a solid foundation for further exploration in whatever style of music interests you. Remember, too, that incorporation of new vocabulary will help you to develop your own style.

[1]*Five Centuries of Keyboard Music,* John Gillespie, p. 2

CHAPTER 5

Music Composition

We have all had the experience of staring at a blank piece of notebook paper while trying to think of the first sentence of an English essay. With music the proverbial mind block is also prevalent. In this chapter we will look at some ways to better define the composition process. In so doing, we will also discover some tricks that can help you to bring a musical idea to fruition in the form of a complete musical composition. Unlike movies you may have seen, composing primarily involves decision making and focus. Although divine inspiration doesn't hurt, you will have a hard time completing a composition if you wait around for it.

The best way to avoid a composing mind block is to work every day. Most good MIDI musicians practice their craft regularly. Understand that a majority of what you sequence and compose may be destined for the virtual recycle bin, but by working every day you can hone your decision making skills. As you get more comfortable with the process of making musical decisions, you will find that mind block is a thing of the past.

LOOKING FOR INSPIRATION

Students often ask me if they should write the melody of a composition before considering the harmony. There is no correct answer to this question. As simple as it sounds, the seed for a composition will be whatever happens to strike your fancy as you compose; it might be a melody, progression of chords, formal structure, rhythmic groove, or even an interesting synthesized sound. The point is that, whatever your original inspiration was, in order to mold this idea into the form of a complete composition, you must make a tremendous number of musical decisions. Other than relying on your ears, one of your best tools in this decision-making process is an understanding of music theory. Although theory is a vast topic (just ask any graduate theory student), the fundamentals, as they relate to mainstream composition, are easy to understand and implement.

Through theory we learn how to analyze and internalize the decisions that were made by other composers. I should stress that, in this context, theory is simply a way of clarifying the decision-making process. Compositions that are based entirely on abstract theoretical principles are rarely successful.

WRITING A MELODY

A good melody is a thing of beauty. It speaks to us, conjures up an image or emotion, and draws us into the song. If you think about music that has stood the test of time (either classical or popular), it is clear how important a good melody can be. It could be said that our entire culture of popular music is based on melody: songs drive the music industry, and songs are simply a vocal expression of a melodic idea. I challenge you to think of a single successful popular music group that has not relied on melody as a primary feature of their music. There are few exceptions.

In my estimation, humans are attracted to melodies in an almost physical way. I recently had the pleasure of hearing a musical trio from southern India. Though the instruments sounded foreign to my ear, the rhythms were complex, and I didn't understand the words, I found myself captivated by the sheer beauty of the melodies. As humans, we are also attracted to rhythm. If you ever have the chance to listen to music from other cultures, it becomes clear that melody and rhythm are the two most important ingredients of a musical composition. You will note that I didn't mention harmony: our concept of harmony and even our system of well-tempered tuning is unique to music that derives from the Western European tradition. Harmony may or may not be germane to a successful composition. Again, if you think of melody and rhythm, it is clear that one of the reasons popular music is so, well, "popular" is that it speaks to the average listener on an almost physical level.

What are the elements that define a good melody? If I knew the answer to that question I would probably be sitting on a yacht right now. Part of the allure of a good melody comes from unexpected or intangible elements that can't be easily analyzed, but we can consider some of the elements that exist in most good melodies. A good melody is often singable.

Though many successful melodies have been written that are not singable, most listeners can't help but be attracted to a melody that they can sing in their head. If we take this concept a step further you will note that singable melodies tend to share certain characteristics:

- They avoid awkward jumps.
- Consider the range: melodies that are too high or low are hard to sing.
- Diatonic melodies are easier to sing than melodies with many chromatic tones.
- Fast moving passages are hard to sing.
- Small jumps, passing tones, and intervalic or rhythmic repetition are often desirable.
- Jumps are often balanced by stepwise motion in the opposite direction.

It is appropriate to point out that singable melodies are not necessarily meant for the voice. A melody that is singable is also attractive to a listener when performed on an instrument such as a piano, violin, or synthesizer. How can you tell if you have achieved a good singable melody? Your voice can be your greatest asset here. As you compose, if you find that you can sing or hum a given melody, you have achieved your goal. The following example illustrates two singable melodies. The first melody is diatonic, the second melody uses some chromaticism (notes that are outside of the key center).

Figure 5.1 Singable melody: diatonic and chromatic versions

AVOIDING TACTILE TENDENCY

If you think about it, nearly everything we do in our lives involves subconscious touching; when you enter a room and flick on a light switch or pick up a ringing telephone you are using subconscious physical movement. I use the term *tactical tendency* to describe the process of using subconscious physical movement when composing and sequencing. In other words, most of us tend to play what our fingers know. Some people refer to this as *muscle memory*. Although muscle memory is desirable when swinging a golf club or playing tennis, it is absolutely counter-productive when composing. If you find that your compositions always sound similar to one another, you may be suffering from this malady. I have already presented a cure: try to get away from your keyboard or guitar and use your voice. Most of us have tons of wonderful melodies inside; your voice is the best tool for getting to these ideas.

IDIOMATIC MELODIES

In contrast to singable melodies, there are nonsingable and idiomatic melodies. An idiomatic melody is one that is comfortable to perform on one specific instrument. Guitar melodies sometimes incorporate pentatonic sounds—a grouping of notes that is comfortable to play on that instrument. Piano-based melodies are often more jumpy than those written on other instruments. In the early part of this century, many classical composers tended to shy away from the use of singable melodies. Though a nonsingable melody can be very effective, I would avoid this approach if your goal is to write the next pop music hit.

Figure 5.2 An idiomatic keyboard melody

FINDING A BALANCE

A difficult concept to master when writing a melody involves the balance between repetition and presentation of new ideas. Though a predictable pattern of notes such as an ascending chromatic scale can be effective (listen to Duke Ellington's "Chromatic Love Affair"), you will tend to lose the listener if your melody is overly repetitive. On the other hand, melodies that sound random are not effective because there is nothing for the listener to latch onto. As you compose, try to find a balance between these two extremes. Of course the style of the music will have much to do with approach you use: classical and jazz composers often write melodies that take more listener attention than popular styles such as rock, pop, or country.

I often find it helpful to consider the shape of a melody as I compose. There is no steadfast rule, but most good melodies have well defined high and low points. The following examples illustrate a few of the common shapes: high to low, low to high, and climax in the middle.

Figure 5.3.1 High to low contour

Figure 5.3.2 Low to high contour

Figure 5.3.3 Climax in the middle

If you are writing a vocal tune, it is also important to consider the relationship of melodic contour and text. Keep in mind that if you are writing a song with words, it is essential to create a melody that best supports the text: you will often want to align a keyword with a melodic climax. The following melody demonstrates one such approach.

Making Music with Your Computer

Figure 5.4 Relationship between melody and words ("My Romance"— Rodgers and Hart)

I CAN MAKE MY MOST FAN - TAS - TIC DREAMS COME TRUE;

Notice how the phrase "fantastic dreams come true" is set, both rhythmically and melodically, to a climactic point in the melody.

A BALANCE OF MOTION

Sometimes it is helpful to consider the relationship of disjunct (skips) and conjunct (stepwise) motion as you compose a melody. Although many great melodies don't fall into this category, many contain a balance of skips and steps. Often, a large ascending leap will be followed by a stepwise descent. A descending leap will often be followed by ascending motion. If your melody sounds too jumpy, it may be helpful to consider adding some contrary stepwise motion to balance the effect of the jump. Similarly, a few well-placed skips can make a stepwise melody more interesting.

Figure 5.5 Jump followed by stepwise motion

PERIOD STRUCTURE

Classical theorists use the term *period* to describe a musical sentence. As the *Harvard Dictionary of Music* so aptly states, a musical period is a "complete musical utterance." A musical period is made up of smaller units called the antecedent and consequent. One way to visualize this concept is to think of the idea of a question and answer. The antecedent and consequent usually share an element such as a rhythmic figure or grouping notes, but the consequent serves to finish the idea presented in the antecedent. Two or more periods may also be used to imply a larger period structure. You might think of this as the relationship between a sentence and a paragraph.

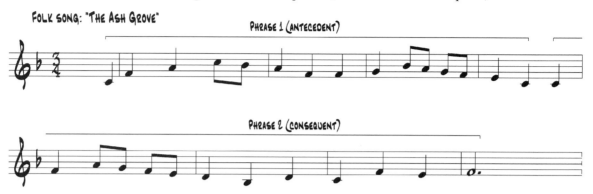

Figure 5.6 Musical period (antecedent and consequent)

To this point we have focused on the concept of creating a melody or tune. The next several paragraphs deal with the concept of a *motive*. Whereas a musical period is a "complete musical utterance," a motive is a musical fragment. A motive should be easily recognizable by the listener, perhaps just two or three notes or a well-defined rhythmic figure. Motives are helpful in that they allow a composer to develop an idea over the course of a composition. By transforming a well-defined motive (either through melodic or rhythmic variation) a composer can create a sense of development that is attractive to the listener. The following paragraphs detail a few of the many ways of manipulating musical motives.

Rhythmic shift. With rhythmic shift, an initial rhythmic motive is displaced either ahead of or behind the beat. Note that with MIDI sequencers this can be an easy concept to investigate. As an experiment, try recording a short motive and use the sequencer to paste a copy of this phrase to various rhythmic offsets in relation to the first statement of the phrase.

Figure 5.7 Rhythmic shift

Augmentation. With regard to melodic composition, augmentation involves expanding the rhythms of a phrase to twice (or more) of their original value.

Figure 5.8 Melodic augmentation

Diminution. In contrast to augmentation, diminution is a halving of rhythmic values.

Figure 5.9 Melodic diminution

Melodic sequence. Theorists use the term *sequence* to describe a phrase that contains repetition of a melodic motive on successively higher or lower pitches. Though a sequence can easily become boring if it employs an inordinate amount of repetition, sequential motives involving two or three repetitions are quite common. Two types of sequential ideas are common. In a *tonal sequence*, the transposition of the initial motive remains diatonic to the key or tonal center. A *real sequence* is simply an exact transposition of the original motive.

Figure 5.10-1 Tonal sequence

Figure 5.10-2 Real sequence

Embellishments. I will let you in on a little secret: one of the best ways to develop skill as a composer is to learn how to develop and manipulate motives. An example I often use with my students is Beethoven's Fifth Symphony. The Fifth Symphony epitomizes the use of concise motives. When you think about it, Beethoven is better known for his ability to mold and manipulate melodic fragments than he is for composing memorable melodies. (Though he certainly wrote many memorable melodies!) For most successful composers, common embellishments can mean the difference between a trite or boring melody and one that is interesting to a listener. In other words, embellishments provide many of the tools a composer needs to manipulate melodic material. Let's have a look at some of the common embellishments that composers use.

Figure 5.11 Common melodic embellishments

To see the power of such a simple concept, take a look at the next example. The following melody certainly wouldn't win any awards for its inventiveness. Notice how, through the application of a few embellishments, the idea becomes much more interesting while still maintaining the simple quality of the original motive.

Figure 5.12 Application of common melodic embellishments

Let's review what we have learned so far with regard to writing melodies and manipulating motives. Singable melodies tend to be the most attractive to a listener. Idiomatic melodies can also be effective, but avoid falling into the trap of tactile tendency. Consider the overall contour of the melody, the relationship of high and low points. Try to find a balance between repetition and new ideas.

The following tips may be helpful to keep in mind as you compose melodies and experiment with manipulating motives:

- Repetition and sequence can be effective but can easily become boring if used too frequently.
- Music with little or no repetition may sound too abstract to a listener.
- Consider the melodic contour: high and low points should not be arrived at in a haphazard way.
- Avoid awkward leaps when writing singable melodies.
- It is often a good idea to balance leaps with stepwise motion in the opposite direction.
- Musical periods are often made up of phrases that contain similar or complementary elements.
- Most melodies contain a unifying element such as a prominent rhythmic figure or interval.

Although it is hard to write a good melody, the results are well worth the extra work involved. Listeners will like your music much more if they find the melodies to be pleasing. Melodies that wander, are unfocused, or are monotonous will tend to lose the listener very fast. Don't be afraid to experiment: many of the masters such as Beethoven sweated through many versions before the melody was deemed to be finished.

RELATIONSHIP BETWEEN MELODY AND HARMONY

As we discussed earlier in the chapter, there are many ways to approach music composition. Whether you start with a melodic idea, a progression of chords, or some other technique, the relationship between the melody and harmony is an important concept to consider. In this section we will consider ways of coming up with an appropriate harmonic progression. I would interject one caveat at this point: though most popular music clearly revolves around traditional harmonic and melodic relationships, most prominent composers utilize composition techniques that go beyond this traditional approach. You may want to investigate composition text books that cover advanced topics such as atonal music, serialism, impressionism, and the like.

Before you start experimenting with chords, it is generally advisable to listen to the melody and try to determine a key center and tonality: does the melody sound like it is in a specific major or minor key? Sometimes this is an easy question to answer. However, some melodies will not imply a specific tonality. In these cases it is a good idea to use what I like to call *descriptive composition*. With descriptive composition, try to describe the type of effect or sound you wish to achieve: happy, sad, mournful, joyous, etc. Each of these terms may help to determine the type of harmonic setting that is most appropriate for a given melody. It is hard, for example, to make a major triad sound particularly mournful. By describing the effect, you can focus on specific ways to achieve the desired effect.

A trick that I find helpful to use when composing a harmonic progression is to consider the wide variety of harmonic choices available for a given note. In short, any note can be harmonized as a chord factor of at least twelve different chords. When you start to look at harmonic progressions in this way, you will realize that a given tonal center can move or modulate to almost any other key, even a distantly related key, in a graceful manner.

Figure 5.13 Twelve of the many possible harmonizations of the note C

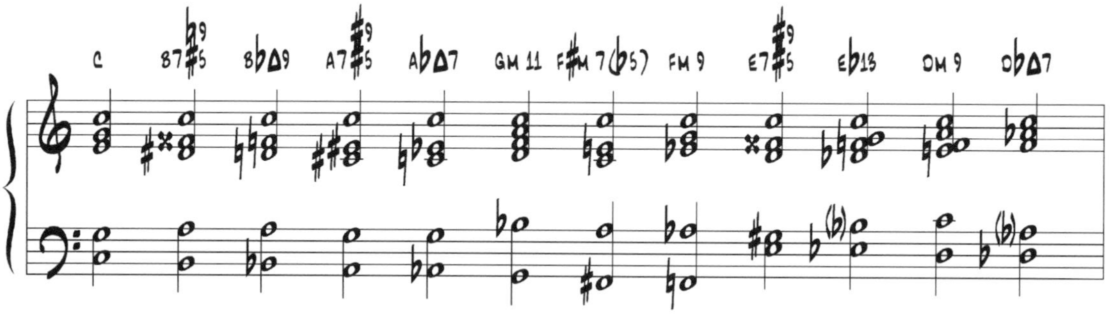

If you are having a hard time finding just the right chord for a particular musical situation, experiment with a variety of roots, as in the previous example. You may or may not find what you are looking for but, at the very least, you will expand your ears to some new options.

HARMONY

We live in an exciting time. As MIDI musicians we have access to all sorts of wonderful software and hardware tools that help us to work more efficiently. We also live in an era that is musically very tolerant. The modern audience can accept new ideas, sounds, and harmonies that are not traditional. Alas, with so many musical choices available to us, how do we narrow the choices to a manageable level? I find it helpful to categorize musical choices (particularly harmonic ones) into two categories: traditional and nontraditional. As you compose a MIDI sequence you can save yourself innumerable headaches by using *descriptive composition* as a problem-solving tool. As you experiment with chord choices ask yourself if the chord you are looking for is "stock," that is to say, should the chord sound natural or familiar to the listener? If the answer is yes, applying some simple theoretical principles can help you to quickly find a possible solution. If the answer is no, descriptive composition can still be helpful in determining what chord to use in a given situation.

An example might be helpful at this point: imagine that you are composing a new song and have run into a problem. You are currently in the key of C major and the melody note is a C. You would like to move to E flat major but are having trouble finding a graceful way to move to the new tonal center. By using the tip from Figure 5.3, you might realize that the note C could function as the fifth of an F minor chord. Because F minor is the ii chord in the key of E flat, a simple ii-V-I progression could be one possible solution. Now let's say that you decide that the chord progression should move directly to a minor tonality in order to provide a more suitable setting for the words. By describing the quality of chord (a minor chord in this case), you can narrow the choices to a manageable level. What minor chords include the note C as a chord factor? Though an A minor, C minor, or F minor might not be the best choice for this situation, you have effectively used theory to begin the process of solving this musical dilemma. Of course, we have not considered the possibility that the note C might simply be a passing tone, anticipation, or embellishment, but the point is that descriptive composition will provide many *potential* solutions to this problem.

We will begin our discussion of harmony by looking at some of the typical solutions that are used in many compositions.

UNSTABLE CHORDS

As the name implies, unstable chords seem to "want" to move: they can help you to get from point A to point B in a composition. Depending on the musical context, almost any chord can have moving tendencies, but the most common form of unstable chords are primary and secondary dominant seventh chords. Major-minor seventh chords contain an interval of an augmented fourth between the third of the chord and the seventh (a very unstable interval), therefore they have a built-in tendency to move. The most common movement for these types of chords is down a perfect fifth or up a perfect fourth.

Figure 5.14 Primary and secondary dominant seventh chords

If you want to increase the unstable tendencies of a harmonic progression, consider using applied dominant seventh chords. Say, for example, that you want to move from the key of C major to its relative minor, A minor. Although it would sound fine to move directly from C major to A minor, a major-minor seventh could be inserted here if the goal is to make the motion to A minor even stronger.

Figure 5.15 Using an E7 to get to A minor

The unstable tendency of the E7 chord in the previous example could be heightened even more by using an altered dominant instead of a simple major-minor seventh chord. Of course, musical context should always be the primary consideration when making these types of choices.

Figure 5.16 Using an altered dominant (E7alt. to A minor)

Diminished chords and minor-minor seventh chords also act as unstable chords. One of the most common examples involves using a diatonic ii7 chord to move to the dominant seventh. The dominant then moves to a I chord to finish the progression. This so-called "two-five-one" progression is common in pop and jazz music.

Figure 5.17 ii-V-I progression

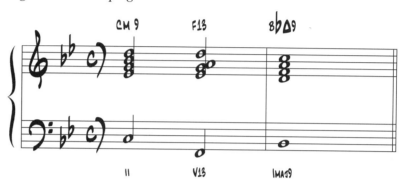

STATIC CHORDS

I like to use the term *static* to describe consonant chords. A consonant chord is a chord that is characterized by a lack of motion. Simple major and minor triads are the most common form of static chords. Obviously, a tonic major or minor chord will provide the least amount of motion in a chord progression. Depending on the musical context, even a moving chord such as a major-minor seventh or minor-minor seventh can sound static. Many blues progressions employ this concept. In some forms of blues, even the tonic chord may be a major minor seventh.

Figure 5.18 Major-minor seventh used as a static chord in blues

NEIGHBOR CHORDS

Neighbor chords are often used to provide interest in a progression. A neighboring tone is a note that is a step above or below a consonant tone. When you combine the concepts of neighbor tones and common tones you have a neighbor chord. The most common form of a neighbor chord is movement from I to IV and back to I. These chords serve to add motion to a static chord; they sound like an embellishment of the primary chord, not an actual change of chords.

Figure 5.19 Neighbor chord (C-F-C)

Making Music with Your Computer

As obvious as it sounds, any chord can work as a surprise chord if it is used in a situation that the listener does not expect. The most commonly used surprise chords are derived by selecting notes that are outside of a given tonal center. In the key of C major for example, an E flat major chord or A flat minor chord will provide this sort of effect.

Figure 5.20 Surprise progression

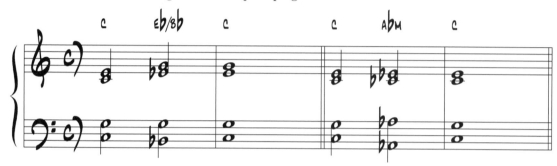

Chromatic mediant and submediant chords are often used for this type of effect. Consider using one of these chords if you intend to make a dramatic musical statement or just simply want to surprise the listener.

Figure 5.21 Chromatic mediant and submediant chords in C major

Another interesting surprise effect involves using a nontraditional resolution of the dominant seventh chord. In the key of C major, you would expect the dominant to move to tonic. If this chord moves to a location other than the tonic, the surprise effect is achieved.

Figure 5.22 Surprise resolution of a G7 in the key of C major

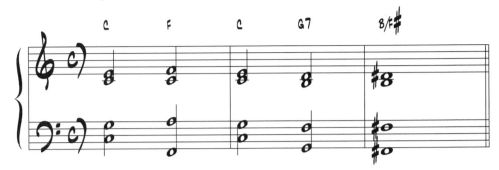

THE POIGNANT CHORD

I like to describe the use of a minor iv chord in a major key as being *poignant*. Though it is easy to overuse this chord, a surprising number of popular music songs utilize this sound. Depending on the musical context, this progression can be pretty or rather dated. Incidentally, traditional music theorists use the term *borrowed chord* to describe chords such as iv that have been borrowed from a parallel minor key. Note that if you are composing a piece that is in a minor key, you can also borrow chords from the parallel major key.

Figure 5.23 The poignant chord C-Am-Fmi6-C

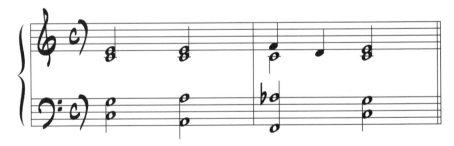

COMMON DIATONIC PROGRESSIONS

When making harmonic decisions it is often helpful to consider some of the many traditional progressions. Keep in mind that, although most compositions do not rely solely on common progressions of chords, these progressions are found in many well-known tunes as well as in traditional musical literature.

The ii-V-I progression I talked about earlier in the chapter is a prime example. In some compositions, ii-V-I's are used to create motion from one key center to another or simply to create motion within an existing tonal center.

Making Music with Your Computer

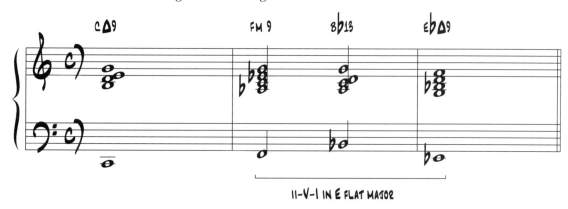

Figure 5.24 Using ii-V-I's to move to a new tonal center

II-V-I IN E FLAT MAJOR

The *turnaround* (sometimes called a *turnback*) is an extension of the ii-V-I concept. A common form of the turnaround utilizes other diatonic chords to create a sense of motion back to tonic. Turnarounds are often used in the last few bars of a tune to move the harmony back to tonic. Some well-known pop tunes are composed entirely around this simple turnaround. Can you think of an example? It is common to use either a I or iii chord as the first chord in a turnaround.

Figure 5.25 Diatonic turnaround

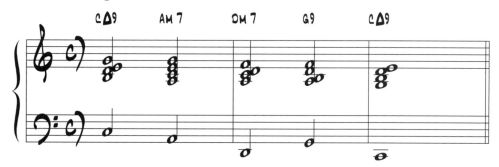

Another variation on the turnaround concept involves using secondary dominant chords instead of diatonic chords. This approach provides a stronger sense of motion than the diatonic version.

Figure 5.26 Using secondary dominant seventh chords in a turnaround

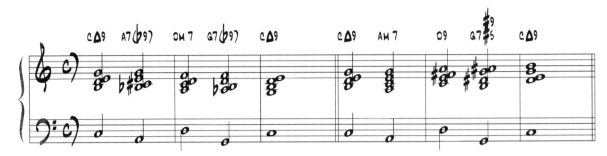

Two other progressions deserve mention in this section. Movement from the tonic to the IV chord or to vi, the relative minor are so common as to be almost clichéd. As you begin to analyze popular songs and compositions you will see that this harmonic motion is surprisingly common. Incidentally, movement to the IV chord in a major key has what I like to term a "feel-good" quality.

Figure 5.27 Relationship of I and vi, the relative minor

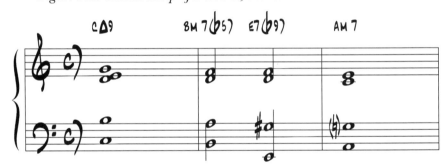

Figure 5.28 Movement from I to IV

Of course, many other harmonic progressions are also common. As you investigate progressions of chords, experiment with both diatonic and chromatic solutions. Obviously you shouldn't always use common solutions when you compose, but as you study and experiment with some of the common progressions, your ear will be that much closer to finding an appropriate chord for a given situation; whether that solution is stock or not is really up to you. As always, your ears should be the final judge. Many wonderful songs have been written that utilize nontraditional harmonic relationships.

LINEAR APPROACH

One of the most exciting concepts available to composers is the idea of linear technique. When using linear technique, consider the melodic tendencies of each of the voices in a progression of chords. Instead of relying solely on vertical chord structures, a linear approach provides a way to look at composition from the standpoint of counterpoint, or "melody against melody." Each of the notes or voices of a given progression may function as a melodically independent unit. When you think in linear terms, a whole world of possibilities is available to you as a composer. Often a melody and/or bass line may help you to determine a linear choice. In the next example, a number of linear solutions are presented for a common progression of chords. Notice how each of the inner voices retains an independent quality. These voices might approach an arrival point using chromatic or diatonic motion, embellishment, or even a jump. The important thing to remember is that each voice retains melodic freedom. The resulting harmonies are often not easily recognizable using traditional analysis, but to the ears of the listener, linear motion can be very pleasing.

Figure 5.29 Linear solutions Fsus4 to Gsus2

As you compose, it is often helpful to consider the formal structure of your work. Musical forms provide a way of looking at the big picture: where does the composition start, how does it develop, and where does it end? Though many composers utilize a freewheeling approach to form, I find that a knowledge of forms helps me solidify my approach to a given composition. Though I don't always start a composition with a well-defined form in mind, I often rely on forms when I run into a serious composition dilemma.

When evaluating the formal structure of a composition, it is helpful to remember that form is determined by the various sections of a piece. Traditionally, these musical sections were characterized by a modulation and/or change of thematic material. Keep in mind, however, that other musical elements such as a change of texture or even a contrast in orchestration could mark the major sections of a composition.

I should point out that a thorough discussion and analysis of musical forms would take an entire book. The comments in this section will be limited to a few of the most common formal structures. It would also be helpful to note that you should not approach the concept of form with a rigid attitude. The terms we use to describe musical forms simply identify common arrangements of musical ideas, but forms are not something you should rigidly adhere to.

Binary and ternary. The two fundamental forms of music are binary and ternary form. A binary form consists of two sections: AB. A typical binary composition starts in the tonic key and moves to a related key (such as the dominant) at the end of the first section. The second section continues with similar thematic material and returns to the tonic. Though it is common to see binary form described as AB, it is sometimes better to describe a binary form as AA[1] because the first and second sections of a binary composition are usually closely related.

Figure 5.30 Binary form

As the name implies, a ternary composition is comprised of three sections: ABA. Ternary forms contrast with binary in that each section of a ternary composition is usually a complete musical unit. Note that the A section may not modulate to a new key. Whereas the A and B sections of a binary composition are often closely related, the B section of a ternary composition usually contrasts with the A sections.

Figure 5.31 Ternary form

Rounded binary. If the second section of a binary composition consists of two subsections and some or all of the first theme returns (*recapitulates*) at the end of the piece, the composition is said to be in *rounded binary* form. Though rounded binary and ternary forms look very similar, the main distinction between the two is the end of the first A section. Remember that, in a ternary piece, each of the sections are self-contained. In a rounded binary composition, the A section will modulate to a new key.

Figure 5.32 Rounded binary form

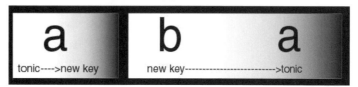

Sonata form. The term sonata can be confusing. On the one hand, a sonata refers to a multimovement composition. On the other hand, sonata form refers to a single-movement form that was developed by Haydn and his contemporaries. On the surface, a sonata form looks much like a ternary form (ABA) but, unlike ternary, the sonata form consists of several sub-sections. The A section (usually called the *exposition*) consists of two themes. A *bridge* is used as a transition between these primary themes. Note that the second theme of the exposition is generally in a closely related key. After the exposition, a development section follows in which the composer manipulates the primary themes from the exposition. Composers such as Beethoven often included new thematic material in the development section as well. A *retransition* is used to move the composition back to a restatement of the first section. This final restatement is called the *recapitulation*. The recapitulation stays in the tonic key (note that the second theme is now transposed to the tonic key) and may be followed by a concluding section called the *coda*.

Figure 5.33 Sonata form

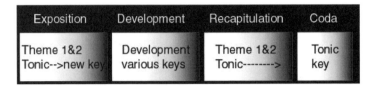

Rondo. In a rondo, the primary theme returns again and again. Classical theorists use the terms *refrain* and *episodes* to describe the primary and contrasting themes in a rondo form. Common forms of rondo are ABACADA, ABACA, and ABACABA. As you might imagine, rondo form is most successful if the A section is truly interesting!

Figure 5.34 Rondo form

Song form. Hundreds of American popular songs utilize the song form: AABA. In most cases, the second A section modulates to the key of the bridge (B). Though some theorists describe the song form as a variation of a ternary form (ABA), the term is not really appropriate because of the repetition of the initial theme.

Figure 5.35 Song form

Theme and variations. In a theme and variations composition an initial theme is varied many times (typically with a change of mode, tempo, meter and the like). The form of a theme and variations composition is $AA^1A^2A^3A^4$, etc. Though theme and variations are not common in most styles of popular music, many jazz recordings fall into this category because jazz performers will typically state the melody of a tune and improvise many variations without changing the underlying formal structure of the piece.

Figure 5.36 Theme and variations

Larger forms. Large-scale compositions fall into one of two categories: single or compound works. Single compositions are self-contained. A compound composition will contain several movements (e.g., a piano sonata may contain a sonata form movement and a rondo movement).

Through composed and narrative music. In the nineteenth century composers started experimenting with writing songs where new material was used for each stanza. The benefit of this approach is that the music can be changed to better support the words. You might think of a through composed composition as a planned improvisation. Themes are presented and manipulated in a nontraditional way. In a similar vein, a narrative composition attempts to tell a story. Though some wonderful symphonic works have been written that can be described as narrative, a narrative composition can be difficult to pull off because of the absence of a recapitulation or restatement of themes. It is easy to lose a listener without at least a minimal amount of repetition. In a narrative composition, the presentation and transformation of motives provides a unifying element.

USING FORMS

I find it helpful to approach the concept of forms in an abstract way. As you probably noticed, all of the forms we have looked at boil down to the concept of a beginning, middle, and end. As you sequence and compose, you may find it helpful to evaluate your composition using these models. I often find that, even if I haven't started a composition with a well-defined form in mind, most compositions will naturally fall into one of these categories.

If the composition seems to wander or perhaps gets overly repetitive, an evaluation of formal structure will often yield a solution that better clarifies the composition. Of course forms can also be a great source of inspiration: use your sequencer to create a rondo or write two themes and try to mold them into a sonata form.

SUMMARY

In this chapter we have learned about many of the helpful theoretical tools that composers use. If the topic of music composition interests you, I suggest that you explore additional resources to learn about other compositional concepts such as atonal music, serialism, impressionism, minimalism, leitmotives, and the like. Granted, we have only scratched the surface, but I think that you will find the concepts of harmony, melodic devices, and formal structures to be helpful as you make composing and sequencing decisions. There may be times, however, when the muse still does not strike. Following is a list of tips to help to get those creative juices flowing. The important thing to remember is to listen to music, perform with other musicians, develop a musical vocabulary, and experiment like crazy.

SEQUENCING STARTERS

- Create a melody to go with lyrics or a poem.
- Create a sequence that conveys a specific mood such as joy, sorrow, or pain.
- Compose a melody or harmonic progression in a mode (e.g., dorian, phyrgian, lydian, etc.).
- Compose a melody that utilizes common melodic embellishments such as changing tones or chromatic approach tones.
- Compose a motive that only uses three or four notes (focus on rhythmic variations).
- Create a motive using a simple one-bar rhythmic motive (focus on melodic variations).
- Create a melody that uses a primary melodic motive: interval or specific grouping of notes.
- Create a new chord progression for a given melody.
- Create a composition using the pentatonic scale (i.e., the interval pattern of black notes on the piano).
- Create a musical setting or texture using quartal (chords built in fourths) or quintal (chords built in fifths) structures.
- Create a harmonic progression that moves to a distant key.

- Compose a melody to fit over an ostinato (a repetitive pattern).
- Listen to a recording and try to emulate some of the musical vocabulary from the album.
- Create a sequence for an unusual grouping of instruments: zither, flute, bagpipe, and koto for example.
- Compose a *style* piece: a composition that sounds like a classical sonata, piano rag, or other such genre.
- Create a sequence that represents a visual image such as a river, storm, garden, etc. (impressionism).
- Create a harmonic progression and sing (then sequence) a suitable melody.
- Experiment with chromaticism: chromatic mediants and submediants, surprise chords, borrowed chords, and the like.
- Create a sequence using a well-defined form such as rondo, binary, or sonata form.
- Compose a piece utilizing the concept of leitmotives (i.e., combine several motives that musically represent a character in a film, book, or opera).
- Use a sequencer to create a minimalist composition (i.e., start with a simple motive and cut, paste, loop, and offset to create a variety of repetitions).
- Create a motive and use the sequencer to transform it: retrograde (backwards), inversion (mirror image), retrograde inversion (upside-down and backwards).
- Use the sequencer to create a four- or eight-bar round (i.e., layer the melody in different tracks starting on subsequent bars).
- Create a sequence using pandiatonic technique (i.e., the composition is in a well-defined key but the notes do not function in the traditional harmonic way).

Real-World Arranging

As computer musicians, a natural extension of our creative work involves arranging material for both electronic and acoustic instruments. In fact, the very essence of sequencing involves arranging decisions: what sounds to use, range and dynamics, style, and harmonic considerations. When sequencing, the lines between composition, arranging, and orchestration become blurred. It is often advisable to rethink a sequence from the perspective of an arranger to come up with the best possible musical statement. Though there are many interpretations of the word *arrange,* in this context I will talk about ways to take an existing composition or sequenced idea and mold it into a complete musical statement.

Arranging involves many elements: orchestration considerations, voicing of harmonic structures, stylization of melody and accompaniment, and elements of form such as introductions, interludes, and endings. Ideally, a successful arranger must distance himself from details of the composition and consider the bigger picture. Most of the suggestions in this chapter will enhance the decisions you make while sequencing. You will also find many techniques that will prove valuable should you be asked to provide an arrangement for traditional instruments or voice—a situation that most MIDI musicians will find themselves in whether playing with a band or producing music for radio, television, or movies. In addition, you will learn many techniques that will apply to playing keyboard instruments or guitar. On a personal note, I have found that, as my arranging chops improve, these improvements apply directly to my playing. In a nutshell, the more solutions and concepts you understand as a computer musician, the more effective and efficient you will be.

One additional word of advice: though the suggestions in this chapter are based on traditional (i.e., acoustic) arranging techniques, these concepts will easily apply to a sequencing environment. Whether you are striving to create an orchestral-sounding score or writing for square wave, sine wave, and lute, the concepts presented in this chapter can help to make your sequences more musical.

I find it helpful to think of arranging in terms of choices. The more choices you have at your disposal as an arranger or composer, the better prepared you will be to find solutions to musical problems. It is easy to get caught up in thinking that the most interesting arrangements and compositions are the ones that utilize new material. In fact, just the opposite is true. I always like to relate music to other arts such as painting or literature. Consider some of the great American authors: Hemingway, Steinbeck, Faulkner, or James Fenimore Cooper. None of these authors is well known for using obscure or obtuse words. Each of these authors was able to put ordinary words together in an extraordinary and poetic way. As arrangers, our goal is often the same. Some of the best arrangers and composers of our time have used a fairly ordinary musical vocabulary. Does this mean you should avoid expanding the boundaries of our musical vocabulary? Of course not. As an artist you do need to find a balance between familiarity and inventiveness. How much inventiveness is too much? That is a question only you can decide. Just remember to consider the listener.

If you have ever attended a college music theory class you know that musical theorists love to think in terms of rules. I prefer to think of the concepts presented in this chapter as suggestions. If you understand the stock solutions to typical arranging situations, you will be that much closer to finding your own voice. By all means, experiment. Go out there and break some rules!

Functional harmony. One of the most common tasks we face as arrangers is the question of harmony: what chords to use, how to voice a melody in four parts, what to do if a note in the melody does not belong to a given chord. Let's begin by looking at some of the underlying harmonic concepts at work in most popular and classical music. Just remember that theory comes after the fact. Composers and arrangers are continually expanding the boundaries of our musical language.

One of the most important concepts relating to popular music theory involves the relationship of tonic and dominant or dominant seventh chords. In any key, the dominant or V chord has a tendency to resolve to the tonic or I chord. To see how this works, play the following sequence of chords.

Figure 6.1 Dominant to tonic relationship

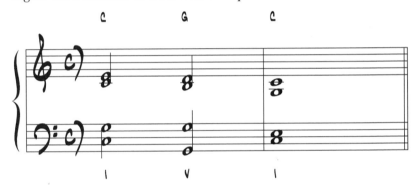

The tendency for dominant chords to want to resolve is even stronger when a seventh is added. Although you will find variations, the most common form of a dominant seventh is the major-minor seventh chord. Play the following example to see how this progression differs from the previous one.

Figure 6.2 Dominant seventh to tonic relationship

The important thing to remember is that root movement down a perfect fifth or up a perfect fourth is strong. Our ear tends to hear this as a natural progression. To see just how strong this progression is, play the following example, which utilizes a surprise resolution. Though the effect of this progression is unusual, it shows just how powerful the dominant to tonic relationship is.

Figure 6.3 Surprise resolution of a dominant seventh

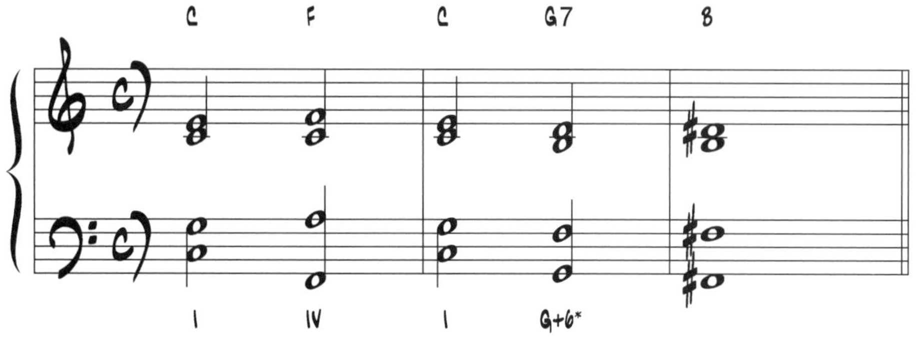

The German augmented sixth (spelled as a V7 here) is a chord that was common in the Classical and Romantic eras. This example illustrates a typical use of this chord: the chord, in this context, moves us to a second inversion B chord.

These tendencies can be used in an arrangement or composition through the process of *tonicization*. Tonicization involves using a dominant or dominant seventh chord to *tonicize* a temporary tonic. In many cases it is possible to modulate from one key to another or move to a distantly related chord by simply inserting a temporary dominant before the chord you wish to arrive at. Say, for example, that you wish to move from an F major chord to A flat major (a distantly related key). Within the context of your arrangement it may sound good to simply move to A flat major without any preparation. If this progression sounds unusual, try inserting a temporary dominant or dominant seventh chord.

Figure 6.4 Tonicization using a secondary dominant

It is often possible to change keys using only a single tonicizing chord. It is even possible to tonicize a tonicizing chord, as in the next example.

Figure 6.5 Using two secondary dominants to change key

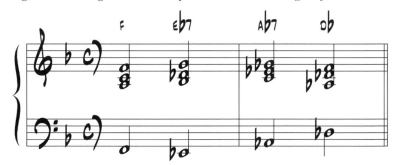

Although the dominant to tonic relationship is very strong, diminished chords can also be used to establish a temporary tonic. The diminished seventh chord built on the *leading tone* works as a tonicizing chord. To find the leading-tone-diminished, build a diminished triad or diminished seventh chord whose root is one half-step below the chord you wish to tonicize.

Figure 6.6 Using a leading tone diminished to tonicize

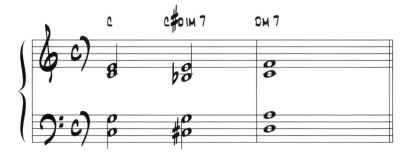

Diminished chords are used infrequently in popular music and jazz. In most contexts they tend to sound antiquated. As you will see later in the chapter, diminished chords can sound great if used in the right way.

Another consideration involves the relationship of chords in a harmonic progression. A simple rule is that diatonic chords (i.e., all the tones of the chord are found in a given key or mode) tend to sound the most natural. Harmony that is chromatic (i.e., contains notes outside the key) will tend to sound foreign to the ear. I am not implying that you shouldn't use chromatic progressions, just understand that chromaticism should not be treated haphazardly. To better understand the concept of diatonic or chromatic harmony, play through the next example. In this case, the A flat would be considered to be a chromatic chord because it contains notes that are out of the key.

Figure 6.7 Diatonic progression vs. chromatic progression

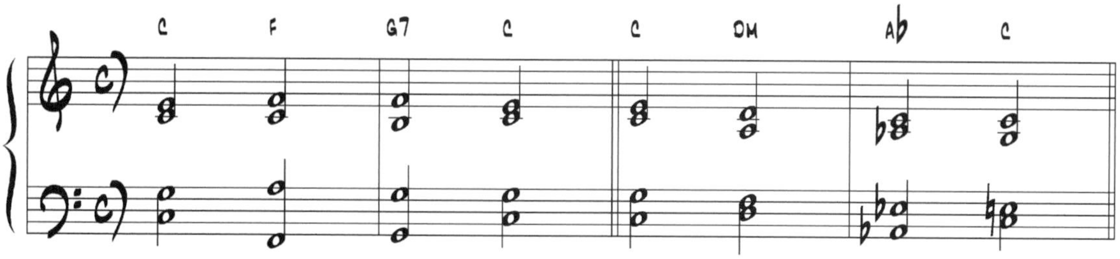

Keep these principles in mind when making choices as an arranger or composer: diatonic harmony tends to sound the most natural, chromatically based harmony tends to "jump out" at the listener.

VOICE LEADING

Classical theorists often emphasize the importance of voice leading. Though voice-leading principles are not rigidly used in popular music, an understanding of these concepts can go a long way in making your music sound better. In a worst-case scenario, poor voice leading can actually wreck a good chord progression.

Although it is possible to devote years of study to the principles of good voice leading, most of the important "rules" can be summarized as follows:

- Avoid jumping around in root position.
- If two chords contain the same note, it often makes sense to keep that tone common to both chords.
- The seventh factor of a dominant seventh tends to want to resolve to the third of a tonic chord.
- The leading tone in a key tends to want to resolve up to tonic.
- Avoid large leaps; if two tones are near to one another in a progression, it usually makes sense to use minimal motion.

Although this list is by no means comprehensive, these simple suggestions will help you to create pleasing voice leading in your sequences. You will find that, with a little work, good voice leading will become a part of your everyday sequencing technique.

Figure 6.8 Poor voice leading

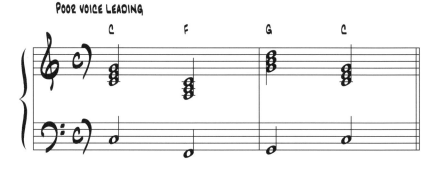

Figure 6.9 Good voice leading

Of course rules are meant to be broken, so remember that if it sounds good to your ear, it probably is good.

A common scenario for arrangers involves voicing a melody for two or more instruments. In the following sections we will look at techniques for voicing a melody from two to five parts. There are a number of goals to keep in mind when doing this type of harmonization:

- The combination of voices should clearly imply the underlying harmonic progression.
- Each of the supporting voices should have a pleasing melodic contour.
- Harmonizations should be appropriate for the style of the music (e.g., extended and altered chords are not usually found in rock music).

Tip: A thorough understanding of chord groups and their related scales will be essential to effectively harmonize a melody in two or more parts. If you have not done so already, be sure to read the relevant chapters on popular music theory and chord-scale relationships.

TWO-PART HARMONIZATION

We will begin by looking at some simple two-voice harmonizations. Note that with each of the examples in this section, the melody will always be on top. Though it is possible to score a melody in a lower voice, the most common scenario involves placing the melody in the top voice. Keep in mind that melodic harmonization may not necessarily be the main melody of the song. It could also be a counter-melody voiced in two or more parts or even a background horn riff.

One of the best ways to voice a melody in two parts is to derive the second voice from an appropriate scale. If the chord of the moment is an Am7, we know that one possible scale choice would be an A dorian scale (or G major if you prefer to think that way). In the following example, the second voice is always a diatonic third below the melody. I use the term diatonic here in reference to the underlying scale: each of the notes in the second voice comes from an A dorian scale. These notes are diatonic to the mode.

Figure 6.10 Two-part diatonic harmonization using A dorian.

It is also possible to arrange this melody in two parts using chromatic tones. Remember that, when referring to chromaticism, we are not necessarily talking about half-steps. Any musical passage that contains notes that are outside of the key, mode, or underlying scale can be said to be chromatic. In this instance, we will start with the same interval (major third) as with the last example. The difference here is that this major third interval will remain constant. The E flat in this example is chromatic: it not found in the A dorian mode. This passage does give an interesting bluesy effect.

Figure 6.11 Chromatic harmonization in two parts

In the previous examples, either a major or minor third interval was used for the second voice, but many other choices are possible. I find it helpful to think of intervals in terms of groups of related sounds. In the following example, the intervals are grouped according to function. Thirds and sixths have a similar quality or effect. Fourths and fifths are also similar. It is interesting to note that each of these groups are simply derived from inverting a given interval. If you invert a perfect fourth, you end up with a perfect fifth. It makes sense then that these groups of intervals provide a similar type of effect to the listener. In the next example, the intervals progress from left to right, with the leftmost intervals being most consonant, and intervals on the right sounding dissonant. It is interesting to note that the term dissonance is subjective: many composers would place fourths and fifths before thirds and sixths in this diagram.

Figure 6.12 Interval groups

UNISON OCTAVE THIRD SIXTH FOURTH FIFTH SECOND SEVENTH TRITONE

Tip: When selecting an interval, consider the type of effect you are after. Thirds and sixths work well for "pretty" melodies. Fourths and fifths tend to sound more modern. Seconds and sevenths can be helpful for creating dissonant or humorous effects.

FOUR-PART HARMONIZATION

Four-part harmonization is perhaps the easiest of all melodic harmonizations. Why? With only four notes it is easy to imply any chord, even a complex one. As you will see, with a few simple guidelines it is possible to easily harmonize a melody in four parts.

One way to approach a four-part harmonization is to select chords from a related chord group, as in the following example.

Figure 6.13 Four-part harmonization using the tonic major chord group

In this example, the chord of the moment is a C6. Our goal is to harmonize the melody so that the harmonic implication of the measure retains a tonic major quality. In this case the note B is not a part of C6, but it is a note found in Cmaj7, one of the other chords in the group. Although this is not necessarily the best way to harmonize the passage, this approach can be very effective. We will look at another possible approach later in the chapter.

What if the given chord contains more than four notes, as with a C13 or C9 chord? One possible solution to this problem involves using rootless voicings. A rootless voicing is, as you might guess, a chord that does not contain a root. Rootless voicings work because, in most cases, the root will be played by the bass.

Remember that we are talking about four-note harmonization of a melody; it is still possible to include bass and rhythm tracks. Even without a bass part, rootless voicings will tend to work: the underlying harmony can still be implied by the musical context of the progression.

Figure 6.14 Rootless voicing of C9

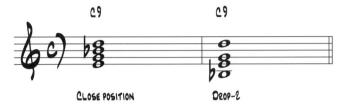

As I mentioned earlier, any chord (even a complex one) can be easily pared down to four parts. The following tips can help you to construct four-part voicings:

- To add a ninth, omit the root.
- To add a thirteenth, omit the fifth.
- To add an eleventh, omit the fifth.

With these simple guidelines it is easy to voice a chord using only four notes. Note that these tips are also helpful for voicing chords on the keyboard or guitar. The following example demonstrates how to omit notes in complex chords. Remember that our goal here is to find a voicing that best implies the underlying harmony using only four notes.

Figure 6.15 Implying complex chords using four notes

What if you want to harmonize a melody or background line using four parts but the underlying harmony is triadic? One possible solution is to double the melody in the lowest voice. Another option might be to use linear techniques—visualize one or more of the voices as an independent melodic line. Yet another solution is to place the root in the lowest voice.

Figure 6.16 Four-part harmonization of a triad

FIVE-PART HARMONIZATION

As with four-part voicings, five-part voicings are fairly easy to implement because almost any chord can be easily implied with just five notes. One common application of five-part voicings is for background pads. It is common to use the root in the bass, but inversions can also be effective.

Figure 6.17 Five-part pad voicings

When voicing simple triadic structures in five parts, it is common to double the top note of the chord. It is also common to double the root when voicing these types of chords but doubling of the third or fifth will also work.

Figure 6.18 Five-part harmonization of simple triads

Another common five-part technique are "Supersax" style voicings. To create a Supersax style voicing, start by creating a four-part harmonization in close position. Simply double the melody note one octave lower for an effective five-part harmonization.

Figure 6.19.1 Supersax voicing

Another common variation is closely related to the last example. After creating a close-position five-part harmonization, drop the second note from the top of each voicing down one octave.

Figure 6.19.2 Supersax voicing (drop two)

THREE-PART HARMONIZATION

I find that three-part harmonizations can be difficult to handle. On the one hand, many chords can be effectively voiced using only three notes. On the other hand, it is difficult to achieve a consistent texture when voicing in three parts. Before we look at some examples of three-part harmony, it would be helpful to look at common three-part structures.

There are three structures that are commonly used for three-part harmonizations: tertian (voicings built in thirds), quartal/quintal (voicings built in fourths or fifths), and clusters (chords built using thirds and seconds).

Figure 6.20 Common three-part structures (tertian, quartal/quintal, cluster)

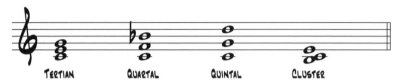

A helpful way to implement these structures is to visualize the great variety of chords would contain the notes of the given structure. A C triad, for example, can be found in the following chords: C, Am7, Dm11, Bb7+11, Fmaj9, Eb13b9, Gb7b9,b5, Gm13, and Abmaj7+5. This list might seem a bit intimidating, but I have found that, with a little experimentation, it is fairly easy to find suitable three-note voicings. Following is an example of a few such choices.

Figure 6.21 Various three-part harmonizations

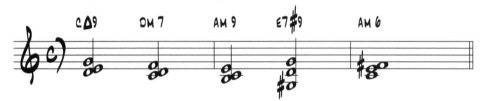

When creating a three-part harmonization, it is generally advisable to be consistent with the approach to vertical structures (e.g., don't haphazardly mix quartal, tertian, and cluster structures). Notice how tertian structures are used to harmonize most of the following melody. In this example, a quartal structure is used to provide a better vertical harmonization of the dominant.

Figure 6.22 Tertian harmonization (with quartal dominant chord)

A common problem that arises when harmonizing a melody in three, four, or five parts occurs when one or more notes of the melody is not a chord tone. In the next figure, the note C does not belong to the tonic major chord group. In other words, it is difficult, if not impossible, to make this note "fit" as a chord tone of any of the tonic major chords. There are a number of common solutions to this arranging problem.

TONICIZATION

If you will recall from earlier in the chapter, tonicization involves inserting a temporary dominant or leading tone diminished chord to *tonicize* a given chord. Quite often, a nonchord tone can be harmonized as a tonicizing chord. Many options are available: "blues" dominant, altered dominant, leading-tone diminished, or even substitute chords that we will talk about in a moment. In the example that follows, the nonchord tone C will be handled using a variety of tonicizing techniques.

Figure 6.23 Voicing a nonchord tone using tonicization

Although the preceding tonicization example digresses significantly from the G6 chord, the tonic-major quality is maintained. The diversion simply leads us back to tonic-major chord. Remember that the key is to think of either a V7 or viidim7 of the chord you are attempting to harmonize: D7 or F#dim tonicizes any G chord, A7 or C#dim7 tonicizes any D chord.

Keep in mind that this technique will not work if the tonicizing chord lasts for a substantial amount of time. Your ear will guide you in this case, but a general rule of thumb is that longer note values such as a half note or dotted half will need to be voiced vertically.

HALF-STEP SHIFT

A half-step shift can provide an interesting solution to a nonchord tone. To implement this technique, visualize a chord that is one half step away from the given chord. For example, if the chord of the moment is a G6, see if the given melody note will work as a chord factor of either Ab6 or F#6.

Figure 6.24 Half-step shift

DIATONIC PLANING

Diatonic planing provides an elegant solution to many nonchord tone harmonizations. To use this technique, carefully consider your arrival points (i.e., the notes that you plan to harmonize vertically). Once you have identified the arrival tones, simply plane each voice through the given mode. This technique will work for any type of chord, even altered dominant or tonic-minor structures.

Figure 6.25 Diatonic planing

CHROMATIC PLANING

Chromatic planing is similar to diatonic planing but, in this case, intermediate structures may include notes outside of the given key or mode. As with the diatonic planing example, be sure to identify melodic arrival points: this technique will only work if the underlying harmonic progression is still clear to the listener. Though chromatic planing can sound unusual, I have found this technique to be very effective.

Figure 6.26 Chromatic planing

We have already talked about linear concepts in Chapter 5, "Music Composition," but it makes sense to revisit this concept as it relates to melodic harmonizations. When approaching a harmonization with linear technique, consider each chord tone as an independent melodic unit. Providing that each of the voices moves in an independent and melodically pleasing fashion, the harmonization will generally work (even if it does not make sense when analyzed vertically). Note that in the next example the upper and lower voices move in contrary motion.

Figure 6.27 Linear approach

CHORD SUBSTITUTIONS

Jazz musicians, in particular, have an affinity for using all sorts of interesting chord substitutions and reharmonizations. Though traditional chord substitutions are used less frequently in popular music, an understanding of these concepts can be a great aid in solving composition and arranging problems. You can hear examples of these chords used in a wide variety of styles.

In Chapter 5, I presented the idea that any tone may be harmonized as a chord factor of at least twelve different chords (see Figure 5.13). This concept is central to our discussion of substitute chords: for any melody note there will be several potential chords that would work with the given note. Though several common substitute chords are often used, many of the most elegant solutions will not fall neatly into a substitution category. That is to say, these solutions depend on the musical context, not substitution "rules."

In my estimation, the goal of reharmonizing a chord progression is to accentuate a key note or phrase in an arrangement. Arrangers often reharmonize songs to provide a suitable setting for their concept of the tune. Avoid the temptation to overuse these sounds. Though substitutions can be very effective, as with any musical device, substitutions will lose their effectiveness if used too frequently.

One of the most common substitute chords is the so called *tritone substitute*. In short, you can consider using tritone substitution for any dominant or temporary dominant seventh chord. The actual substitute chord is found by counting up three whole steps (hence the term *tritone*) from the root of the dominant. Tritone substitution works because the third and seventh of the dominant are enharmonically equivalent to the seventh and third of the substitute chord.

Figure 6.28 Tritone substitute

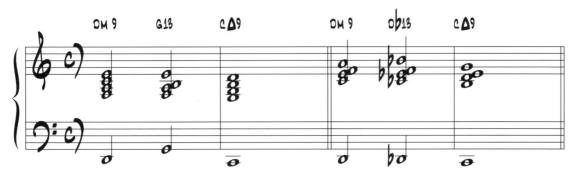

MINOR-THIRD SUBSTITUTION

Though many musicians refer to minor-third substitution, the term is not very appropriate. This relatively rare form of substitution is really a reharmonization technique: it will only work in places where the melody is appropriate for the substitution chords. A common implementation of this technique involves transposing both the ii and V chords up a minor third at a ii-V-I cadence.

Figure 6.29 Minor-third substitution

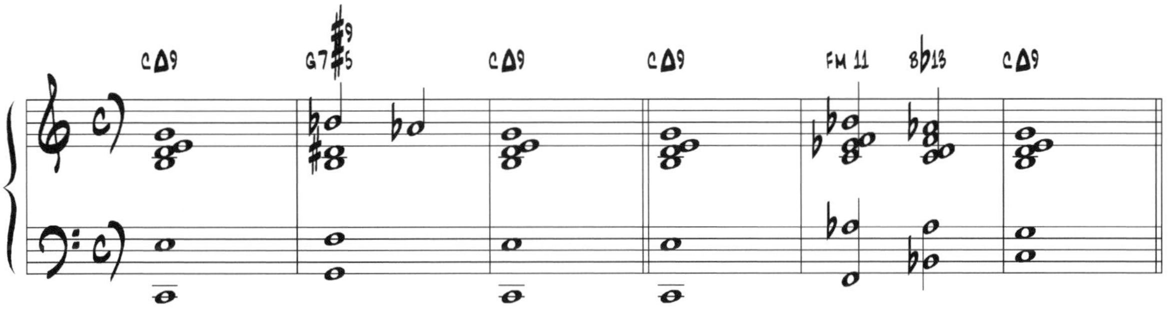

In a diatonic scale, alternate chords share two or more common tones. In a C major scale for example, Cmaj7 and Em7 share three common tones. It often makes sense to make diatonic substitutions when you wish to retain the underlying function of a chord but vary the progression of chords (e.g., use IV-V instead of ii-V, or iii-vi instead of I-vi).

Figure 6.30 Diatonic substitution (turnaround)

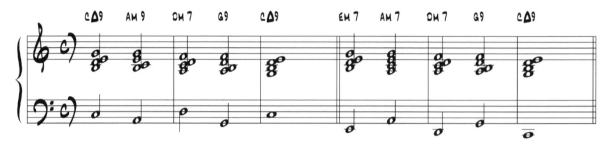

CHORD MUTATION

Classical theorists use the term chord mutation to refer to a chord that mutates over time (i.e., notes of the chord change, altering the quality of the chord). With regard to substitution, I use the term mutation to reflect a common arranging technique. If a sequence of chords functions in a predictable way, arrangers will sometimes change the quality of chord while retaining the underlying root movement. I found a striking example of this technique in the Chopin *Mazurka, Opus 24, No. 1.* Chopin substitutes a major-major seventh chord for a traditional dominant seventh chord in this piece, and the effect is very unusual. The next example illustrates a common modern-day version of the technique.

Figure 6.31 Variation on tritone substitution

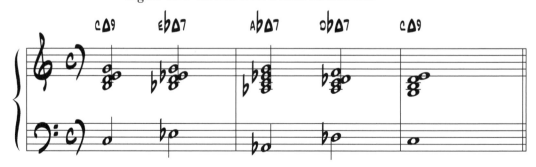

DIMINISHED CHORD SUBSTITUTION

As I mentioned earlier in the chapter, diminished chords can sound dated, but they are sometimes used for linear substitution. A common example involves substituting a diminished chord for a major-major seventh chord. This technique works because the inner voices move in a linear fashion; the resulting diminished chord is simply an embellishment of the underlying major chord.

Figure 6.32 Diminished chord used to embellish a major-major seventh chord

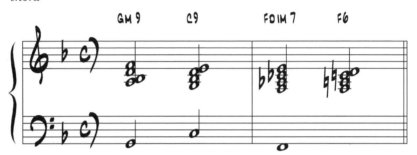

Tip: Diminished chords are also used as passing chords. They often function as passing chords between the ii and iii chords in a major key (either ascending or descending).

STYLIZING A MELODY

A key consideration when creating an arrangement is the treatment of the melody. Let's use something familiar: "Happy Birthday." I find it helpful to consider the underlying "groove" as a first step in stylizing a melody. Though "Happy Birthday" is clearly a waltz, the melody could work fine if we stylize it for a bossa nova groove as in the next example.

Figure 6.33.1 "Happy Birthday" bossa nova

In a similar vein, this tune could also work as a swing tune or even a funk melody. Obviously there are no steadfast rules but do consider changing rhythms and articulations in a way that is appropriate for the given musical context. The next example is a not-too-serious swing version of the tune.

Figure 6.33.2 Swing version of "Happy Birthday"

STRIVING FOR CONSISTENCY

When I arrange music, I strive for consistency. Though the term is not easily defined when applied to music, a consistent arrangement is one that makes sense to the listener. Evaluate your arrangement on several levels. Does the harmony work in a convincing way? Do voicings relate to one another? Are substitutions used to accentuate the arrangement, or do they distract the listener? Is the melody appropriately stylized for the given musical context? Does the introduction and ending make sense in context of the entire arrangement? Though it would be impossible to quantify these concepts into a set of rules, let your ear guide you when making these types of decisions. As you work, be sure that the various components of the arrangement such as form, melody, dynamics, articulations, orchestration, and harmony work together to create a unified musical statement.

CONSIDERATIONS OF FORM

One of the most important considerations facing an arranger is the issue of form. Arrangements that tend to work best provide subtle variations of form that keep the listener interested. As you listen to music, evaluate the music from the standpoint of form. You will find that good arrangers are not afraid to use repetition. Arrangers will often use devices such as interludes or modulations to keep the music interesting to the listener. The following suggestions may be helpful as you evaluate the form of your arrangement.

Introductions. Though it is certainly not necessary to include an introduction in an arrangement, introductions can be helpful in that they help to set the "vibe" of the arrangement. An introduction may provide the arranger with motivic material that may be repeated later in the arrangement. Though there are as many introductions as there are compositions, most provide the following characteristics:

- Introductions set the mood of the arrangement.
- Introductions draw the listener into the arrangement.
- Introductions often establish the tonal center.
- Introductions often provide motivic material for an interlude or ending.

Interludes. Interludes are often used to provide variation between the sections of an arrangement. Arrangers will often insert an interlude between choruses of a song or to provide a vamp for a solo. I find that it is often helpful to create interludes that provide a textural change: if the preceding section of music is dynamically loud, a soft bass and drum vamp or stop-time section can be very effective.

Endings. Obviously, all arrangements must end. Your approach to the ending will have much to do with the success of the arrangement. Arrangers will often utilize material from an introduction or interlude in the ending. This approach is helpful when you want to give a sense of symmetry to the arrangement. Though the listener might not be aware of it, they will appreciate the sense of order that comes from reusing material in the arrangement. In contrast, some arrangements benefit by the addition of new material such as a key change, tempo change, or ending riff. In most cases, you will want to set up the ending in a deliberate way so that the ending does not catch the listener unawares. A dynamic change or restatement of a few bars of the tune is a common way to set up the ending.

Avoiding "chunks." Earlier in the chapter I stated that a consistent arrangement is one that makes sense to the listener. With that in mind, it is sometimes helpful to blur the boundaries between the sections of an arrangement. Though sudden changes can be very effective, you will probably want to avoid making the arrangement overly sectionalized. For example, imagine that you are sequencing a funk tune and wish to add a saxophone background figure on the bridge. Consider inserting the saxophones in the last bar or two of the chorus. An ascending scale or repetitive figure could help to connect these two sections of the piece.

Creating interest. If your goal is to keep the listener's attention, you will want to evaluate the textures in your arrangement. Static textures, while appropriate for some musical settings, will tend to tire the listener. Arrangers often utilize contrasting textures in order to keep the interest of the audience. The following list illustrates some of the many musical elements that you can use to create effective texture changes:

- Dynamics
- Voicing (complex vs. simple)
- Rhythm (active vs. static rhythms)
- Range
- Tonality (major vs. minor, atonal, chromaticism, etc.)
- Harmonic progression
- Articulations

OTHER CONSIDERATIONS

Key changes. Key changes can provide a refreshing change in an arrangement. Though key changes can easily sound trite, a change of key in the final chorus of a song can provide a new level of intensity. Arrangers will often implement a key change in an unexpected place such as the last eight bars of the song or in the bridge.

Reusing material. Consider creating a musical hook that can provide a unifying element in your arrangement. It is common for arrangers to use a well-defined bass line or rhythmic pattern in an introduction, interlude, and ending.

Solo sections in popular music. Though most of us enjoy jamming, consider the audience as you compose and arrange. It is common to hear improvised solos on pop, rock and country recordings, but most recordings that get airplay do not include lengthy solo sections. Solo sections should be of a length that is appropriate for the genre. I also find it helpful to consider solos as they relate to texture: if your arrangement if fairly active rhythmically, consider creating a solo section that provides a change of texture (e.g., long tones and softer dynamic level).

Sequencing parts. When sequencing, a common mistake is to treat a group of instruments such as a saxophone section as a single keyboard sound. Even though it takes a bit more work, consider setting up several MIDI channels and sequence each voice separately. The slight imperfections in performance will provide a natural feel to the sequence. Of course, this approach will also allow you to select individual sounds for each voice and utilize sonic placement (panning, delay, and volume) that will add an additional level of realism. This is even true when using synthesized sounds.

Making a statement as an arranger. One of the things I enjoy about arranging is that it can be a fun challenge to create a new version of an existing song. When arranging a cover tune, consider making a personal musical statement with the arrangement. There are many tools at your disposal such as instrumentation, reharmonization, stylization and the like. Consider doing a techno version of "Amazing Grace" or creating a "soundscape" of "Lush Life"—there are many possibilities.

CONCLUSION

There are many things to consider when arranging a song: harmonic progression, reharmonization, stylization of the melody, orchestration, groove, formal structure, introductions, endings, modulations, and the like. As you explore the many options available to you as an arranger, keep an ear open to the big picture. Most successful arrangements provide a sense of continuity: the various sections work together to provide a cohesive whole.

One final note: consider working with other musicians. Collaboration can often yield new insights into the arranging and composing process. I also find it helpful to get feedback from friends and musicians as I work on a new arrangement or composition. Constructive criticism can go a long way in helping you to refine a musical statement in the form of a successful arrangement.

Electronic Orchestration

Orchestration involves the study of the various capabilities and ranges of instruments and the utilization of combinations of instruments. As computer musicians, the issue of orchestration is a dichotomy: on the one hand, synthesizers provide us with an almost unlimited palette of timbral possibilities. On the other hand, the use of synthesizers to realize traditional orchestrations generally provides marginal results. In this chapter, we will investigate the concept of orchestration from a traditional approach. While our approach is traditional, the reader is encouraged to explore the application of these techniques in a purely synthetic setting. Synthetic orchestration and sound design can be very rewarding from an artistic standpoint, but as computer musicians we are often called upon to create "realistic" orchestrations for jingles, industrials, and other commercial productions. Practicality of cost and expediency dictates that a significant portion of commercial productions are realized with synthesizers and computers. My goal is that, though the concepts presented in this chapter will help you to effectively use MIDI technology to realize traditional orchestrations, these same concepts will also enhance your approach to synthetic orchestration.

IS MIDI A SUITABLE SUBSTITUTE FOR ACOUSTIC INSTRUMENTS?

When we listen to a live acoustic music performance, something magical happens: we actually become physically connected to the music. As the performers use their instrument or voice to create sound vibrations, these vibrations interact with the hall, and our ears eventually translate these signals into something the brain recognizes as music. The inevitable question that arises in a chapter on electronic orchestration is the validity of attempting to mimic acoustic instruments. The reader is encouraged to ponder the validity of this question, but I suggest two ideas regarding the subject. As a performance medium, MIDI instruments are not well suited to accurately mimic acoustic instruments. Though sound production techniques and real-time control of MIDI instruments has improved, there are several obvious limitations. First, electronic instruments must be amplified, and amplification involves transduction: the conversion from electronic energy to kinetic energy or vice versa. For this reason alone, MIDI instruments face a distinct disadvantage. When a saxophonist blows into a mouthpiece and sets a reed in motion he is creating kinetic energy that connects, in a very direct way, with the audience. A second disadvantage relates to the issue of real-time control. Though some synthesizers provide the means to manipulate a sound in real-time by changing embouchure, air pressure, filters, and other parameters, a synthesizer that could accurately model a wind instrument would require dozens (if not hundreds) of real-time controllers. Such controllers would include not only parameters for embouchure and air pressure, but parameters to control position of the lips on the reed, type of reed, varying position of the tongue and teeth, shape of the mouthpiece, and myriad other features. Obviously, a MIDI musician with only four appendages and one mouth would be hard pressed to control such an instrument. As new forms of MIDI controllers evolve, this gap may lessen. Does this mean that MIDI instruments cannot be used as artistic performance instruments? Of course not. But I suggest that such instruments are better suited for production and performance of nontraditional timbres than replication of traditional sounds.

With regard to emulation of recordings of acoustic instruments, digital synthesizers are better suited to the task. Though most would agree that synthesized productions of a symphonic music are still less than accurate, synthesized orchestrations can be a suitable illusion of the real thing. For obvious financial reasons, this illusionary aspect of digital synthesis has been recognized by many film and record producers. I will leave the artistic debate of such practices to other philosophers and conclude by saying that, with regard to music, the better prepared you are to handle both traditional and nontraditional orchestrations, the more marketable you will be as a computer musician.

OTHER RESOURCES

It goes without saying that a single chapter of introduction to orchestration will not do justice to such a vast topic. If the topic interests you, I suggest that you study well-regarded texts on the subject by authors such as Samuel Adler, Walter Piston, and Cecil Forsyth. I am also fond of the Henry Mancini book *Sounds and Scores*. Though Mancini's comments and analysis are brief, the score excerpts and recordings are very helpful.

In pre-Baroque eras, orchestration was not a consideration. Instruments were used in an ad hoc fashion; in a sense, the ensemble was determined by who showed up for the gig. In the Baroque era, composers such as Bach and Handel began to write for specific combinations of instruments, though the approach was not refined in the sense that we think of orchestration today. Key developments in orchestration coincided with the invention of valved brass instruments in the early nineteenth century. Prior to the invention of valves, valveless instruments such as the trumpet and French horn were relegated primarily to an accompanying role. With these *natural* instruments it was impossible to accurately play chromatic tones—these instruments could only produce notes from the overtone series. The invention of valves (and coincident advancements in manufacturing technology) made it possible for composers such as Beethoven and Berlioz to utilize brass instruments as melodic resources on a par with the strings and woodwinds. By the mid-to late nineteenth century, Romantic composers were writing for large orchestras, and orchestration was an integral part of the composition process. In the twentieth century, composers have continued to expand the concepts of orchestration to include new instruments and the use of extreme instrumental ranges and innovative playing techniques.

SELECTING APPROPRIATE SOUNDS

One of the difficulties facing computer musicians is the relationship between orchestration and composition. In a typical sequencing environment, you must consider not only the composition and instrumentation but the actual design of the sounds. If you have ever spent time designing sounds you know that this aspect of synthesis can be a time consuming task. Though there is no correct or incorrect way to approach this problem, I have found that it is often beneficial to separate these tasks. As you begin a new composition, select sounds that are close to your vision of the final production. As the composition takes shape, you can start to focus on the design of more appropriate sounds.

It is also helpful to evaluate sounds from the standpoint of textural setting: avoid the temptation to always select the most "interesting" synthetic sounds. In many cases, a combination of more subtle instruments can create a composite effect that is very interesting. Also note that the goal of a synthesizer manufacturer is to sell synths. I have noticed that, while default patches often sound great as solo sounds, many manufacturers will create demonstration sounds that are artificially brilliant. These sounds may help to sell synthesizers, but they are often of marginal value when used in a thick orchestration.

THE FINE LINE BETWEEN ORCHESTRATION AND COMPOSITION

As I mentioned previously, early orchestral composers were less concerned with orchestration than with harmony, melody, and motivic development. As MIDI musicians, we have a distinct advantage in that we can actually hear our orchestrations as a part of the composition process. Though this direct feedback is generally helpful, take care that the selection of sounds does not interfere with the composition process. It is very tempting to simply adjust the notes and articulation of a musical passage to make them fit with a sound that may be inappropriate for the current musical setting. As you compose, if you find yourself making musical decisions based on an arbitrary selection of sounds, consider taking time to select or edit new sounds. More than once I have witnessed students rerecord a beautiful legato style melody as a series of staccato notes because the currently selected sound was not appropriate for the melody or didn't cut through a mix.

ORCHESTRAL CHOIRS

The instruments in a traditional orchestra are categorized as belonging to one or more of the following orchestral choirs: percussion, woodwinds, brass, and strings. Though this classification system is not entirely accurate (a piano is both a stringed instrument and a percussion instrument, and a contemporary flute is not made of wood), it is a helpful way to organize the instruments of a modern-day orchestra. In the next several pages we will look at each of the orchestral choirs and consider some of the idiosyncrasies of instruments in each group. Though this chapter deals primarily with traditional orchestral instruments, consider the application of these techniques to nontraditional sounds: a square-wave synthesizer patch could be a suitable functional substitute for an oboe. Likewise, a synthetic string pad can provide similar functionality to a traditional string choir. By learning to mimic traditional sounds, we can improve the approach to musical performance of nontraditional sounds.

It takes a great deal of work to successfully mimic acoustic instruments. After all, orchestral players spend years learning to master their instruments! When attempting to emulate these instruments, take time to set up your equipment to allow for the maximum amount of musical nuance. Synthesists often use a variety of continuous controllers simultaneously when doing this type of work. It is not uncommon for a MIDI musician to assign a breath controller for volume changes, modulation wheel or aftertouch for vibrato, data slider for timbral changes, and so on. Some physical modeling synthesizers will even allow for control of elements such as embouchure, breath, tonguing, and throat. (Listen to the *Silicon Dream* recording on the accompanying CD for an example of these techniques.)

If your goal is to emulate traditional instruments, it is essential that you consider the idiosyncrasies of the instruments you are trying to emulate. To effectively emulate traditional instruments, you must develop an idiomatic playing style. In a sense, you need to approach a passage of music in much the same way as the instrumentalist you are trying to emulate. For example, while woodwind players can usually execute fast arpeggiations quite comfortably, a similar passage would be very difficult on a brass instrument. Similarly, it is easy for a saxophonist to play softly in a high register, but a trumpet player will have a hard time controlling the dynamics of notes in the upper register of the instrument.

EMULATING WIND AND BRASS INSTRUMENTS

Though it may be obvious, remember that brass and wind instruments are monophonic. To accurately mimic these instruments, it is often advisable to sequence brass and wind parts monophonically. Though it may be tempting to sequence a trumpet section as a series of three- or four-note chords, this type of approach defeats the goal of playing in an idiomatic playing style. At best, such an approach will miss the slight variations in dynamics and articulations that would be achieved through monophonic sequencing. In a worse case, this approach will sound like a keyboardist playing a brass or wind sound. As you work through the remainder of the chapter, consider how you can best emulate the playing style of each of the instruments in the orchestra and work on developing an idiomatic style of playing that accurately imitates the real thing.

BREATHING

One of the problems associated with keyboard sequence entry is that we tend to forget about basic elements such as breathing and articulation. Obviously, a brass or woodwind player cannot hold notes indefinitely. Though it is easy to hold a 50-second high G on a synthesized trumpet, this type of passage will sound entirely unnatural to the listener. One of the techniques I use to overcome this tendency is to sing lines as I sequence them on the computer. A singable approach yields several benefits. Singing can help you to interpret a melody in a musical fashion (i.e., phrasing a melody with dynamic contours). It can help you to articulate a melody in an appropriate way (you will tend to be more attuned to accents, short and long notes). Finally, singing will, out of necessity, help you to utilize a natural approach to breathing. When approaching a passage of music in an idiomatic style, consider the size of the instrument you are emulating. Because low-pitched instruments necessarily require a greater length of tubing than high-pitched instruments, it is understandable that a low brass player will need to move more air through the horn than an instrument such as the trumpet or French horn. In general, you will need to phrase in smaller units when sequencing low brass or woodwind parts. In a similar vein, double reed instruments such as bassoon or oboe can be more taxing to play than single reeds such as clarinet or saxophone. As with brass instruments, consider these idiosyncrasies as you sequence.

RANGE

Each instrument is unique with regard to range, but a general rule concerning brass instruments is that higher notes are more difficult to play than lower notes. Understand that, if textural considerations dictate a soft passage, orchestrating a brass instrument in an extreme high register will not yield suitable results. It is easy to fix this type of problem with MIDI by scaling velocities or lowering channel volume, but such a solution would not be entirely accurate. When orchestrating this type of passage, remember that a brass mute might be a potential solution. In a similar vein, it is very easy for a saxophonist to play high notes (within the traditional range). On the other hand, it is difficult for a saxophonist to play the lowest few tones of the instrument at a soft dynamic level. Note that the clarinet is unique in that most clarinetists are quite comfortable playing in the entire range of this instrument. Though the clarinet has three distinct timbres dependent on the given range, the instrument is often scored in any or all of the three registers: low (dark), mid (throat), and high (shrill).

When sequencing brass and woodwind parts, I find it helpful to consider the "sweet range" of each instrument. The sweet range can be defined as the range in which the instrument can be played effortlessly and with a tone that is natural and pleasing to the ear. The easiest way to visualize the sweet range of brass and wind instruments is to consider the written (vs. concert) pitch of the instrument. In general, the sweet range will fall in the staff in a transposed part. For example, though the range of a baritone and alto saxophone differs greatly, each of these instruments has a written (transposed) sweet range from around E-3 (MIDI numbering) to G-4.

When emulating acoustic instruments, you must consider both the upper and lower limits of any instrument you intend to emulate. An instrument that falls grossly out of range will sound unnatural to an attentive listener. Of course, one of the great things about MIDI is that you can easily extend the range of a given instrument, and I do extend ranges on occasion. Just remember that if your goal is to accurately create the illusion of a traditional orchestra, these types of inaccuracies can be a problem. I remember being very proud of one of my first synthesized orchestral pieces. I will never forget playing this recording for a percussion friend: my friend only heard two notes before he informed me that my timpani part was way out of range! Since then I have been much more attentive to the concept of instrumental ranges.

ARTICULATION

A fundamental problem associated with most synthesizers is that it is difficult (and often impossible) to emulate articulations of traditional instruments. Obvious as it might seem, it is impossible for brass and woodwind players to tongue extremely fast passages of notes. You should consider using a *legato* (connected) approach for these types of passages. Some synthesists will design a "composite" sound in order to activate or deactivate the tongued portion of the sample as needed. I suspect that, as *physical modeling* technology improves, synthesists will enjoy greater flexibility and accuracy with regard to articulation of brass and wind parts.

When articulating accents, realize that accents generally produce a change in timbre when executed on an instrument such as the trumpet. (This makes sense when you consider that a brass player will need to increase the amount of air going into the horn when performing an accent.) In a sequencing environment, you may want to design your sounds to reflect this natural musical phenomenon: try editing a sound so that higher velocities slightly increase the cutoff point of a low-pass filter. Even if you are not trying to emulate an acoustic instrument, these types of details will help your sequences to sound much more musical. Though many synthesizers do not support the feature, application of release velocities can also add an element of musicality when articulating music. As with attack velocity, you could assign release velocities to trigger a timbre change for more realistic staccato passages.

DYNAMIC CONTOUR

One of the best ways to create musical sequences (whether emulating traditional instruments or using synthetic sounds) is to implement the concept of dynamic contour. A clarinetist, for example, will rarely play a sequence of notes in a dynamically static fashion. It is natural for acoustic musicians to shape the dynamics of a passage in a musical way (even if the part is inconsequential). Though dynamic contour can be difficult to execute on a MIDI keyboard or guitar controller, the use of a dedicated volume pedal, aftertouch, or data slider can help you to naturally phrase in this way. Though dynamic changes are usually very subtle, they can provide very musical results. Note that it is also common for performers to add a touch of vibrato at the end of a long note or the climax of a melody. Classical musicians often add a nearly continuous vibrato throughout a musical phrase. Again, the use of a modulation wheel can add much to the musicality of this type of passage. One technical solution to this problem is to invest in a relatively inexpensive breath controller. Note that many synthesizers provide a breath controller port. If your synthesizer does not support this feature, you can still add this capability by purchasing a third-party breath controller interface. These devices are connected to an instrument via a MIDI cable and provide the ability to connect an external breath controller. This will allow you to use breath to alter channel volume in real time.

Mutes are almost exclusively used for brass and string instruments. (An interesting exception is the rare saxophone bag mute.) Mutes are used most often by trumpet and trombone players, but most brass instruments use them occasionally. Mutes are primarily used for two reasons: they can help to fix dynamic imbalances between instruments, and they are also used to change the timbre of an instrument. A few of the common mutes include the harmon, cup, bucket, and straight mute. In jazz styles, trumpet players and trombonists often use a plunger for wah-wah types of effects.

The following examples list both the sounding pitch (concert) and written ranges for common brass and woodwind instruments. Transposition will not be an issue (unless, of course, you decide to prepare parts for acoustic instruments). I have included the transpositions for each of the instruments because the written range often provides a hint as to the "sweet range" of the instrument. In general, the sweet range will fall in the staff when a concert note is transposed for a given instrument.

Figure 7.1 Bb clarinets

Figure 7.2 Flutes

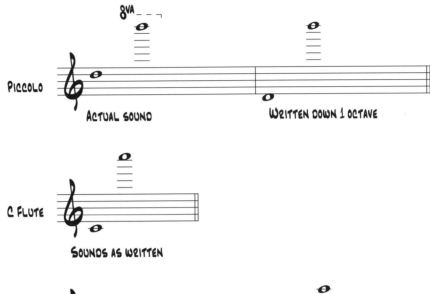

Piccolo

8va
Actual sound   Written down 1 octave

C Flute
Sounds as written

Alto (G) Flute
Actual sound   Written up a perfect 4th

Figure 7.3 Double reeds

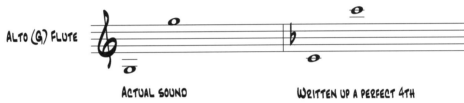

Oboe
Sounds as written

English Horn
Actual sound   Written up a perfect 5th

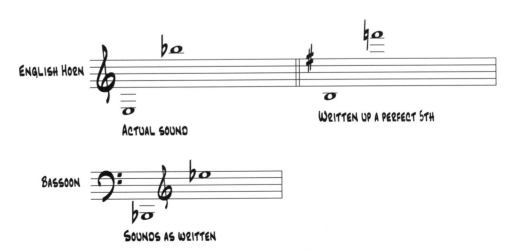

Bassoon
Sounds as written

Figure 7.4 Saxophones

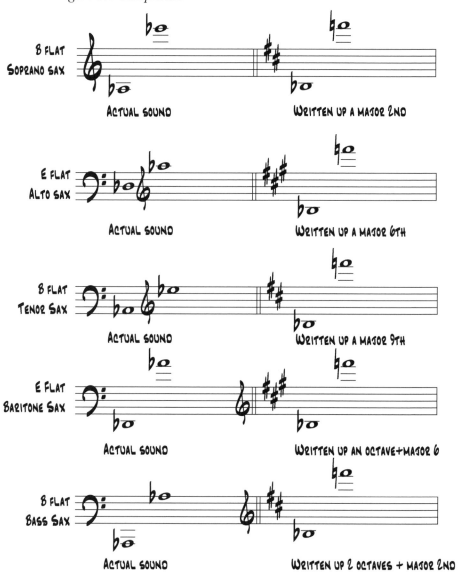

Making Music with Your Computer

Figure 7.5 Brass

STRINGS

Strings have long been a mainstay of the symphonic orchestra. Strings are attractive to composers because they are capable of great dynamic contrasts. The string choir is a largely homogenous group of instruments, meaning the timbre of each or these instruments is very similar. Strings are also unique in that they can sustain notes indefinitely. Though strings are used for almost any musical situation, they often function as melodic instruments or as harmonic pads. The following example illustrates the open tunings for each or the primary string instruments.

Figure 7.6 Range of string instruments

When sequencing string parts, it is helpful to consider the variety of bowing techniques common on these instruments. Though this list is not comprehensive, it should get you started with writing for most typical situations. Note that composers often indicate frequent changes in bowing technique in a composition. In MIDI terms this means that you will probably need to set up a variety of string sounds to have an appropriate pallet of bowing sounds for a given orchestral composition.

Figure 7.7 String bowing and color techniques

Détaché	The most common bowing stroke-player changes the direction of the bow for each note (i.e., nonlegato).
Louré	A legato (connected) style but with slight separation between notes.
Staccato	Short notes that are played with one bow stroke.
Spiccato	A style of playing where the bow "bounces" on the string.
Pizzicato	The strings are plucked.
Sul ponticello	Playing near the bridge to create a "metallic" sound.
Sul tasto	Bow is placed over the fingerboard to create a soft tone.
Col legno	The bow is turned upside down and the instrument played with the wooden portion of the bow.
Tremolo	Although string players utilize several types of tremolos, most synthesized tremolo sounds are unmeasured, bowed tremolos (as contrasting with a fingered or measured tremolo).
Con sordino	Mute is placed on the bridge. Creates a softer sound and an interesting change in timbre.

One of the things you will want to avoid when sequencing string parts is to approach these tracks as a keyboardist. In the next example, though the musical concept is sound, when applied to a string ensemble effect it is very unnatural.

Figure 7.8 Unnatural keyboard-string approach

When orchestrating string (or brass or woodwind) music, consider using a more symphonic approach. Notice how, in the next example, each of the voices functions in more natural fashion. Though each of the voices are simple, the combination of rhythmic elements produces the desired rhythmic feeling. You will find that this type of linear approach to orchestrating electronic instruments will yield outstanding results.

Figure 7.9 Linear version of a keyboard pattern

There are two categories of percussion to consider when creating a traditional orchestration: nonpitched and pitched instruments. Nonpitched instruments include the bass drum, snare drum, toms, triangle, cymbals, Latin percussion, tambourine, whip, whistle, anvil, wood blocks, and gong. Pitched percussion includes the xylophone, vibraphone, marimba, glockenspiel, chimes, crotales, and timpani. Of course, many world and ethnic percussion instruments are also available as sonic resources.

Nonpitched percussion. A common mistake made by many MIDI musicians is an over-reliance on nonpitched percussion. Remember that, in particular, gongs and cymbals are generally used for grand musical gestures. As with any sound, percussive sounds lose their effectiveness if used too frequently. I tend to gravitate to these sounds because percussion sounds are often some of the most accurate samples in my library. This makes sense when you consider that, unlike wind, brass, and string instruments, percussion sounds produce a fairly consistent attack and decay. This predictability lends itself to accurate reproduction in a sampling environment.

When sequencing drums, it is helpful to understand that, while the instrument may or may not produce a definite pitch, the pitch of the instrument will change depending on the force with which it is struck. Consider designing drum sounds that emulate this feature. One way to achieve this effect is to map velocity levels to pitch. As you increase the velocity of your attack, the pitch of the instrument will change in a natural fashion.

Some of the more difficult techniques to master when sequencing percussion parts are the performance rudiments such as rolls and flams (the percussion version of a grace note). If you don't have access to a percussion controller such as a MIDI drum set, these rudiments can be comfortably performed using special keyboard mapping. The best way to execute these types of passages on a keyboard is to map the same sound to several adjacent keys. By practicing a variety of trills and tremolos, it is possible to achieve fairly natural-sounding drum rolls. Another option is to use an arpeggiator for a similar effect. Sequence a percussive pattern such as a paradiddle or ratamacue and use your arpeggiator to trigger these patterns in real time.

It is easy to forget the limitations of some percussion instruments when sequencing. Though drums and suspended cymbals have a large dynamic range, remember that crash cymbals are called crash cymbals for a reason. Using velocity scaling or volume changes to adjust a dynamic imbalance of a loud crash cymbal may produce artificial results.

Pitched percussion. Pitched percussion instruments are used for a wide variety of effects. The xylophone, for example, is often associated with comical musical effects. In contrast, the wonderfully mellow tone of a marimba can provide a beautiful accompaniment for a wind melody or be featured as a solo instrument. When imitating pitched percussion instruments, it is helpful to visualize the playing technique common to these instruments. The xylophone is typically played with two hard mallets. When sequencing xylophone parts, consider using both hands just as a xylophonist would do. While it might be more natural to perform these passages using traditional keyboard fingering, a two-handed approach may help you to play in a more idiomatic style. Vibraphone and marimba performers generally use from two to four mallets when performing. When mimicking these instruments, consider the limitations of using two hands to control four mallets. Though marimba virtuosos can perform amazing feats of dexterity, there are limitations with regard to the independence of the mallets and execution of fast runs in a four-part mallet texture.

Marimba players use a tremolo mallet technique to achieve sustained notes. Though slow tremolos are usually comfortable to perform using a keyboard controller, you might want to consider temporarily slowing the tempo of a sequence in order to perform a natural sounding marimba tremolo. As with snare rudiments, an arpeggiator can also be helpful. For single-note sustained passages, try setting your arpeggiator to repeat twenty-fourth or thirtysecond notes—the effect can be fairly natural. Step-time entry can also be effective in that it will allow you to implement slight variations of dynamic level. On a recent project, I set up my sequencing environment so that when I pressed the damper pedal it triggered my arpeggiator. This technique was effective in allowing me to perform a fairly natural sounding mallet part—complete with graceful single-note tremolos—in real time.

Figure 7.10 Common pitched-percussion instruments

TIMPANI

Timpani are often used as an exciting percussive element in symphonic music, but note that the timpani can also be used as a melodic instrument. In orchestral music, four timpani are typically used. Each of the timpani can be tuned to a variety of pitches but if your goal is to mimic a real timpanist, you must provide space in the score for the timpanist to retune the instruments should you want more than four pitches. Although most synthesized timpani sound rather bombastic, these instruments have a huge dynamic range and can also be utilized in softer, lyrical types of passages. The ranges of the four timpani are as follows.

Figure 7.11

MISCELLANEOUS

Although we have looked at ranges for most of the common orchestral instruments, there are several other instruments that you may want to use in an orchestral setting.

Guitar. Notice that the guitar is similar to electric bass and double bass in that the instrument sounds an octave lower than the written pitch. When trying to mimic a guitar, remember that the tuning of this instrument makes some types of voicings awkward to play. In talking to many guitarists I have learned that drop-two style voicings (see Chapter 4, "Contemporary Keyboard Techniques") are common. The open-string tunings for six-string guitar is shown in the next example.

Making Music with Your Computer

Figure 7.12 Open-string guitar tunings

Celesta. The celesta is a keyboard instrument that sounds very brilliant. The celesta is much like a piano in that notes can be sustained with a damper pedal. This instrument can be interesting as a solo voice or used to add a "metallic" quality when doubled with winds, brass, or string instruments.

Figure 7.13 Celesta

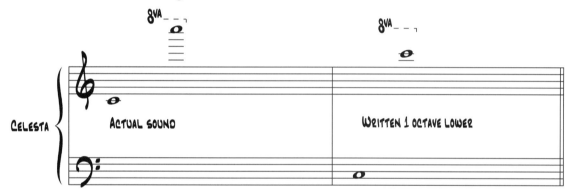

Harp. The harp can be wonderfully effective as a melodic voice or when used in a rhythmical background texture (listen to the *Orchestral* track on the accompanying CD). Of course, the harp may also be used for the glissando figures that are so common. When sequencing a harp glissando, you may want to execute a white or black note glissando on the keyboard. Use your sequencing software to transpose the glissando to an appropriate key.

Figure 7.14 Harp

PUTTING IT ALL TOGETHER

Now that you have learned about some of the common instruments, ranges, and playing techniques, it is time to consider using these instruments in an orchestral setting.

It is often helpful to think of the concept of *foreground* and *background* when orchestrating music. An instrument may come to the foreground in several ways. An obvious example is volume; an instrument that is louder than other instruments will catch the ear of the listener. In MIDI music, however, a reliance on volume can be problematic. By adjusting note velocities or channel volume, it is easy to make a flute sound louder than a full brass section. If your goal is to realistically mimic an acoustic orchestra, you will want to consider other methods for establishing a foreground theme.

Timbre can be one of the most helpful elements in establishing a foreground voice. In the previous example, doubling a flute melody with an oboe could help to make the melody stand out more effectively. This can be particularly helpful when trying to bring out an inner voice in a thick orchestral texture. Again, listen to the *Orchestral* example and note how clarinet and French horns are used in several sections to bring out an inner string voice. The modern symphonic orchestra provides an amazing amount of timbral possibilities. My best advice is to listen to the masters and experiment. Allow yourself to think across sections (i.e., various combinations of woodwinds, strings, brass and pitched percussion). One of the things I love about MIDI is the ease with which you can experiment with various combinations of instruments.

Making Music with Your Computer

DYNAMIC CONTOUR

The modern orchestra provides a huge dynamic range. One of the best ways to get your orchestral sequences to "breathe" is to take advantage of dynamic contour. You will probably want to get in the habit of using real-time volume control as you orchestrate traditional or nontraditional music. As you sequence, try to match to the volume of a foreground instrument in the same way that a symphonic player would blend with other musicians in the orchestra.

THINK AHEAD

Although it can be a time-consuming process, you will want to do a fair amount of planning before you attempt to sequence a traditional orchestration. Consider writing out the piece before you begin the sequencing process. The *Orchestral* demonstration is one such example. I don't think it would have been possible for me to create a multitexture piece such as this orchestral demonstration without writing it out first. It can be difficult (if not impossible) to create a convincing orchestral composition using the "bottom up" approach common to popular music sequencing. For me, I find that taking the time to write and orchestrate before sequencing allows me to make better orchestration decisions. Of course, MIDI provides wonderful opportunities for experimentation, so don't be afraid to break some rules.

PART TWO: TECHNOLOGY

8. All About Computers

9. Introduction to MIDI

10. Sequencing Concepts

11. Synthesists' Delight

All About Computers

Humans have long been interested in automating or enhancing the process of performing mathematical calculations. One of the earliest forms of a simple computer was the abacus. In 1642, Blaise Pascal developed one of the first automated computers, an adding machine that used toothed wheels to handle carries from one digit to another. Though Charles Babbage and others worked on the concept of an *analytical engine*, it was not until 1890 that Herman Hollerith developed the first important data processing device. He developed the punched card for the U.S. Census Bureau to help tabulate the census of 1890. Punched cards were used to enable faster processing of data than would have been possible by traditional (human) means. In 1945, John von Neumann developed the concept of a stored program computer. This modern development was important because it set the stage for the concept of using computer memory to store programs and data. The first electronic digital computer was developed for the U.S. Army in 1946. This ENIAC (Electronic Numerical Integrator and Calculator) was primarily used to calculate ballistic tables.

As with early synthesizers, early computers such as the ENIAC were huge and prone to breakdown. The ENIAC consisted of rooms full of vacuum tubes. The invention of the transistor in the late 1940s and continued improvements in integrated circuits enabled a newer generation of computers that were smaller and more reliable. The first microcomputers were developed in the mid-1970s. Microcomputers set the stage for the revolution in personal computing because they were small and relatively inexpensive. Many businesses and even hobbyists were now able to have access to a computer.

INTERNAL HARDWARE COMPONENTS

Though computers have continued to improve and, thankfully, decrease in cost, all personal computers still contain several basic hardware components. Let's take a moment to learn what really makes a computer tick.

Making Music with Your Computer

Microprocessor. The microprocessor is the heart of any digital computer. It is an integrated circuit that contains the "brains" of a computer on one chip. The computational logic of the computer (i.e., how the computer computes using *and, or,* and *not* gates) is a key component of the design of the micro-processor. The microprocessor represents the entire *central processing unit* (CPU) of the computer on one chip. Only memory and input and output devices need to be added for the computer to function.

Microprocessors allow digital computers to run at increasingly faster rates. In the days of early computers, large integrated circuit boards were used instead of microprocessors. A truism in computing is that the farther a bit of data must travel, the slower the data will be processed. Obviously, data that must travel from one room to another will travel much slower than data that moves about in a tiny microprocessor. Scientists are now experimenting with new metal alloys and temperature control (e.g., refrigerated processors) to get past physical limitations regarding how small these processors can actually get.

It is interesting to note that, though processor speed is an important factor regarding the speed of a computer, the design of the microprocessor also affects speed of operation. Put another way, two computers with the same clock speed may not actually process data at the same rate due to differences in microprocessor design. The speed at which a microprocessor runs is primarily dependent on two factors: the number of bits on the data bus and the internal data registers and clock speed. In general, larger data registers and faster data bus will allow the computer to work more efficiently (e.g., a 32-bit system would, all things being equal, be faster than a 16-bit system).

Clock speed is another important issue regarding the speed of a microprocessor. Microprocessor clock speed is measured in megahertz (MHz). A 1MHz microprocessor would work at a speed of 1 million cycles per second. Though we still use clock speed to compare the speed of various computers, the number can be misleading. Each computer instruction may actually use up several clock cycles, so megahertz is more of a theoretical concept. A poorly implemented microprocessor will run more slowly than a well-designed microprocessor even if the two units run at the same clock speed. Note that other factors such as the speed of the hard drive will also affect the actual speed of the computer.

Bus. The system bus is used to move data to and from the microprocessor. As with microprocessors, the speed of the bus is dependent on the number of bits that can be simultaneously handled as well as the clock speed of the bus. A 120MHz microprocessor may actually use a 66MHz system bus. To understand how the bus is used, it would be helpful to consider how a typical instruction such as addition is handled by the computer. If the CPU (central processing unit) intends to store a number in a memory register, it sends the data down the data wires on the system bus. The CPU also sends a number representing the requested memory location down the address wires. This number is then "written" to memory at the requested position. If two numbers are stored in this fashion, it is then possible for the computer to store yet another number representing a mathematical operation involving the previously stored numbers. This concept of moving and manipulating numbers is the very essence of modern-day computers. As amazing as computers seem to be, they are really rather simple. (We're talking addition, subtraction, multiplication, and division here.)

Motherboard/system board. The system board, or motherboard, contains the system bus and is used to connect the various components of a computer system. The motherboard will include plugs to connect storage devices such as hard drives and floppy drives, a connection to the power source to actually run the various components, slots for RAM (random access memory), ROM (read-only memory) chips for enabling the boot procedures, connections for I/O devices such as a mouse, keyboard, device cards, monitor, and a fan to cool the internal components. As with microprocessors, the design of a motherboard has much to do with the speed and reliability of the computer as a whole.

ROM. ROM is the acronym for *read-only memory*. ROM chips are used to store instructions that do not need to be modified, such as the initial bootup instructions that need to be performed when a computer is first switched on. The *toolbox,* an important part of the Macintosh operating system, is also encoded on ROM chips. The Macintosh toolbox has grown from a few hundred functions to several thousand. As new features are added to the toolbox, users of older Macintosh computers are still able to take advantage of new features by updating the *system file*—a software version of the functions found in the ROM-based toolbox.

RAM. RAM is the acronym for *random access memory*, the main memory of a computer. RAM is used to store (temporarily) user input data such as text entered by a keypad or the numbers representing a digital audio recording. In the early days of computers, most systems had less than 1 megabyte (MB) of RAM. Today, modern operating systems require a minimum of 32 to 64MB of RAM just to function efficiently. Many power computer users and professionals use 128MB of RAM or more. It is important to note that, in the event of a power failure, any data residing in RAM will be lost, so it is important to remember to frequently save your work. It is also a good idea to save several versions of files as you work in them—if the power goes out while you are saving to disk, chances are that the file will be corrupted and rendered useless.

Hard drive. The hard drive is a storage device that contains one or more disks or platters. Digital data is stored on a hard drive by magnetic means much like a tape recorder uses magnetism to record an audio performance. In fact, early computers used tape drives for storage of data. Tape is still a low cost (albeit slow) way to archive data. The bulk of the operating system is stored on a hard drive. When you use a software program such as a sequencer and save your work, temporary data that resides in RAM is copied to the hard disk. The operating system may "swap" memory to and from the disk if the system runs out of RAM. Computer programs, the series of instructions that tell the computer what to do, are also stored on the hard drive. Because hard drives use magnetism to store data, they are prone to failure after repeated use. As computer technicians will point out, it is not a matter of *if* your hard drive will fail, it is a matter of *when* the drive will fail. Get in the habit of backing up important data to another drive to avoid a nightmare should your drive fail at an inopportune time.

One of the hardest computer-related decisions involves what size and type of hard drive to purchase. With the rather bloated software programs and operating systems available on current computer systems, a minimum of 4 gigabytes (GB) will be needed. I suggest that you invest in 10GB or more if you plan to do digital audio recording. (Remember that a stereo recording takes up 10MB of space per minute.) Another option is to add a second hard drive that is dedicated to recording digital audio information. Most professionals advise that you use a dedicated drive for this type of work because digital audio programs will work most efficiently on a drive that is uncluttered and frequently defragmented. I do not want to open up a Pandora's box regarding what type of drive to purchase; many options are available including IDE, EIDE, SCSI, Ultra SCSI, and the like. Each of these technologies has pros and cons when you consider performance vs. cost. Before you invest in a hard drive, you would do well to ask the software manufacturer what hard drives they suggest for the software you intend to run. With that said, hard drive performance is primarily dependent on the rotational speed of the platter (i.e., the faster the platter rotates, the better performance you can expect from the drive), and continuous data transfer rates. Transfer rates are measured in megabytes per second. The higher the number, the better. Another specification to look at is MTBF (mean time between failure). In short, the MTBF gives an indication of how long the drive will last with normal use. As with rotation speed and transfer rates, the higher the number, the better. Because hard drives are expensive, it may be tempting to try to use a removable device such as a Zip disk for digital audio recording. Though some removable hard drives provide performance that is similar to internal hard drives, do not attempt to use a slower removable drive such as a Super disk or Zip disk. These drives are mainly intended as storage solutions; they simply do not transfer data at a fast enough rate to be useful as real-time drives.

Floppy drive. As you probably already know, floppy drives are removable drives that work much like a hard drive. Though modern floppy disks are no longer flexible, the earlier 5.25-inch disks were flexible, hence the term floppy disk. Though floppy drives can be helpful for storing data such as word processing documents and sequencing files, they are relatively slow and will only hold about 1.4MB of data. Because of these limitations, floppy drives are becoming less helpful for storing digital data. A one-minute stereo CD recording would require seven or more floppies to archive this data! Several new technologies have been developed to address this limitation. Super disks and Zip disks are two removable storage media that provide around 100MB of storage on a disk that is about the same size as a floppy disk.

Power supply. Of course, digital computers only work when power is applied to the system. I mention this because power problems can cause several difficulties for computer users. As I mentioned previously, a loss of power can cause a loss of data if you have not recently saved your work. Other power supply problems such as brownouts can be more insidious as they may actually damage your system. By way of example, a friend of mine, after replacing three hard drives over a period of six months, traced the problem to a defective power cord. This example illustrates the importance of using high-quality cables and maintaining an adequate supply of power to your system. Many computer users also elect to use an *uninterruptible power supply* (UPS). Such a device can be beneficial in that it will allow you a few minutes of time to backup your work in the event of a power failure. These devices can also be helpful in protecting your gear from a temporary loss in power during a brownout.

Fan. Newer microprocessors generate a great deal of heat during normal operation. Fans are used to keep the internal components of your computer operating at a reasonable temperature. It is important to always allow adequate ventilation for your system. Though it might be tempting to enclose your computer in a box to minimize noise in a studio environment, improper ventilation can cause your system to overheat and malfunction. If noise isolation is an issue, you may want to consider purchasing an isolation box that is specifically designed to minimize computer noise while maintaining an appropriate operating temperature.

EVALUATING A COMPUTER: WHAT THE NUMBERS REALLY MEAN.

If you are thinking about investing in a new computer or upgrading your existing computer, it would be prudent to learn what to look for in a computer system. There are several terms and numbers that you will want to consider before you spend money on a system. Although "less is more" may apply to other areas of your life, most computer experts advise that you invest in the most powerful system you can afford. As operating systems and software continue to evolve, more and more processing power is required for a computer to run at a reasonably efficient level. Keep in mind that one downside of these advancements is that any money you spend on a computer system is not an investment. An unfortunate reality is that the money you spend on a cutting edge system today will not be reclaimed should you decide to sell your computer in the future. Most people find that a computer will only provide one to three years of acceptable performance. If technology continues to improve at the current rate, your current system will be a virtual dinosaur in as little as a year or two.

A key consideration when buying a computer is the microprocessor speed. Most of the current crop of computer systems run at a speed of 500MHz to 1.5GHz. Is it really necessary to spend the extra money on a cutting edge microprocessor? That all depends on what you intend to do. Basic sequencing does not require a tremendous amount of power. Some of the first generation of software sequencers such as *Performer, Cakewalk,* and *Vision* ran at perfectly acceptable rates even on the early computers (i.e., 8 to 33MHz). You will need to consider a faster processor if you intend to do digital audio work. Real-time digital audio effects require a tremendous amount of processing power. Though a 200MHz system would work fine for most sequencing software, you will definitely want to consider a faster processor if you want to run more than a couple of channels of digital audio. Remember, though, that a slower (read: inexpensive) machine should work just fine for basic notation and sequencing applications. Do keep in mind that, though many sequencers such as *Performer* or *Logic* can run in "MIDI-only" mode, these programs still require a reasonably fast computer. Be sure to evaluate the system recommendations provided by software manufacturers before you invest in *any* computer system. Also keep in mind that, in general, the minimum system requirements provided by software manufacturers are driven more by economic considerations than actual performance. In a word, invest in a system that well exceeds the minimum software requirements, or you will be frustrated with your computing experience.

RAM is another important consideration. Though, until recently, computers ran at acceptable rates with only 32MB of RAM, you will want to purchase at least 64MB-128MB of RAM. Fortunately, RAM is currently a cheap commodity and adding 128MB of RAM will only cost about a hundred dollars. For a total price of around $1,500, many vendors will even include 128MB of RAM as part of the cost of the system. Extra RAM generally provides improved system performance because the operating system will not need to page memory out to the hard disk (a relatively slow process). Digital audio and video applications will use a tremendous amount of RAM so, again, the relatively small investment in additional RAM will be well worth it. Finally, additional RAM may result in improved reliability of your system. Software programs, extensions, and the operating system all compete for available resources. If more memory resources are available, chances are that you will have fewer problems with memory conflicts.

I/O connections. You will also need to evaluate the number and type of connections and hardware slots. For many years, Macintosh users have relied on the venerable serial port to connect MIDI devices, printers, and the like. Newer Macs such as the iMac only provide one to two USB (universal serial bus) connections.

Though many USB MIDI and audio devices are now available, you will need to add an additional serial card should you want to use one of these computers with older serial devices. Most PCs still provide support for legacy devices in the form of serial and parallel ports, but look for USB to become a new standard for connectivity of peripherals such as keyboards, mice, and MIDI interfaces.

FireWire is a relatively new technology that will be of interest to you if you want to do digital audio recording on your computer. FireWire (also called IEEE 1394) is a high performance serial bus for connecting devices such as digital audio recorders to your computer. The main advantage of FireWire is speed. Where a USB device can transfer data at a rate of 12 megabits (Mb) per second, FireWire runs at a rate of 400Mb per second. As hardware manufacturers begin to develop more FireWire devices, look for this to be a viable and fairly painless solution to connecting digital recording devices to your computer.

Many users will want to connect external storage devices using a SCSI connection. Again, the newer Macintosh computers do not, without adding additional hardware, provide a SCSI connection. (For a complete discussion of SCSI, see Chapter 11, "Synthesist's Delight.") FireWire will most likely make older devices obsolete. It provides faster speed and greater bandwidth, allowing the user, with appropriate hardware, to send digital video and audio directly over a FireWire port.

Hardware slots are another important consideration. PCI slots have been popular for many years. You can install an upgrade card such as an audio, video, or SCSI card into an open PCI slot. Keep in mind that the number of available slots will become an issue should you plan to add several cards. Newer Macintosh computers provide four expansion slots. Most PC computers provide four to six slots. Depending on the type of work you intend to do, you may need to add three or more cards for audio and digital-video applications. Also, some computers such as the iMac, G4 Cube, and some small footprint PCs do not provide any PCI slots, which will be a serious limitation should you decide you need to install professional audio cards or other devices.

The operating system. Whereas the computer microprocessor is the brains of the computer, the operating system provides the intelligence of a computer system. It enables a user to run programs, handles tasks such as file management, and generally provides an interface between the user and the various components of the computer system. In the early days of computing, operating systems such as MS-DOS relied on key commands entered by the user. Today, most operating systems such as the various versions of the Macintosh or Windows operating systems use a GUI (graphical user interface) as a more "friendly" way for a user to interact with the operating system.

The great debate. The issue of selecting a computer platform is a topic that rivals politics and religion in its ability to get people riled up. There are two viable platform options (with some slight variations) that are currently available to MIDI musicians: Apple Macintosh or Wintel[1]. Although some other options are available such as Linux or the BeOS (an operating system that works on some Macintosh and PC computers), all of the mainstream software that is currently available runs on either the Mac or PC. My goal for this discussion is not to point you to one system over another. (I happen to use both; each has its strengths and weaknesses.) What you will learn from this discussion is how to evaluate software and computers and make logical purchase and upgrade decisions.

Before you spend time debating the merits of one operating system over another, you should consider a key issue: software. A computer is only as good as the applications you intend to run on it. Although many outstanding programs are available for both operating systems (*Logic Audio, Cubase,* and *Finale* to name a few), many of the most popular programs are written for a single operating system. *Performer* and *Cakewalk* are sequencing programs that run only on Macintosh and Wintel computers, respectively. Similarly, *Pro Tools* and *Sound Forge* are digital audio applications that were written for specific operating systems. As you ponder what type of system to invest in, take a hard look at the types of things you plan to do with your computer and make a list of the software that would best serve your needs. After completing your list, the issue of what operating system to choose will probably be moot: if you have your heart set on running *Performer* or *Vision,* you must select a Macintosh computer. If you feel that applications such as *Cakewalk* or *Sound Forge* would best serve your needs, your choice will clearly be a Wintel computer.

It is also a good idea to ask friends and professionals about their choice of computer and software. How often does their system crash? What types of applications do they use, and how is the tech support for these applications? Is peripheral hardware (and more importantly, software drivers) available for their operating system? Is in-house compatibility an issue (i.e., can they easily exchange files with colleagues)? How stable is the user-base for software applications they use (e.g., are Web sites and list servers available where users can exchange tips and ideas)? Also, be sure to read current trade magazines (both electronic music and computer-specific publications). What types of software and hardware are being used in the real world? If you take the time to do some homework, you will be able to make a choice that works best for you.

Multitasking. For musicians, an important concept regarding the operating system is the process of *multitasking*. Humans often multitask without giving it much thought. If you have ever made coffee in the morning while you talked on the phone and listened to the news, you have engaged in the multitasking process. In a multitasking operating system, it is possible to run several applications at once. You might, for example, start a download from a Web site, print a musical score, and begin to sequence a new song. Although it appears that these tasks are being performed simultaneously, this is not actually the case. In a multitasking operating system, each program or process uses a brief slice of time. This type of "round robin" approach makes it appear to the user that the programs are running simultaneously.

Figure 8.1 Multitasking (round robin)

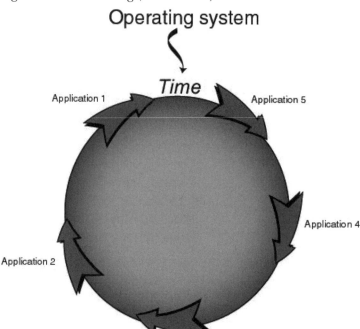

The two basic types of multitasking are *preemptive multitasking* and *cooperative multitasking.* In a preemptive multitasking operating system such as Windows 95/98/2000, the OS itself handles the allocation of time given to each application or process. In a cooperative multitasking system such as the Mac OS prior to OS X, each program is required to yield time to the system for other programs to run. If each program plays by the rules, a cooperative multitasking can work well. In such a system, if a program fails to yield time due to a programming bug or other problem, the entire system can hang. Though a preemptive system can provide better stability (i.e., the operating system may still work even if a program crashes), a downside is that preemptive operating system can be problematic when dealing with sophisticated timing issues such as recording and playback of MIDI data. Many people who upgraded to Windows 95 were dismayed to find that the MIDI timing routines of this system were less than accurate. Programmers have solved this problem by forcing their programs to run in the older cooperative multitasking mode of Windows 3.*x.* Microsoft has developed another workaround in the form of the DirectX extensions that allow programmers to specify an application cooperation level. Such a program may specify a low level of cooperation and thereby retain better control over timing sensitive processes such as recording and playback of MIDI and digital audio data.

Multiprocessing will become an important term for computer musicians. In a multiprocessing system, several microprocessors can each run a different program or process simultaneously. I mention this because multiprocessing may well become common as the price of microprocessors continue to fall. If you have a dedicated graphics accelerator card or digital audio card, you are already experiencing a form of multiprocessing: each of these hardware devices contains a minicomputer capable of handling a specific task such as graphics or digital audio processing, thereby lessening the burden on the operating system itself. Note that Apple has recently released dual-processor G4 computers that function as true multiprocessing machines. With such systems calculations such as digital audio processing can be handled simultaneously by a second processor. Several popular music applications have already been rewritten to take advantage of multiprocessor architecture.

HOW A COMPUTER WORKS

It is helpful to visualize a computer system as a series of hardware and software levels. At the lowest level, *firmware* provides machine language instructions that bring hardware components to life and enable the mechanisms for loading the operating system. Firmware is an instruction set that resides in ROM chips or EPROM. The operating system and device drivers provide an interface between the hardware and the user. At the highest level, programmers create applications that run within the specific operating system. The following diagram illustrates this concept.

Figure 8.2 Levels of a computer system

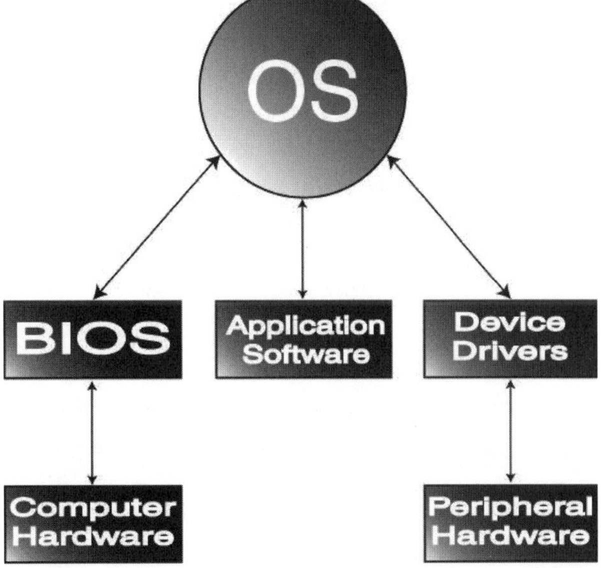

In summary, a computer system consists of the following:
- Hardware (microprocessor, hard drives, etc.)
- BIOS ("wakes up" the computer hardware)
- Device drivers (provide an interface between the hardware and the operating system)
- Operating system (provides an interface for user interaction with the hardware and manages system resources and device drivers)
- Application software (unique programs that run on a specified OS and handle specific tasks such as sequencing or word processing)

When a computer boots up, several things happen. When power is first applied to the system, special instructions encoded on ROM chips take control of the computer hardware level. The term *BIOS* stands for basic input-output system and refers to this initial bootup procedure. The BIOS performs several hardware tests to make certain that hardware is functioning properly. If you have ever added extra RAM to a Wintel computer, you probably noticed that, during the booting procedure, your computer already knows about the upgrade. This is the BIOS at work. The BIOS then looks for special programs that actually load the operating system from a floppy drive or hard disk. Once these programs are found, the BIOS passes control over to the loader programs. Once the operating system has completed loading, the OS takes control over the system.

DEVICE DRIVERS

Device drivers are an important component of any modern computer system. A device driver is a form of software whose job is to provide an interface between hardware, such as a sound card or MIDI interface, and the operating system itself. Device drivers are used on both Wintel and Machintosh machines. Appropriately, a *device manager* allows the user to change the properties of a device driver. Device drivers are part of the OS *kernel*, which is the main module of the operating system.

Device drivers can be a source of frustration for computer users for several reasons. First, your hardware is only as good as the device drivers that are available for it. If you are trying to use an older device and the manufacturer has not provided a new device driver for your current operating system, chances are that the device driver may work haphazardly or may even cause a system crash. Second, device drivers are at the mercy of other device drivers and the operating system itself. Another device driver or part of the operating system can, in a worst-case-scenario cause the driver to fail and crash the system.

A welcome trend in the area of device drivers has been provided by both Microsoft and Apple. Newer operating systems such as OS 8+ and Windows 98/2000 utilize the concept of a *device model.* A device model is a virtual representation of the characteristics of a given device driver. With device model technology, hardware manufacturers are free to develop devices using any method they choose. The operating system specifies the types of services it requires, and the hardware manufacturer simply provides a driver fulfilling the requested services. In the early days of personal computers, software designers had to write programs to interact with many different devices such as MIDI interfaces and sound cards. Because each manufacturer developed different device drivers with different communication methods, developing programs to work with a plethora of devices was a real pain. The unified device model greatly simplifies this process. The programmer simply requests a service from the operating system and the operating system asks the given device, via a device model driver, to execute the requested service.

HOW COMPUTERS THINK

It is interesting to note that, though computers are complex systems that can do many wonderful things, microprocessors are only capable of doing relatively simple tasks such as addition and subtraction. The instructions that a microprocessor can perform are defined in its basic *instruction set.* At the most primitive level, *machine language* is used to specify the instructions that a computer should execute. Machine language is a binary language in which each binary instruction refers to a specific action of the machine. At a slightly higher level, *assembly language* is used to describe machine language instructions using symbolic (text) code that is much easier for humans to read. Thankfully, programmers rarely need to program directly in assembly language anymore. Many higher level languages provide an easier development cycle, but I will provide a bit of assembly code here, as it nicely illustrates the types of operations that go on behind the scenes in any computer system. I wrote the following code several years ago for a graphical program that ran under MS-DOS. The following code simply clears video memory with a specified color.

Figure 8.3.1 Assembly code example

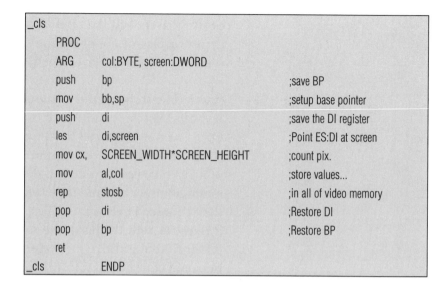

```
_cls
        PROC
        ARG     col:BYTE, screen:DWORD
        push    bp                              ;save BP
        mov     bb,sp                           ;setup base pointer
        push    di                              ;save the DI register
        les     di,screen                       ;Point ES:DI at screen
        mov cx, SCREEN_WIDTH*SCREEN_HEIGHT       ;count pix.
        mov     al,col                          ;store values...
        rep     stosb                           ;in all of video memory
        pop     di                              ;Restore DI
        pop     bp                              ;Restore BP
        ret
_cls            ENDP
```

Today, *high-level computer languages* are typically used to create programs that run on a given operating system. When writing programs using a high-level language, the programmer does not need to know about all of the inner workings of the computer. A compiler or interpreter is used to translate a high-level language such as Pascal, Basic, or C++ into relevant machine language instructions. The following code illustrates the ease with which a program might be developed using a high-level language. The following hypothetical function was written in the C language. Notice how simple the syntax is. This function simply adds two numbers and returns the sum.

Figure 8.3.2 C language function

```
int Add(int a, int b)
{
        return a+b;
}
```

I find it helpful to visualize software programs as a list of instructions for a computer. Computer programmers use programming languages to help them organize the complex logic that goes into organizing any program. Complex tasks are broken down into manageable miniprograms called functions or procedures.

Being a hobbyist programmer, I have always been fascinated by the battle that has been waged by competing hardware and operating system manufacturers. Unlike electronic music manufacturers who devised the MIDI standard in the 1980s, computer and software manufacturers have been slow to develop standards. Though consumers generally benefit from competition, the often dog-eat-dog world of computer and software developers has created a climate that is less than stable. If you have wondered why some software designers do not always create versions of their software for both the Macintosh and Windows platform, the reason is that, because of the high level of competition between vendors, recoding an application for a new operating system (and maintaining the code once it has been released) can be a very expensive proposition. As I stated earlier in the chapter, our computers are only as good as the software and operating system that is available for it. I mention all of this because Java, a relatively new technology developed by Sun Microsystems, may change all of this. While Java is primarily used to develop applets for delivery over the Web, many programmers are starting to look at Java as a potential way to develop cross-platform applications.

What is Java, anyway? Java is a language that might be described as a cross between Pascal and C++. Sun's goal with this language was to make it easy to create applications for any modern operating system. Where a high level language such as Basic or C++ distances the developer from the internal workings of a computer, Java helps to distance programmers from the many quirks of a given operating system. Java is unique in that it not only interprets code, it provides a virtual computer called the *Java virtual machine.* Java virtual machines have been developed for Windows, Macintosh, and many other operating systems. When a Java programmer writes a line of code, he or she doesn't need to worry about the syntax of the command for a specific system or if the particular function such as graphical output is available on a specific platform. The Java virtual machine interprets the command and, behind the scenes, makes the appropriate system calls on the given operating system. Although there are currently some serious limitations with this technology (Java applications run about 20 percent slower than native applications), I anticipate that, with the introduction of *native* code compilers, Java technology may well be an attractive solution for many developers. A native compiler, when fed the appropriate source code, creates machine language that is "native" to a specific processor.

With regard to Java, native compilers have the potential of improving the performance barrier that currently exists. If developers embrace this technology, you can expect many of the single platform applications that you currently run may well be available on multiple platforms.

WHY COMPUTERS CRASH

We have all experienced the frustration of losing work due to a computer malfunction or system crash. Although it is easy to demonize a computer or operating system, it is certainly advisable to understand how and why computers crash. With an understanding of the inner workings of the computer, you may be able to lessen the chances of future crashes. The first thing to understand is that a computer system is an assortment of many software programs, system extensions, device drivers, and the like. Each of these components compete for time and resources. Some components, such as a MIDI interface, need to occasionally interrupt the system to handle a time-sensitive task. Each of these programs process data, allocate and deallocate memory, read and write from disk, and do all of the things we generally expect our software to handle. With computers, an unfortunate reality is that we, as users, are at the mercy of all of the hundreds and perhaps thousands of programmers who have worked on each of the components of our system. When you consider the fact that a modern operating system may contain over a million lines of computer code, it is evident that many malfunctions are simply the result of programming bugs and logic errors.

Even though development tools have continued to improve, it is still difficult for programmers to gracefully handle each of the potential problem scenarios that result in a multitasking environment. To give you an idea of some of the potential problems that might occur, it would be helpful to demonstrate a few real-world examples. A common error involves allocation and deallocation of memory. Due to a flaw in programming logic, an application might, for a variety of reasons, neglect to deallocate a portion of memory. Such a memory leak can, over time, cause a substantial loss of available system resources. In the worst case, system resources may be minimized to the point that the operating system runs out of memory. Such a scenario will surely result in a system lockup.

Another common scenario involves interrupt-handling code. An interrupt is a signal from a device that temporarily interrupts the system. Imagine that you have just completed work on a new sequence. Your sequencing software is constantly managing system resources in order to store user data and track the current sequence of instructions of the computer code itself. In order to handle all of these complex tasks, the software frequently requests, uses, and deallocates system memory. Imagine that this process is temporarily interrupted by an interrupt message. The interrupt handler, software that is designed to handle such an interrupt, responds to the message. The interrupt handler might, because of some unforeseen event, accidentally write over some of the "saved" data or, worse, may trash the memory location where computer code resides. When the system passes control back to the sequencing application, the program has effectively been "trashed" and will surely be rendered unstable. Although these scenarios are extreme, they do represent the types of problems that might arise. Unfortunately, these types of problems may be extremely hard if not impossible to detect. The offending device driver or application software may even work perfectly fine when it leaves the manufacturer but you, as a user, end up with an unstable system due to the unique combination of components on your system.

To minimize these types of problems, I suggest the following recommendations to improve the reliability of your system:

- Minimize the number of system extensions when possible. Though that cool-looking screen saver or key commander might be nice to use, each of these extensions will provide a higher potential for system faults. (Remember that you are at the mercy of the many programmers that have worked on the various components of your system.)
- Always use current drivers. As operating systems change and evolve, code that previously worked well may now be marginally stable or even downright dangerous to system reliability.
- Don't push the resources of your system. If you are running a system with minimal RAM, it is generally best to not max out these resources by trying to run several RAM-hungry applications at the same time.
- Avoid running time-sensitive tasks while doing time-intensive work. Though it is usually fine to run background tasks such as audio processing while sequencing, these types of multitasking activities can result in a higher chance of a crash.

- Do not expect your software to respond to unusual circumstances (e.g., after beginning work on a digital audio project, don't expect your software to intuitively know that you have removed and inserted a new disk in your removable hard drive).
- Give your system a chance to complete its work (e.g., avoid trying to start a new application or shut down the current application during a lengthy write-to-disk procedure).
- When possible, limit the installation and use of additional hardware devices to those that are really essential. Though write tablets, joysticks, digital cameras, computer television cards and the like might be fun to use, they do increase the likelihood of a potential conflict between the various components of the system.
- Frequently perform disk scans and defragment your drives to find potential problems before they become catastrophic. Drives that are severely fragmented can cause two problems: first, the system will run more slowly as the computer needs to work harder to store and retrieve information. Second, a fragmented drive will increase the likelihood of write errors. If a system file has been damaged and you don't know about it, a crash will certainly result when the system tries to read data from the file. It is always a good idea to make regular backups of important system files in the event that one of these files might be damaged.
- Use caution when removing or deleting files. System files such as DLLs (dynamic link libraries) on a Wintel or files in the system folder on the Macintosh are needed for the operating system and some application programs to work properly. If you are not sure that such a file can be safely deleted, place it in a temporary folder for a few weeks. If a program or the system crashes because it cannot find the given file, it is then a simple matter to copy the file back to its original location.
- Do not upgrade your operating system or application programs if you *must* rely on the system for an upcoming or current project. While upgrades can improve system reliability, they can also cause system instability. It's usually best to save a major upgrade for a time when you don't need to rely on the stability of your system because many users will experience problems as a result of the upgrade. When possible, take steps to back up your data and, if the installation software provides the option, keep the older version of the application backed up on disk so that you can revert to a previous version should the need arise.

- Save your work often. Though this will not help with the reliability of your system, the above discussion should scare you enough to remember that your work is only as current as the last save and backup. Computers do fail, and it is up to you as a user to take some precautionary measures. You can lose the ability to save your work in the event of a power failure or catastrophic system crash.

PERIPHERALS AND EXPANSION CARDS

MIDI interfaces. If you plan to make music with your computer, you will want to consider investing in additional hardware to increase the capabilities of your system. An obvious first choice is to invest in a MIDI interface. As an educator, one of the most common questions I field relates to the type of MIDI interface to buy. Let's start with some inexpensive solutions. If you own a Wintel computer, chances are that you can add MIDI capability for as little as $15. Nearly every newer PC contains a sound card. In general, a joystick port will be provided on the back of the computer on the soundcard. In many cases, an inexpensive *breakout* cable, when connected to the joystick port, will provide basic MIDI in and out to the computer. Note that you will need to change the MIDI devices settings in your MIDI software to take advantage of this inexpensive solution. For Macintosh users, a simple MIDI serial device will provide an inexpensive solution for MIDI input and output. Note that a serial device will only be an option for Macs that have a serial port. None of the newer Macs include this port, so you will want to check this out before you spend your money on a serial device.

If you own a newer PC running Windows 98/2000 or a newer Macintosh such as the iMac, G3, or G4 you will want to consider investing in a USB MIDI interface. Though USB interfaces are still more expensive than the entry level serial devices, USB provides several benefits including larger *bandwidth* (the amount of data transmitted in a given period of time) and the ability to *hot-plug* a device without first powering down the system. Though some of the early USB devices have been problematic, I expect these to be a viable solution as manufacturers work to improve USB device drivers. Some manufacturers are now developing products that take advantage of the higher bandwidth of USB to enable more accurate recording and playback of MIDI data than would be possible using a traditional serial port.

If you intend to regularly use more than one synthesizer, you may want to consider investing in a *multiport* MIDI interface. A multiport interface provides several (two to eight) discrete paths of MIDI data. As you will learn in Chapter 9, "Introduction to MIDI," one MIDI port provides sixteen channels, so a 2-port interface would provide thirty-two channels (2x16). Similarly, an 8-port interface would provide a whopping 128 channels of MIDI. The benefits of a multiport interface are twofold: First, more complex streams of MIDI data may be sent and received using such a system. Second, multiport systems are generally easier to use in that each synthesizer may be dedicated to a single port. This frees you from having to enable and disable MIDI channels on each of your synthesizers each time you create a new sequence. Two -port MIDI interfaces start at around $100. A professional 8-port interface may cost $400 or more.

One other MIDI expansion option is available. Several single and multiport interfaces are available as internal expansion cards. The downside of this option is that you need to open up the computer to install the card. Also note that not all MIDI interfaces are cross-platform compatible. Before you purchase a MIDI interface, be sure to carefully read the specifications to make sure it will work with your computer and operating system.

Soundcards. Soundcards have evolved to address the need for audio and MIDI playback in multimedia systems. Providing your needs are simple and your means are few, a soundcard will provide decent fidelity as a first synthesizer. Some of the software synthesizers such as Seer Systems' *Reality Synthesizer* or Roland's *Virtual Sound Canvas*, sound surprisingly good even on consumer soundcards. If you plan to do serious digital audio work, you will need to think about investing in a professional model audio card. I make a distinction here between multi-media soundcards that are generally designed for the consumer market and full-fledged commercial audio cards designed for professional work. While it is certainly possible to do digital audio recording with a consumer sound card, you generally get what you pay for in this regard. Professional audio cards will cost several hundred to several thousand dollars. As with MIDI inter-faces, be sure to carefully research brands to find one that will be most appropriate for your computer, operating system, and software. Also note that even though the card promises digital output, the fidelity of your recordings may be less than pristine. In short, not all DACs (digital audio converters) are created equal. Many audio cards provide a combination of an internal card and an external unit to actually connect line-level signals to your computer. Because the inner workings of a computer are notoriously noisy, an external device may provide better fidelity. With that said, I have used several internal cards and have been generally pleased with the results.

Printers. If you plan to prepare musical scores for other musicians or need to print documents or label CDs, you will need to invest in a printer. A new printer can cost anywhere from $50 to several thousand dollars. Though laser printer technology has long provided superior print quality, advancements in bubble jet/inkjet technology has blurred these lines somewhat. There are two primary things to consider when evaluating a printer. Dots per inch (dpi) refers to the number of dots used in one square inch to represent an image. A 1,200 dpi printer will provide much cleaner output than a 600 dpi printer. Note that some manufacturers will specify both a vertical and horizontal resolution such as 720x320 dpi. Another number to look at is pages per minute (ppm). As the term implies, ppm indicates the number of pages that may be printed in one minute. If you don't plan to do an inordinate amount of printing, a 4 ppm printer may provide acceptable results. If you plan to do lots of printing (e.g., you are writing a book like this one), you will want to consider investing in a more powerful printer. If you intend to create your own CD labels, you may also want to consider investing in a color printer. Picture-quality color printers have become surprisingly affordable in recent years (many of them cost around $100). One other issue you should look at before investing in a printer is the cost of the ink or toner replacements. Many ink and toner replacements cost $25 or more, so you will want to do a little math to see what your actual per-page cost will be for printing. It may well be that, while more expensive initially, a laser printer will provide a substantial savings in per-page costs over the long haul.

Video cards. Although video cards are marginally useful to musicians, I mention these here because they can be very helpful for creating QuickTime or AVI files from a video or when you want to capture a still picture for use on an album cover or in a publication. Personal computers are so powerful these days that is also possible to do digital video editing in your home studio. With the proper hardware it is possible to digitally record data from a video camera and use specialized software such as an Avid system to manipulate and edit the video. This could be a great option if you want to create an MTV-style video of your band. As with digital audio recording, digital video editing requires a tremendous amount of hard drive space and RAM. If you plan to do much of this, you will also need to think about investing in an additional hard drive(s). Note that many digital video solutions are now available that take advantage of USB (low end) and FireWire (high end) connections.

Speakers. Multimedia audio monitors have really improved over the past several years. Many monitors are available that, for a few hundred dollars, provide reasonably accurate playback. It is important to note that many of these systems are designed for gamers (i.e., the speakers are not accurate enough for serious music monitoring work). If you want to do serious mastering work, you will need to invest in a professional referencing system. Such a system may cost well over a thousand dollars but will provide more accurate playback of your music. With the advent of USB, another interesting trend has been the development of digital speakers. With a digital speaker, you don't have to worry about the signal being degraded by interference that finds its way into the signal chain. Of course, a digital signal doesn't do much good if the speakers do a poor job of transducing the signal into the audio domain. Put another way, inferior speakers will still sound inferior even if they are digital.

Computer monitor. One of the more expensive yet essential pieces of hardware is your computer monitor. If you plan to spend a great deal of time in front of a computer monitor, I advise you to spend the extra money to get a high-quality monitor. Nothing is worse than striving to beat a deadline and looking through blurry eyes at a low-quality monitor. Buying a monitor that supports a high *refresh rate* will minimize eye strain that is a result of monitor flicker. Monitor size is another important consideration. Large monitors allow you to work at higher resolutions and provide more "real estate" for applications. If you run the current crop of sequencing and notation software, you will really appreciate having some extra space onscreen. It is not uncommon to find yourself running dozens of MIDI tracks, with additional windows open for editing and audio processing.

Tip: If money is no object, an LCD monitor can be very easy on the eyes. LCDs have the added benefit of a small footprint. If you have ever tried to find space for a 19- or 20-inch monitor, you will appreciate how slim an LCD really is. Though LCDs are still relatively expensive ($800 or more), look for prices to fall as manufacturers develop more cost effective production of these monitors. I would also suggest that you spend some *time trying out a variety of monitors before you make a purchase decision. Though the specifications can be helpful in determining an appropriate monitor for your needs, nothing beats hands-on experience for determining the monitor that will provide the best price/performance ratio for you.*

Storage devices. As I mentioned previously, expect your hard drive to eventually fail. With this in mind, it becomes necessary to back up important projects and documents. Thankfully, many relatively inexpensive solutions are now available. For many computer users, a removable drive is a handy solution. Zip and Super disks provide inexpensive backup of data, but note that these technologies are limited in size. If you don't plan to do digital audio work, these disks should provide adequate storage for most situations. If you need to regularly back up large digital audio or video files, you will need to invest in a device such as a *magneto-optical* drive or recordable CD. For musicians, the recordable or re-recordable CD (CDR) solution is obviously attractive. A CD recorder will allow you to back up data such as audio files just as if the CD were a removable floppy or hard disk. An added benefit is that you can also use a CDR to record an audio CD. Note that CDRs have two distinct disadvantages over other archiving solutions: CDRs are still fairly slow (4x speeds are still the norm), and that as opposed to a CD rewriteable (CD-RW), you can't add additional data to a disk once the CDR has been "burned." Still, at around $1 per 650 MB of removable storage, a CDR can be a cost effective data archiving solution.

Optimizing your system. To this point we have learned much about computer hardware, software, operating systems, peripheral devices, and the like. To conclude this chapter we will consider ways to improve the performance of your system.

As I mentioned previously, one of the best things you can do to tune your system and improve reliability is to remove any extraneous extensions or drivers. If your goal is to run an efficient music producing system, you will want to take the time to disable things that may be clogging your system resources such as screen savers, calendar and reminder programs, system resource meters, and the like. In short, *any* programs that run concurrently with your primary application program has the potential for slowing things down. If you are running low on RAM, I suggest that you avoid software RAM doublers. These days RAM is so inexpensive that I recommend adding more RAM instead of trying to get by with a doubler.

It is a good idea to regularly defragment your hard drives. When a drive is fragmented, the many files on the drive are spread about in a haphazard fashion. Defragmenting moves the files to consecutive positions on the drives and allows the computer to find files more quickly. It also takes less time for the drive to find empty space when writing new data to disk.

Depending on your setup, you may want to get in the habit of temporarily disabling some types of extensions when you do heavy computing such as digital audio recording. Extensions that establish network connections or device drivers that communicate with peripheral devices can certainly slow down a system. In general, disable everything that you don't regularly use to achieve maximum efficiency with your system.

Finally, you should periodically clean house to remove old program and data files that you no longer use. I recently took a few hours to delete and backup files on my trusty laptop computer. I was shocked to find that I had more than 800MB of files that were not really necessary for my music and office applications! Just remember that any unneeded files take up precious hard disk space and can cause your system to work slower. Just as it takes time for a human to sort though a huge stack of files, the computer also needs extra time to wade through lots of extraneous data on disk.

Tip: An unfortunate reality of modern computing is that computer viruses do exist. Though not all viruses are malicious, any virus is undesirable in that it may cause your system to become unstable. Most viruses propagate by attaching themselves to "healthy" executable files. When an unsuspecting user runs an infected application, the virus loads itself into memory and attempts to infect other files. There are two primary ways of avoiding infection by a computer virus. Virus protection software can help to minimize the risk of catching a virus, but note that virus protection software needs to be regularly updated to be effective against new forms of viruses. Also note that virus protection software may need to be disabled during time-intensive tasks such as digital audio recording. You can also minimize your risk by avoiding downloads from questionable sources. Unfortunately, even these precautions may not be enough to protect against a virus: two of the major sequencing vendors have released products with infected disks in the last two years! As always, backup your work regularly to avoid a catastrophe.

[1]Wintel: a hybrid of Windows (an operating system for PCs) and Intel (a microchip found in many PCs).

Introduction to MIDI

How things change. In 1978, I purchased my first synthesizer. It could play a single note at a time, the sounds had to be programmed each and every time I used the instrument, and it had to be retuned every hour or so because the oscillators floated out of tune. The cost: around $1,000. Today, that same $1,000 could buy a synthesizer capable of playing 64 notes at a time with 16 to 32 simultaneous sounds. The same synthesizer would provide 500 to 1000 realistic timbres and plenty of stunning nontraditional sounds as well. Unlike most of the rest of the world, MIDI musicians can count on wonderful advancements in technology and good value for the money.

In this chapter, we will explore some of the exciting technologies available to musicians today. A primary focus will be the Musical Instrument Digital Interface, or MIDI. In other chapters we will look at related topics such as computers and operating systems, MIDI software and hardware, sequencing environments, synthesizers, and digital audio. Let the fun begin.

INTRODUCTION TO MIDI

In pre-MIDI days, keyboard and synthesizer manufacturers competed in an environment without well-defined standards. To be viable in the marketplace, each synthesizer had to function as a stand-alone machine (usually in the form of a keyboard controller, sound source, and several modifiers). In order to add new functionality to their setups, synthesists of this period had to purchase (and lug around) another self-contained synthesizer. Although communication protocols existed, no standards were in place. Each manufacturer provided proprietary communication between their own systems. This all changed in the 1980s with the advent of MIDI.

MIDI is a communications protocol. Through MIDI, a keyboard manufactured by one company can communicate with a synthesizer manufactured by another company. This same keyboard can also send or receive data from a computer or any other type of MIDI hardware. You could make a comparison to a standard phone line: when you call a friend, you don't care who manufactured the phone on the other end or what carrier they use, all that is important here is that the conversation be audible. The same goes for MIDI. MIDI allows for complex networks of synthesizers, computers, and other devices to communicate seamlessly with one another.

It is hard to fathom the huge impact MIDI has had on the music industry. Virtually every facet of music production has been affected: MIDI is used in the production of a majority of television shows, feature films, popular music recordings, television and radio spots, industrial films, and in live performance as a way of automating light shows, mixing sound, and a plethora of other applications.

Although MIDI has proven to be a valuable aid to many musicians and producers, it has a negative side. In pre-MIDI days, all of the major television and film studios employed a staff of many orchestral musicians, writers, and arrangers. The decline of the studio orchestra coincides perfectly with the advent of MIDI technology. Although most would agree that this is a sad scenario, MIDI is used in many of these situations as a simple matter of practicality. A lone synthesist can produce a complete soundtrack for a television show in a matter of days and much more economically than productions utilizing dozens of musicians and arrangers. It is true that musicians have lost jobs to MIDI, but it is also clear that MIDI will never be a replacement for a real orchestra. It should also be said that this same technology is also available to these musicians as well. Many fine woodwind, string, and brass players have found success providing MIDI soundtracks with the added advantage of being able to provide the "real thing" when needed.

It is clear that MIDI is here to stay. Let's look at some of the specifics that allow this marvelous technology to work.

PERFORMANCE DATA

A key concept to understand with regard to MIDI is the idea of *performance data*. When a pianist records a MIDI performance using a MIDI *sequencer*[1], nearly every nuance of the performance is recorded by the sequencer: what notes were played at what time, how strongly each key was struck, when the note was released, the exact point in time when the damper pedal was pressed and released. Many other types of performance data may be recorded. The MIDI specification provides for a wide variety of messages that describe performance data as well as system related functions. Some of the messages are standardized (the damper pedal, for example). Other types of data are available for the performer to define. We will look at performance messages in more detail later in this chapter.

It is important to note that what is not recorded as a part of a MIDI performance are the actual sounds. Unlike a traditional tape recording, a sequence only records performance data. This performance data may be used to "play" any type of MIDI instrument. For example, a pianist might decide to change the sound from an acoustic piano to an electric piano. The performance data remains the same but the actual sounds we hear will depend on how the receiving instrument is set up. The bottom line is that a MIDI performance is represented by a series of numbers, not actual sounds. These numbers, when they are recorded, can be sent to any MIDI device. These same numbers may also be manipulated with appropriate hardware or software to fix mistakes or edit the performance in much the same way that a word processor is used to edit or manipulate words and characters.

THE MIDI NETWORK

Five-pin DIN MIDI is the most common method for connecting a network of keyboards and computers. Although MIDI is often used to create music with a complexity that rivals or even surpasses that of the modern symphony orchestra, it is interesting to note that the MIDI network is a *serial* network. That is to say that performance data (the numeric messages that represent a performance) travels down a MIDI cable one message at a time. How then is it possible to record and play back chords (i.e. two or more notes played simultaneously)? Technically speaking, it is not possible to play simultaneous notes through MIDI. In practical terms, we will perceive a chord if the individual notes are struck nearly simultaneously. To better understand this concept, let's look at some numbers.

MIDI messages are transmitted at a fixed rate of 31,250 bits per second (bps). A MIDI byte contains eight bits plus a start and stop bit for a total of 10 bits. At this rate, a maximum of 3,125 10-bit words can be transmitted each second through a MIDI cable. Therefore, a MIDI byte requires around 320 microseconds (ms) for transmission. Although it has been documented that humans can hear time delays in the range of 1 to 2ms under optimal conditions[2], in a musical context, we tend to hear sounds with a delay of 20 to 30ms as being synchronous. An average multibyte MIDI message requires 960 microseconds for transmission—10 times faster than the 20 to 30ms threshold. Simply put, we perceive these sounds as being produced simultaneously.

Unlike many computer messages that utilize two-way connections such as a modem or serial cable, MIDI messages only travel in one direction. In order for a synthesizer to send and receive MIDI messages, it is necessary to connect it using two MIDI cables connected to the In and Out *ports*. A common scenario involves connecting a *master* controller keyboard to a *slave* synthesizer or sound module[3]. In this instance, the MIDI Out of the master is connected to the MIDI In of the slave.

Figure 9.1 Master keyboard connected to slave synthesizer

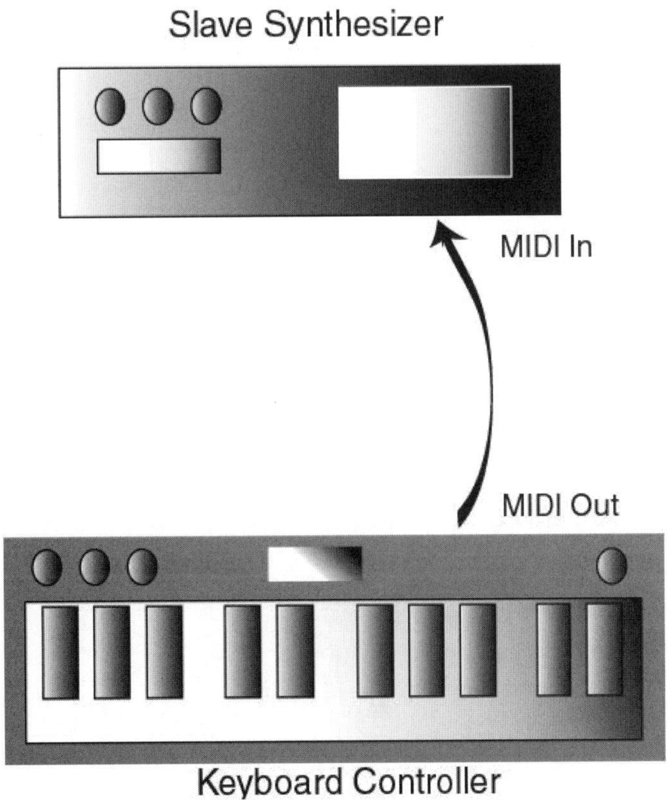

Slave Synthesizer

MIDI In

MIDI Out

Keyboard Controller

A third type of port—the Thru port—is often a source of
confusion for beginning MIDI musicians. The Thru port sends
an exact copy of any data that arrives at the In port. Although
the Thru port doesn't send data on its own, you can think of the
Thru port as a type of Out port. It is used to *daisy-chain* several
MIDI devices together. Imagine that you would like to connect a
master keyboard with two slave synthesizers. Connect the master
to the slave as usual using an Out to In connection. Connect the
first slave to the second slave using Thru to In. In this case, any
data sent to the first slave will be passed along to the second
(remember that the Thru port sends an exact copy of any data
that arrives at the In port).

Figure 9.2 Master keyboard connected to two slave synthesizers

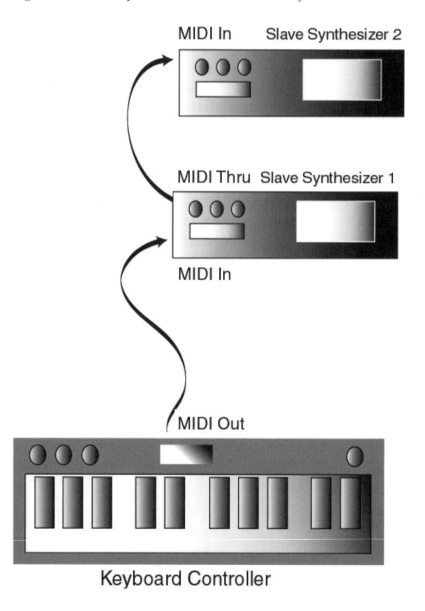

Making Music with Your Computer

What would happen if you connected the Out of slave 1 to the In of slave 2? Nothing—slave 2 would not receive any of the messages from the master keyboard. In this instance, slave 1 would not pass any data from the master keyboard to the second module. The Thru port would be the only way to pass along a copy of the data to slave 2.

Some synthesizers provide only an In and Out port. These types of instruments usually allow you to specify whether the Out port functions as a true Out port or a Thru port. It is rare to find only two ports on a modern synthesizer or other type of MIDI device.

Another common setup involves the connection of multiple sound modules and a controller to a sequencer. In this scenario the modules must be able to respond to both real-time keyboard data as well as playback of sequenced messages. In this case, the master keyboard will also need to respond to sequenced messages. Note that some keyboard controllers can not "play" any sounds. They are specifically designed only to "control" other devices. It is not usually necessary to connect the output of the sequencer to the input of this type of device, since it can not produce any sounds.

Figure 9.3 Hookup of master keyboard, modules, and sequencer

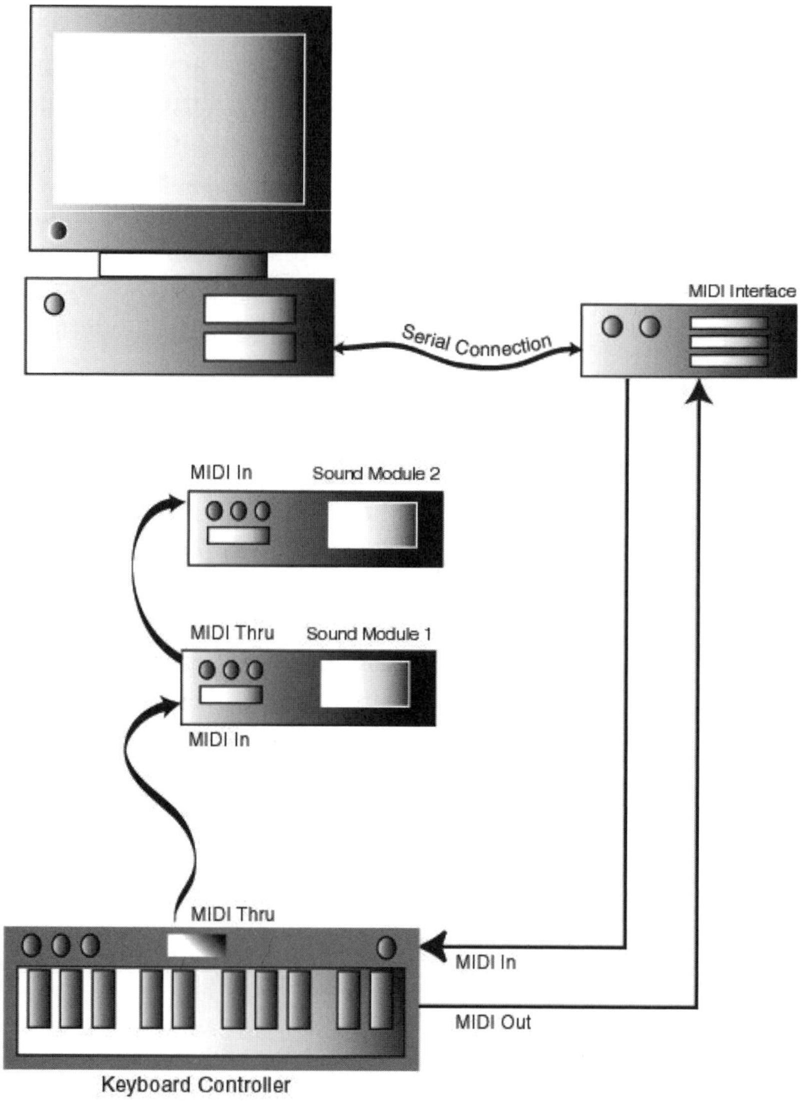

In this example, a message that initiates from the master keyboard will travel to the sequencer where it will be processed (and recorded if the sequencer is set to this mode). Depending on the configuration of the sequencer, the message will be sent via the Out port (a form of Thru that can be turned on or off from the sequencer). The message will return to the In port of the master keyboard. A copy of this incoming message will be sent along to the modules via the Thru port on the master keyboard.

There are many variations on the previous scenarios. If you plan to develop an extensive MIDI network, you might want to consider investing in *a MIDI Thru box*. A Thru box provides a more elegant method for connecting several MIDI devices than the daisy-chaining method just described. The previous setup, however, will work fine for a modest MIDI studio without the need for additional hardware.

LOCAL ON/OFF

You may have noticed one problem with the previous example. In its default setup, the keyboard would produce a tone when the keys are struck. Depending on how MIDI channels are assigned, the keyboard might also rearticulate the note when the note-on message returns to the keyboard from the sequencer. The local on and off setting is used to alleviate this problem. When Local is turned to off, the connection between the keyboard and the internal synthesizer is broken. MIDI messages are sent as usual, but the internal synthesizer will only respond to incoming messages. This is exactly what you want. In effect, the master keyboard functions as a slave to the sequencer.

CHANNELS AND TRACKS

To this point we have concerned ourselves only with a single timbre. But what if you want to create *multitimbral* sequences? Enter the concept of a MIDI channel. The MIDI specification allows for transmission of sixteen separate channels of data to be sent and received by a MIDI instrument. MIDI channels are analogous to channels on a cable television set. The TV can be set to respond to any of a number of channels. Although there are many channels, each of the channels arrives at the television through a single cable. With MIDI, all sixteen channels of messages are sent on a single MIDI cable.

Sixteen channels felt luxurious to musicians used to dealing with monophonic synthesizers, but today it is common for MIDI musicians to use more than sixteen channels. This is achieved through the use of special hardware and software called *multiport* or *multicable* systems. A multiport interface generally provides two to eight independent paths of data (sixteen separate channels for each device). This type of setup is easier to use and maintain than a network with many daisy chains and will provide the added benefit of allowing you to devote as many as sixteen MIDI channels to each of the MIDI instruments in your rig.

A sequence *track* represents a collection of MIDI performance data. Hardware or software sequencers provide from sixteen to many hundreds of tracks. In most cases, a track may be assigned to any MIDI channel but only sixteen possible channels are available. Why would anyone need more than sixteen tracks then? The answer has to do with flexibility and convenience. A pianist might, for example, record the right hand of a piano selection on track one. The left hand could be recorded on track two. Both tracks could be assigned to play back the piano sound on channel one. Here's another example: if you have ever watched a good drummer in action, you know what it means to be ambidextrous. It is often helpful to allocate many tracks to drums: hi-hat, snare, kick, etc. Although many tracks might be used, the entire drum kit would still take up only one of sixteen possible channels.

MIDI MATH 101

You have already learned that MIDI involves the transmission of digital performance data. What types of numbers are actually transmitted? Before we delve into the intricacies of MIDI messages, let's review some basic math.

If you have ever looked at the back of a MIDI instrument manual, you may have wondered what the strange looking numbers such as F-7 or x11110111 mean. For MIDI musicians, three types of numbering systems are relevant: decimal (what you and I are used to), hexadecimal, and binary.

The term bit stands for a binary digit. A binary digit can only be one of two numbers: one or zero. You can represent large numbers using only ones and zeros (providing you use enough digits). The base-2 binary number system is well suited for use with computers because of the simple on/off mechanisms associated with logic gates and other electrical devices. Although it's difficult for most of us to count in binary (don't worry—you don't need to do this to be a MIDI musician), binary numbers are the basis for the computer revolution. In fact, even though their operation seems complex, computers really can only count using ones and zeros! The greater the number of bits, the larger the number that can be represented in binary. Let's count from zero to three using a 2-bit binary number to see how this works.

binary	decimal
00	0
01	1
10	2
11	3

A 4-bit binary number can represent decimal numbers in the range of 0 to 15.

binary	decimal
0000	0
0001	1
0010	2
0011	3
.	.
.	.
.	.
1111	15

A 7-bit binary number can represent decimal numbers in the range of 0 to 127.

binary	decimal
0000000	0
0000001	1
0000010	2
0000011	3
.	.
.	.
.	.
1111111	127

As you can see, the greater the number of bits used, the greater the numeric range.

Hexadecimal is a numbering scheme that is often used with MIDI. Many software applications such as *Performer* or *Cakewalk Pro Audio* allow you to send special MIDI system exclusive messages using hexadecimal notation.

Figure 9.4 Cakewalk Pro Audio (hexadecimal entry)

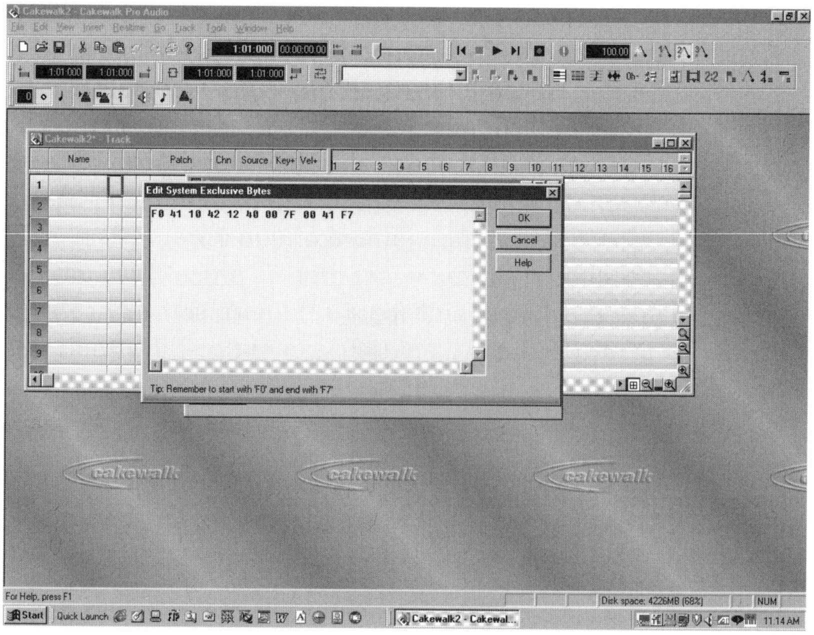

It is interesting to note that, in the hexadecimal system, the numbers from 0 to 15 can be represented using only a single character. Let's see how this works.

hex	binary	decimal (base 10)
0	0000	0
1	0001	1
2	0010	2
3	0011	3
4	0100	4
5	0101	5
6	0110	6
7	0111	7
8	1000	8
9	1001	9
A	1010	10
B	1011	11
C	1100	12
D	1101	13
E	1110	14
F	1111	15
10	10000	16

etc.

Hexadecimal notation is often used in MIDI applications because it is a convenient shorthand for representing binary numbers. By looking at binary numbers four digits at a time, you can easily convert between binary and hexadecimal.

binary number (one byte)	1111	1011
hexadecimal equivalent	F	B

1111011=FB

Though hexadecimal notation may look strange at first, just remember that in this numbering system, the letters *A* through *F* are equivalent to decimal numbers 10 to 15.

Do you need to be able to count in binary or translate from decimal to hexadecimal in order to use MIDI technology? Probably not. There are times, however, that an understanding of the underlying numbering schemes is helpful. Advanced users often use these numbering schemes to extend the functionality of software to include system exclusive dumps, creation of patch lists, remote control of advanced MIDI networks, and the like. Many fine freeware and shareware calculators can help you when it is necessary to make this type of conversion.

Tip: Windows 98/2000 includes a free calculator that can be set up to convert decimal, binary, and hexadecimal numbers. You can find this in the Start menu under the accessories menu. Run the program and select the View menu. Toggle the scientific option to on and you will have a handy binary and hexadecimal converter.

WHAT'S FOR LUNCH? BITS, BYTES, OR NIBBLES?

In computer jargon, a grouping of eight bits is termed a *byte*. To be more precise, a byte refers to the amount of memory space needed to store a single character on a given system (typically eight bits). A related term *word* is also used to describe a grouping of bits, though the term is not well defined. In some circles numeric words may be made up of eight, sixteen, thirty-two, or even higher numbers of bits.

If eight bits make up a byte, half a byte (four bits) is of course a *nibble*. Remember that the greater the number of bits, the greater the range of possible values. A byte (eight bits) can represent numbers in the range of 0 to 255. In MIDI, eight bit bytes are used. The first bit, appropriately termed the *most significant bit,* is used to specify the type of byte; either *status byte* or *data byte*. The following example should clarify this concept.

Figure 9.5 An eight bit word

Eight bit byte (eight ones and zeros)	
Leftmost bit=most significant bit (0 in this example)	
0100	0000
first nibble	second nibble

Can you calculate the decimal value of this byte?

INTRODUCTION TO MIDI

MIDI Manufacturers Association. Many of the tables in this section have been adapted from information available on the MMA Web site. You can purchase *The Complete MIDI 1.0 Detailed Specification* from MMA for about $50. Although the MMA encourages the dissemination of this information, the MIDI specification is periodically revised, so you may wish to contact them to purchase a current version of the MIDI spec.

MIDI Manufacturers Association
PO Box 3173
La Habra, California 90632-3173
http://www.midi.org

MIDI STRUCTURES

Let's look in greater detail at one of the most common MIDI messages, a simple note-on message. A note-on message is comprised of an 8-bit status byte and two 8-bit data bytes. How does a receiving instrument tell the difference between status bytes and data bytes? The answer lies in the concept of the *most significant bit*. The first bit of any status byte will be equal to one. The first bit of any data byte will be equal to zero. Because the first bit of any MIDI byte is reserved, only seven remaining bits are available to represent the actual numeric value. Therefore,

MIDI values will typically fall in the range of 0 to 127 (the largest number that can be represented using seven bits of data). It is important to understand that some MIDI messages may require more than one data byte. The extra data byte(s) will provide additional information (e.g., the note number and attack velocity for a note-on message). For other types of data such as a pitch bend message, the bytes are handled in groups: two or more data bytes are used to describe a summative value greater than 127. Consider the following note-on message.

Figure 9.6 Note-on message

	Status byte	Data Byte 1	Data Byte 2
Data (in binary)	1001 0001	0011 1100	0111 0000
	Status/Channel #	Note #	Attack Velocity
	note-on, ch. 2	MIDI note=#60	velocity=112

The note-on message consists of a status byte and two data bytes. You can think of the status byte as a description byte: it alerts the receiving device as to the type of message and to what MIDI channel this message relates. The first bit identifies the byte as a status byte. The next three bits describe the type of message, in this case a note-on command. The remaining four bits identify the MIDI channel. The observant reader has probably already noticed an inconsistency. If the largest possible value that can be represented using four bits of data is fifteen, how is it possible to identify all sixteen MIDI channels? The solution is that a one is always added to the second nibble in a channel message. MIDI channels always fall in the range of one to sixteen (zero is not used). This is always handled automatically by the receiving device, so it's nothing to worry about.

The first bit of the first data byte identifies it as a data byte (value of zero). The remaining seven bits of this byte describe the MIDI note (0 to 127). It is helpful to remember that middle C on the piano is equal to MIDI note number sixty.

As you have probably already guessed, the final byte of the note-on message describes the attack velocity—how loud or soft the note was struck. Once again, the first bit describes this byte as a data byte. The remaining seven bits describe the velocity in a range of 0 to 127.

If a MIDI synthesizer could talk (some of them do), it might describe the previous note-on message as follows:

"I am sending a status byte. This byte describes a note-on event on channel two. I will now send two data bytes to further clarify this message. The first data byte will tell you to play note number 60 (middle C). The second data byte will tell you how loud to play the note (value of 112). Be ready for another status byte that describes my next message..."

MIDI MESSAGES

The MIDI specification provides for a great variety of messages that enable performers to capture and play back performance data. MIDI also allows for transmission of nonperformance data such as system messages and mode messages.

MIDI messages fall into two categories: *channel voice messages* and *system messages.* You have already seen an example of a channel voice message. The note-on message is one example. Channel messages relate to performance data. These messages describe various types of performance data that relate to a specific MIDI channel. *Channel mode messages,* a subset of channel voice messages, relate to how a receiving device will respond to MIDI channel messages. System messages, as the name implies, relate to the operating system of the receiving device and do not contain actual performance data. Before we get into each of the specific types of messages it might be helpful to look at a list of all the possible types of MIDI messages. Look closely at the first four bits of the status byte.

Figure 9.7 List of possible status bytes

Status Byte	Type of Message	Number of Data Bytes
	Channel Voice Messages	
1000cccc[1]	note-off	2: note and release velocity
1001cccc	note-on	2: note and attack velocity
1010cccc	polyphonic after touch	2: note and pressure
1011cccc	control change	2: controller ID (0-120) and value
1100cccc	program change	1: program (patch) number
1101cccc	channel after touch	1: pressure value
1110cccc	pitch bend	2: pitch bend LSB and MSB[2]
	Channel Mode Message	
	(see control change above)	
1011cccc	channel mode	2: controller ID 120-127 and value
	System Exclusive Messages	
11110000	system exclusive message	?: variable number of data bytes

System Common Messages		
11110xxx[3]	system common	0-2: type of message
11110010	song position pointer	2: song position pointer LSB and MSB
11110011	song select	1: specifies song to be played
11110110	tune request	0
11110111	end of exclusive	0
System Real-Time Messages		
11111xxx	system real time	0
11111000	timing clock	0
11111010	start	0
11111011	continue	0
11111100	stop	0
11111110	active sensing	0
11111111	reset	0

[1] cccc=channel number 0-15 equals 1-16
[2] LSB=least significant byte, MSB=most significant byte
[3] xxx=three-bit numeric value

Do you see the pattern that exists in the first nibble? As you have already learned, the first bit of any status byte is always one. The remaining three bits of the first nibble determines the type of message. Values of zero to six (000 to 110 binary) identify the message as a type of channel voice message. (The channel mode message is a variation of the control change message). If these three bits are equal to seven (111 binary) the message is a system message. For system messages, if the second nibble is equal to zero, the message is a system exclusive message (commonly described in hexadecimal as F0). If the first bit of the second nibble is zero, the message is a system common message. If this bit is one, the message is a real-time message.

What does this all mean? MIDI is an elegant network that provides performers with a wide variety of messages to accurately describe performance data and take control of a complex MIDI setup! Do you need to know what each of these messages means to be a proficient MIDI musician? Well, yes! The more you know about these types of messages the more expressive you will be as a performer. Let's take a look at what these messages actually mean to a MIDI musician. The remainder of the chapter will familiarize you with all of the possible MIDI messages: channel voice messages, channel mode messages, and system messages.

All channel messages consist of a status byte and one or more data bytes. The channel number is encoded as a part of the status byte (the least significant nibble of the first byte). There are seven possible channel voice messages: note-off, note-on, polyphonic aftertouch, channel aftertouch, program change, pitch bend, and control change.

Note-on. The most common of all MIDI messages. A note-on message consists of a status byte and two data bytes. The first data byte contains the MIDI note number. The second data byte is used for attack velocity.

Figure 9.8 Note-on message

Status Byte	Data Byte 1	Data Byte 2
1001cccc	note number (0-127)	attack velocity (0-127)

Note-off. The note-off message complements the note-on message. Like the note-on message, this message consists of a status byte and two data bytes. The first data byte represents the MIDI note number. The second data byte indicates release velocity. Though release velocity is not always implemented in synthesizers, this parameter can be potentially very expressive. You might, for example, experiment with assigning filter cutoff or other parameters to this release value. Note that in some sequencers the note-off message is not used. A note-on with a velocity of zero is often used as an equivalent to the note-off message.

Figure 9.9 Note-off message

Status Byte	Data Byte 1	Data Byte 2
1000cccc	note number (0-127)	release velocity (0-127)

Tip: When a note-off message is lost, the result is a stuck note. One way that you might lose a note-off message is by changing a channel assignment or patch while holding down a key. Most sequencers include a panic button that will fix a stuck note. You can also try playing a chromatic scale on the offending channel to find the stuck note.

Aftertouch. This is used to alter a note after it has been struck but before the note is released. Aftertouch is usually added by applying additional pressure to a key after the note has been played. It can also be applied using a mod wheel or data slider. Not all synthesizers respond to or transmit aftertouch messages.

The two forms of aftertouch are polyphonic and channel. With polyphonic aftertouch, each note of a chord can respond to differing amounts of aftertouch pressure. Polyphonic aftertouch is the least-common form of aftertouch. Channel aftertouch affects all notes on a given channel.

Polyphonic aftertouch. Polyphonic aftertouch messages consist of the usual status byte and two data bytes. The first data byte carries the note number. The second data byte transmits the amount of aftertouch pressure.

Figure 9.10 Polyphonic aftertouch message

Status Byte	Data Byte 1	Data Byte 2
1010cccc	note number (0-127)	amount of pressure (0-127)

Channel aftertouch. Channel aftertouch is the most common form of aftertouch. With this message, an increase in aftertouch pressure on *any* key will increase the amount of aftertouch for all notes currently playing on the given channel.

The channel aftertouch message requires only a status byte and a single data byte. The data byte provides the amount of aftertouch pressure for the entire channel (any currently playing notes.)

Figure 9.11 Channel aftertouch message

Status Byte	Data Byte
1101cccc	amount of pressure (0-127)

Program/patch change. Program change messages (sometimes referred to as patch change messages) are used to select sounds. It is important to understand that the program change message is simply a number. The number will mean different things to different receiving devices. A program change message with a value of five might, on one instrument, call up a piano patch. On another MIDI instrument this same message might call up a bass sound. How an instrument responds to a specific patch change message is up to the manufacturer and/or user of the instrument. There is one exception to this rule: *General MIDI* instruments are designed to call up a predefined sound for specific patch change messages. We will learn more about General MIDI later in this chapter.

Program change messages can be a source of confusion for musicians new to MIDI. Although most software sequencers allow a user to select patches by name, the names are just a pretty face for an underlying program change message. If the software and synthesizer are not properly configured, the names onscreen probably won't match the sounds coming out of your synthesizer.

Figure 9.12.1 Program change message

Status Byte	Data Byte 1
1100cccc	program (patch) number

Pitch bend. If you have ever listened to a great blues guitar player, you know how important fluctuations in pitch or "bent" notes can be. The pitch bend message allows a performer to adjust the pitch of a tone in real time. This message requires two data bytes. Both bytes, taken together, provide a number that is greater than our usual 7-bit single data byte. By combining the two bytes, the pitch bend message has a resolution of 14 bits (+/- 8192). By adjusting pitch bend sensitivity, it is possible to bend notes in a range of sixty-three semitones above or sixty-four semitones below the standard pitch.

A word of advice: in its default setting, the pitch bend wheel or lever will reside at zero—the middle position. If you ever have problems with strange and sudden transposition while sequencing, check the pitch bend lever. If you record a series of bends and end the recording before the lever is reset to zero, the synthesizer will sound as if it is in the wrong key. Also note that pitch bend levers generally transmit a flood of information into the MIDI stream. It may be wise to filter some of these messages while recording or thin them after recording pitch bend data. Data thinning is analogous to a comb or hair brush: you could remove every other tooth on a comb and the comb would still work. Most sequencers provide options for filtering and thinning data. Pitch bend will usually sound convincing even with a fair amount of thinning.

Figure 9.12.2 Program change message

Status Byte	Data Byte 1	Data Byte 2
1110cccc	least significant 7-bits	most significant 7-bits

Control change. Easily the most complicated and extensive MIDI message, control change messages are used to transmit and play back physical control devices such as wheels, levers, foot pedals and many other devices. You might think of control changes as a message within a message. With a control change message, the first data byte specifies the controller ID number. This number represents a type of control device such as volume, modulation, or panning. The fun of control change messages is that they can be incredibly expressive. You can also program synthesizers (and even set up software) to reassign these numbers. You could, for example, use the modulation wheel to control panning in real time.

Note that in the following table some controller functions are *switch* controllers: they are either on or off. Controller ID numbers 64–69 are examples of switch controllers.

Status Byte	Data Byte 1	Data Byte 2
1011cccc	controller ID number	value

Figure 9.13 Controller and Mode Changes (Status Bytes 176–191)
© 1991, 1994 MIDI Manufacturers Association, used with permission

2nd Byte Value			Function	3rd Byte	
Binary	Hex	Dec		Value	Use
00000000=	**00=**	**0**	**Bank Select**	**0-127**	**MSB**
00000001=	**01=**	**1**	**Modulation Wheel**	**0-127**	**MSB**
00000010=	02=	2	Breath control	0-127	MSB
00000011=	03=	3	Undefined	0-127	MSB
00000100=	**04=**	**4**	**Foot Controller**	**0-127**	**MSB**
00000101=	05=	5	Portamento Time	0-127	MSB
00000110=	06=	6	Data Entry	0-127	MSB
00000111=	**07=**	**7**	**Channel Volume (formerly Main Volume)**	**0-127**	**MSB**
00001000=	08=	8	Balance	0-127	MSB
00001001=	09=	9	Undefined	0-127	MSB
00001010=	**0A=**	**10**	**Pan**	**0-127**	**MSB**
00001011=	0B=	11	Expression Controller	0-127	MSB
00001100=	0C=	12	Effect Control 1	0-127	MSB
00001101=	0D=	13	Effect Control 2	0-127	MSB
00001110=	0E=	14	Undefined	0-127	MSB
00001111=	0F=	15	Undefined	0-127	MSB
00010000=	10=	16	General Purpose Controller #1	0-127	MSB
00010001=	11=	17	General Purpose Controller #2	0-127	MSB
00010010=	12=	18	General Purpose Controller #3	0-127	MSB
00010011=	13=	19	General Purpose Controller #4	0-127	MSB
00010100=	14=	20	Undefined	0-127	MSB

00010101=	15=	21	Undefined	0-127	MSB
00010110=	16=	22	Undefined	0-127	MSB
00010111=	17=	23	Undefined	0-127	MSB
00011000=	18=	24	Undefined	0-127	MSB
00011001=	19=	25	Undefined	0-127	MSB
00011010=	1A=	26	Undefined	0-127	MSB
00011011=	1B=	27	Undefined	0-127	MSB
00011100=	1C=	28	Undefined	0-127	MSB
00011101=	1D=	29	Undefined	0-127	MSB
00011110=	1E=	30	Undefined	0-127	MSB
00011111=	1F=	31	Undefined	0-127	MSB
00100000=	**20=**	**32**	**Bank Select**	**0-127**	**LSB**
00100001=	21=	33	Modulation Wheel	0-127	LSB
00100010=	22=	34	Breath Control	0-127	LSB
00100011=	23=	35	Undefined	0-127	LSB
00100100=	24=	36	Foot Controller	0-127	LSB
00100101=	25=	37	Portamento Time	0-127	LSB
00100110=	26=	38	Data Entry	0-127	LSB
00100111=	27=	39	Channel Volume (formerly Main Volume)	0-127	LSB
00101000=	28=	40	Balance	0-127	LSB
00101001=	29=	41	Undefined	0-127	LSB
00101010=	2A=	42	Pan	0-127	LSB
00101011=	2B=	43	Expression Controller	0-127	LSB
00101100=	2C=	44	Effect Control 1	0-127	LSB
00101101=	2D=	45	Effect Control 2	0-127	LSB
00101110=	2E=	46	Undefined	0-127	LSB
00101111=	2F=	47	Undefined	0-127	LSB
00110000=	30=	48	General Purpose Controller #1	0-127	LSB
00110001=	31=	49	General Purpose Controller #2	0-127	LSB
00110010=	32=	50	General Purpose Controller #3	0-127	LSB
00110011=	33=	51	General Purpose Controller #4	0-127	LSB
00110100=	34=	52	Undefined	0-127	LSB
00110101=	35=	53	Undefined	0-127	LSB
00110110=	36=	54	Undefined	0-127	LSB
00110111=	37=	55	Undefined	0-127	LSB
00111000=	38=	56	Undefined	0-127	LSB
00111001=	39=	57	Undefined	0-127	LSB
00111010=	3A=	58	Undefined	0-127	LSB
00111011=	3B=	59	Undefined	0-127	LSB
00111100=	3C=	60	Undefined	0-127	LSB
00111101=	3D=	61	Undefined	0-127	LSB
00111110=	3E=	62	Undefined	0-127	LSB
00111111=	3F=	63	Undefined	0-127	LSB
01000000=	**40=**	**64**	**Damper Pedal On/Off (Sustain)**	**<63=off!**	**>64=on**
01000001=	41=	65	Portamento On/Off	<63=off!	>64=on
01000010=	**42=**	**66**	**Sustenuto On/Off**	**<63=off!**	**>64=on**

01000011=	**43=**	**67**	**Soft pedalOn/Off**	**<63=offl**	**>64=on**
01000100=	44=	68	Legato Footswitch	<63=offl	>64=on
01000101=	45=	69	Hold 2	<63=offl	>64=on
01000110=	46=	70	Sound Controller 1 (Sound Variation)	0-127	LSB
01000111=	47=	71	Sound Controller 2 (Timbre)	0-127	LSB
01001000=	48=	72	Sound Controller 3 (Release Time)	0-127	LSB
01001001=	49=	73	Sound Controller 4 (Attack Time)	0-127	LSB
01001010=	4A=	74	Sound Controller 5 (Brightness)	0-127	LSB
01001011=	4B=	75	Sound Controller 6	0-127	LSB
01001100=	4C=	76	Sound Controller 7	0-127	LSB
01001101=	4D=	77	Sound Controller 8	0-127	LSB
01001110=	4E=	78	Sound Controller 9	0-127	LSB
01001111=	4F=	79	Sound Controller 10	0-127	LSB
01010000=	50=	80	General Purpose Controller #5	0-127	LSB
01010001=	51=	81	General Purpose Controller #6	0-127	LSB
01010010=	52=	82	General Purpose Controller #7	0-127	LSB
01010011=	53=	83	General Purpose Controller #8	0-127	LSB
01010100=	54=	84	Portamento Control	0-127	SourceNote
01010101=	55=	85	Undefined	0-127	LSB
01010110=	56=	86	Undefined	0-127	LSB
01010111=	57=	87	Undefined	0-127	LSB
01011000=	58=	88	Undefined	0-127	LSB
01011001=	59=	89	Undefined	0-127	LSB
01011010=	5A=	90	Undefined	0-127	LSB
01011011=	5B=	91	Effects 1 Depth	0-127	LSB
01011100=	5C=	92	Effects 2 Depth	0-127	LSB
01011101=	5D=	93	Effects 3 Depth	0-127	LSB
01011110=	5E=	94	Effects 4 Depth	0-127	LSB
01011111=	5F=	95	Effects 5 Depth	0-127	LSB
01100000=	60=	96	Data Entry +1	N/A	
01100001=	61=	97	Data Entry −1	N/A	
01100010=	62=	98	Nonregistered Parameter Number LSB	0-127	LSB
01100011=	63=	99	Nonregistered Parameter Number MSB	0-127	MSB
01100100=	64=	100	Registered Parameter Number LSB	0-127	LSB
01100101=	65=	101	Registered Parameter Number MSB	0-127	MSB
01100110=	66=	102	Undefined	?	
01100111=	67=	103	Undefined	?	
01101000=	68=	104	Undefined	?	
01101001=	69=	105	Undefined	?	
01101010=	6A=	106	Undefined	?	
01101011=	6B=	107	Undefined	?	
01101100=	6C=	108	Undefined	?	
01101101=	6D=	109	Undefined	?	
01101110=	6E=	110	Undefined	?	
01101111=	6F=	111	Undefined	?	
01110000=	70=	112	Undefined	?	

01110001=	71=	113	Undefined	?	
01110010=	72=	114	Undefined	?	
01110011=	73=	115	Undefined	?	
01110100=	74=	116	Undefined	?	
01110101=	75=	117	Undefined	?	
01110110=	76=	118	Undefined	?	
01110111=	77=	119	Undefined	?	
01111000=	78=	120	All Sound Off	0	
01111001=	79=	121	Reset All Controllers	0	
01111010=	**7A=**	**122**	**Local Control On/Off**	**0=off**	**127=on**
01111011=	7B=	123	All Notes Off	0	
01111100=	7C=	124	Omni Mode Off (+ All Notes Off)	0	
01111101=	7D=	125	Omni Mode On (+ All Notes Off)	0	
01111110=	7E=	126	Poly Mode On/Off (+All Notes Off)	*	
01111111=	7F=	127	Poly Mode On	0	
(incl mono=off +all notes off)					

* This equals the number of channels, or zero if the number of channels equals the number of voices in the receiver.

As you can see in the above table, there are many possible control change functions. Many of the functions are undefined: you can program synthesizers to respond in a unique way to these messages. Many of the control change ID numbers are standard: channel volume=cc#7, sustain pedal=cc#64 are two such examples. Some control change messages are more common than others. Volume and modulation are used in most sequences, while portamento or breath control might be less common in a sequence. Ten of the most common messages are listed in bold-face type. Do keep in mind that thoughtful use of control change messages can add a great deal of nuance and musicality to a MIDI performance.

The following are some tips on using control change messages.

Volume vs. velocity. Understand the difference between volume and velocity. You can think of the volume change message as a *master fader* for the given MIDI channel. With this message you can adjust the volume of a note after it has been struck to effect a crescendo or diminuendo. Velocity relates to how hard or soft the initial attack of the note is. Note that velocity relates to a single note, not all of the notes on a given channel. It is easy to get into a *tail-wagging-the-dog* syndrome when using volume change messages. A typical example involves recording a fade out on one or more MIDI channels using volume change messages. This, in effect, turns off the volume on the given

MIDI channels. The problems arises when you try to play back the sequence from the beginning: no sound will be heard. One solution is to record volume change messages at the beginning to reset the synthesizer to maximum volume. The MMA suggests that *expression* be used for in-song volume changes. With this approach, you can reset default values after the song ends without affecting the overall channel volume. Expression can also be helpful when distributing sequences. By using expression instead of channel volume, a listener can make channel volume adjustments without affecting crescendos and other volume changes in a sequence.

Tip: Some software programs will automatically reset controller values each time you stop and start a sequence. This may or may not be helpful depending on the type of work you are doing. If your synthesizer develops strange behavior, this might be something to check. I recently purchased a new synthesizer and was perplexed to find that it didn't work properly. After several minutes of confusion, I found that my sequencing software was closing down the filters on the instrument when it sent an automatic controller reset message.

Bank select. We have talked in some detail about the limitations of 7-bit binary numbers. When selecting sounds using a program change message, the maximum range is 0 to 127. Today, most synthesizers have a few hundred to a few thousand sounds. How do you select sounds (or automate a sequence) when the limit for program change messages is 0 to 127? The *bank select* method is used. Unfortunately, manufacturers have interpreted the MIDI spec in different ways regarding bank select. You will need to check your instrument manual to see how bank select works on your instrument. The standard bank-select method involves sending two control change messages. Control #0 is sent along with #32 as the least significant byte. This method allows for a whopping 16,384 banks of 128 sounds!

A common nonstandard bank select message involves sending a single control change message (controller #0 or controller #32, depending on the manufacturer and/or setup of the instrument). The data byte of this message selects the *active* bank. Any subsequent program change messages will call up the appropriate sound in that bank.

Figure 9.14 Nonstandard bank select and program select example

Message 1		
Control Change	Data Byte 1	Data Byte 2
1011cccc	0 (bank select)	5 (bank 5 is active)
Message 2		
Patch Change	Data Byte 1	
1100cccc	62 (selects patch #62 in active bank)	

In this example the first message, a control change message, sets the fifth bank as the *active* bank of sounds. The next message, a patch or program change message, selects patch number 62 within bank 5.

Channel Mode Message. Control change numbers 120 to 127 are reserved for channel mode messages. You can think of these messages as *mode of operation* commands. These messages are used to set a MIDI device to function in a particular way. The mode messages function as follows.

• *All sound off:* When an instrument receives an all sound off message, the oscillators are turned off and volume envelopes are set to zero.

• *Reset all controllers:* This message is used to reset controllers such as damper pedal, volume, etc. to a default state.

• *Local control:* Local control in the off state disconnects the keys of a synthesizer from the sound source of the instrument. The most common reason for doing this is when using the keyboard in a sequencing environment. "Local off" ensures that the sound produced by the keyboard will be driven by the sequencer, not the keyboard.

• *All notes off:* If a note-off message is lost due to malfunction or user error, the all-notes off message can be a lifesaver. Most sequencers include a panic button to this message, but remember that some instruments might not respond.

• *Omni mode on/off:* When omni is set to on, the synthesizer will respond to MIDI data on all channels. The synthesizer will only respond to messages on a single channel when omni is set to off.

• *Mono mode or poly mode:* In poly mode, a synthesizer will respond polyphonically to incoming note messages. In mono mode, the synthesizer will respond to only one note on the given channel.

Tip: If the previous explanation of omni and poly modes seems confusing, don't fret. Most synthesizer manufacturers provide more user-friendly terms for setting up the proper operating mode. Today, most synthesizers will default to omni off/poly mode (usually termed multimode). The omni mode can be helpful if you use a module that is not multitimbral (e.g., a piano or drum module that will respond to incoming messages on any channel).

SYSTEM MESSAGES

To this point we have concerned ourselves with channel messages—performance data that applies to a specific MIDI channel. MIDI also provides for a number of system messages. System messages apply to the entire MIDI network. System messages can be organized into three groups: *system common, system exclusive,* and *system real-time* messages. Note that the first nibble of any system message is 1111 in binary, 15 in decimal, or F in hexadecimal. The transmission format for system messages is as follows.

Figure 9.15 System messages

Status Byte	Number of Data Bytes	Type of Message
11110000	variable	system exclusive
11110xxx	0 to 2	system common
11111xxx	0	system real time

The most important system common messages to know about are the *MTC quarter frame* and *end of exclusive* messages.

MTC quarter frame. *MIDI time code* quarter frame messages are used to translate SMPTE time code into a time code that is meaningful for MIDI devices. With SMPTE time code, time is organized into hours, minutes, seconds, and frames. For example:

Figure 9.16 SMPTE time code

```
00:05:09:01
hh:mm:ss:ff
```

MIDI time code quarter frame messages are used to translate each of the quarters of SMPTE code (i.e. hours, minutes, seconds, and frames) throughout the MIDI network.

End of exclusive. The *end of exclusive,* or EOX, message signals the end of system exclusive data transmission. We will explore system exclusive messages in a moment.

Song position pointer. The SPP message is used to allow a device such as a drum machine or hardware sequencer to synchronize with an external source such as a tape machine. SPP is an incremental counter: this message increases by a count of one for every six MIDI clock messages. In short, SPP is used to tell relevant MIDI devices the current location in a sequence.

Song select. The primary use for the song select message is for live performance. It is similar to a program select message. Instead of selecting a specific sound, the song select message requests a specific song from an external sequencer or drum machine. Once a song has been selected, the device will respond to start, stop, and continue messages.

Tune request. This message is rarely used in modern MIDI networks. In the days of analog synthesizers, the synthesizers would sometimes float out of tune as the oscillators heated up. The tune request message is an attempt to combat this problem. A tune request message asks MIDI devices to initiate their internal tuning routines. Such a message would be moot to a digital synthesizer because digital oscillators can't float out of tune.

System real-time messages are used to provide accurate timing messages to allow for synchronization of MIDI devices. These messages are unique in that they can occur at any time, even in the midst of other MIDI messages.

Timing clock. This message is used to synchronize timing clocks of MIDI devices throughout the MIDI network. It is transmitted at a rate of 24 pulses per quarter note (ppqn).

Start. The start, stop, and continue messages relate to the system-common *song select* message. If a song select message has been received by a device such as a drum machine, the start message will initiate playback of the given song.

Stop. As the name implies, the stop command will stop playback of a song that has been previously selected with the *song select* system-common message.

Continue. This message is similar to the start message, but playback will continue from the current position, wherever the sequence was stopped.

Active sensing. Active sensing is an optional message. The idea of active sensing is to provide a means for determining if a MIDI device is still connected to a MIDI network. When in stop mode, an active sensing message may be transmitted every 300 milliseconds. If the receiver fails to get an active sensing byte every 300 milliseconds, it will shut down all active notes. This can be helpful in preventing stuck notes. Note that some synthesizers do not provide active sensing. This command simply is not very helpful other than to track setup errors in a MIDI network.

System reset. This message is used to reset a MIDI device back to its power-up settings (e.g., local on, all notes off). Like active sensing, this message is rarely used.

The system exclusive (SysEx) message is one of the most helpful of all system messages. SysEx provides a way to transfer data that is unique to a particular MIDI device. SysEx messages are typically used to transfer banks of sounds, sample data, or any other data that is unique to a particular device. The interesting thing about SysEx messages is that these messages only make sense to the intended device; they are ignored by all other devices in the system. SysEx messages are helpful in that they allow manufacturers to transmit messages that were not thought of in development of the original MIDI specification.

System exclusive messages, like all MIDI messages, start with a status byte. The status byte (11110000 in binary, F0 in hexadecimal) alerts the network that system exclusive data is about to be transmitted. A unique manufacturer ID or general use Universal SysEx ID is included in the SysEx header. If the receiving device "understands" the manufacturer ID (i.e., the message is intended for this device), it will know what to do with the remaining data bytes. If the ID number is not recognized by a device, the remainder of the system exclusive message will be ignored. Any number of data bytes will follow. The *end of exclusive* message signals that the SysEx message is complete. An example of a typical SysEx message follows. Note that, other than the status byte (F0), ID byte, and end of exclusive byte (F7), *any* number of data bytes may be transmitted. Additional data bytes are used to describe the specific product (i.e., what model of synthesizer), and a device ID number (in case you have more than one of these same devices connected to your MIDI network). The following example is a system exclusive message for an E-mu Proteus.

Figure 9.17 System exclusive message (in hexadecimal)

F0	system exclusive status byte
18	E-mu ID byte
04	product ID byte (e.g., Proteus synthesizer)
dd	device ID byte (if more than one is connected to MIDI network)
.	
.	any number of data bytes that mean something to this synthesizer
.	(patch dump, program map, etc.)
F7	(EOX-end of exclusive)

In plain English, the above message might read: *"Transmitting a system exclusive message. This message is intended for a device manufactured by E-mu. This message is intended specifically for an E-mu Proteus synthesizer that is set to the given device ID number. This message will be complete when you receive an end of exclusive data byte."*

One caveat: SysEx messages can take a long time to transfer over a 5-pin DIN MIDI network (from a few seconds to many minutes). It is almost always a good idea to avoid transmitting these messages while time-sensitive data is being transmitted. In other words, don't try to send a bank of SysEx patches to a synth during playback of a sequence: timing errors will certainly occur. Simple SysEx messages may be sent without worry. Some manufacturers use these messages as a way of controlling the device in real time, adjusting parameters that couldn't be controlled using continuous controller messages. Universal SysEx messages are divided into real and non-real time messages. You can expect real-time universal SysEx messages to respond appropriately during playback.

GENERAL MIDI

To conclude our chapter of introduction to MIDI, let's look at a fairly recent development in the MIDI specification: *General MIDI*. General MIDI (GM) provides a means of translating a sequence prepared on one synthesizer to another synthesizer. A General MIDI–capable synthesizer simply provides a standardized selection of sounds and control change assignments. If, for example, you have recorded a GM sequence with a fretless bass on channel one, any GM-compatible synthesizer will play back with a similar sound (some version of a fretless bass) on this channel. General MIDI is not very helpful for MIDI musicians who like to program their own sounds: the General MIDI palette of sounds is somewhat limiting. It does, however, provide an easy, organized way to distribute sequences. A GM sequence prepared on a GM synthesizer will sound roughly the same on any GM-compatible synthesizer. Note that with General MIDI sequences, percussion will always be assigned to channel ten.

Figure 9.18 General MIDI instrument patch map
The General MIDI instrument sounds are grouped by families. In each family are eight specific instruments.

PC#	Family	PC#	Family
1-8	Piano	65-72	Reed
9-16	Chromatic Percussion	73-80	Pipe
17-24	Organ	81-88	Synth Lead
25-32	Guitar	89-96	Synth Pad
33-40	Bass	97-104	Synth Effects
41-48	Strings	105-112	Ethnic
49-56	Ensemble	113-120	Percussive
57-64	Brass	121-128	Sound Effects

PC#	Instrument	PC#	Instrument
1	Acoustic Grand Piano	31	Distortion Guitar
2	Bright Acoustic Piano	32	Guitar harmonics
3	Electric Grand Piano	33	Acoustic Bass
4	Honky-tonk Piano	34	Electric Bass (finger)
5	Electric Piano 1	35	Electric Bass (pick)
6	Electric Piano 2	36	Fretless Bass
7	Harpsichord	37	Slap Bass 1
8	Clavi	38	Slap Bass 2
9	Celesta	39	Synth Bass 1
10	Glockenspiel	40	Synth Bass 2
11	Music Box	41	Violin
12	Vibraphone	42	Viola
13	Marimba	43	Cello
14	Xylophone	44	Contrabass
15	Tubular Bells	45	Tremolo Strings
16	Dulcimer	46	Pizzicato Strings
17	Drawbar Organ	47	Orchestral Harp
18	Percussive Organ	48	Timpani
19	Rock Organ	49	String Ensemble 1
20	Church Organ	50	String Ensemble 2
21	Reed Organ	51	SynthStrings 1
22	Accordion	52	SynthStrings 2
23	Harmonica	53	Choir Aahs
24	Tango Accordion	54	Voice Oohs
25	Acoustic Guitar (nylon)	55	Synth Voice
26	Acoustic Guitar (steel)	56	Orchestra Hit
27	Electric Guitar (jazz)	57	Trumpet
28	Electric Guitar (clean)	58	Trombone
29	Electric Guitar (muted)	59	Tuba
30	Overdriven Guitar	60	Muted Trumpet
61	French Horn	95	Pad 7 (halo)

62	Brass Section	96	Pad 8 (sweep)
63	SynthBrass 1	97	FX 1 (rain)
64	SynthBrass 2	98	FX 2 (soundtrack)
65	Soprano Sax	99	FX 3 (crystal)
66	Alto Sax	100	FX 4 (atmosphere)
67	Tenor Sax	101	FX 5 (brightness)
68	Baritone Sax	102	FX 6 (goblins)
69	Oboe	103	FX 7 (echoes)
70	English Horn	104	FX 8 (sci-fi)
71	Bassoon	105	Sitar
72	Clarinet	106	Banjo
73	Piccolo	107	Shamisen
74	Flute	108	Koto
75	Recorder	109	Kalimba
76	Pan Flute	110	Bag pipe
77	Blown Bottle	111	Fiddle
78	Shakuhachi	112	Shanai
79	Whistle	113	Tinkle Bell
80	Ocarina	114	Agogo
81	Lead 1 (square)	115	Steel Drums
82	Lead 2 (sawtooth)	116	Woodblock
83	Lead 3 (calliope)	117	Taiko Drum
84	Lead 4 (chiff)	118	Melodic Tom
85	Lead 5 (charang)	119	Synth Drum
86	Lead 6 (voice)	120	Reverse Cymbal
87	Lead 7 (fifths)	121	Guitar Fret Noise
88	Lead 8 (bass + lead)	122	Breath Noise
89	Pad 1 (new age)	123	Seashore
90	Pad 2 (warm)	124	Bird Tweet
91	Pad 3 (polysynth)	125	Telephone Ring
92	Pad 4 (choir)	126	Helicopter
93	Pad 5 (bowed)	127	Applause
94	Pad 6 (metallic)	128	Gunshot

Figure 9.19 General MIDI percussion key map
Assigns drum sounds to note numbers. MIDI Channel 10 is for percussion on General MIDI instruments.

Key#	Drum Sound	Key#	Drum Sound
35	Acoustic Bass Drum	59	Ride Cymbal 2
36	Bass Drum 1	60	Hi Bongo
37	Side Stick	61	Low Bongo
38	Acoustic Snare	62	Mute Hi Conga
39	Hand Clap	63	Open Hi Conga
40	Electric Snare	64	Low Conga
41	Low Floor Tom	65	High Timbale
42	Closed Hi Hat	66	Low Timbale
43	High Floor Tom	67	High Agogo
44	Pedal Hi-Hat	68	Low Agogo
45	Low Tom	69	Cabasa
46	Open Hi-Hat	70	Maracas
47	Low-Mid Tom	71	Short Whistle
48	Hi Mid Tom	72	Long Whistle
49	Crash Cymbal 1	73	Short Guiro
50	High Tom	74	Long Guiro
51	Ride Cymbal 1	75	Claves
52	Chinese Cymbal	76	Hi Wood Block
53	Ride Bell	77	Low Wood Block
54	Tambourine	78	Mute Cuica
55	Splash Cymbal	79	Open Cuica
56	Cowbell	80	Mute Triangle
57	Crash Cymbal 2	81	Open Triangle
58	Vibraslap		

DOWNLOADABLE SOUNDS

Downloadable Sounds (DLS) is a recent development that provides game and Internet developers with a way of expanding the palette of General MIDI sounds. Developers can use this technology to download custom sounds to RAM. DLS provides a standard playback engine that guarantees a "universal" playback experience.

[1] A sequencer is a device (either hardware or software) that records performance data. The term sequence comes from the fact that the sequencer orders or *sequences* the notes in precisely the same order and time as the original performance.

[2] *Synthesizer Performance and Real-Time Techniques,* Jeff Pressing, p. 118

[3] A sound module is a type of synthesizer that provides the functionality of a keyboard without a controller (keyboard). A controller such as a MIDI keyboard, guitar, drum, or wind controller is used to "play" the sounds in the module.

Sequencing Concepts

In this chapter, we will consider some tips that will help you to get the most out of your sequencing experience. In general, a sequencing session is characterized by the following activities: selection of sounds, setting parameters (e.g., tempo and key maps, track assignments, and panning), entry of data, and manipulation of data. As you work with your sequencer, evaluate your effectiveness with each of these tasks. If you find that you spend an inordinate amount of time on any of these tasks, it might be time to crack open the software manual and consider an alternate method. In a worst-case scenario, you may need to consider investing in new software that better supports your style of working.

SELECTING SOUNDS

Most sequencers allow you to organize lists of sounds and select synthesized sounds via a patch name instead of relying on program change numbers. Although this method is certainly intuitive, you may want to consider using program change numbers if you roll your own sounds or if you use a synthesizer where you regularly import new patches or samples. This is the method that works best for me. I set up my software to represent all synthesizer presets with a patch name. I use program change numbers to access any of the "user" banks in my synthesizers. Many musicians will elect to invest in patch management software such as *Sound Diver* by Emagic or *Unisyn* by Mark of the Unicorn. Patch management software can be a great help in finding, editing, and archiving sounds.

Figure 10.1 Sound Diver *screen*

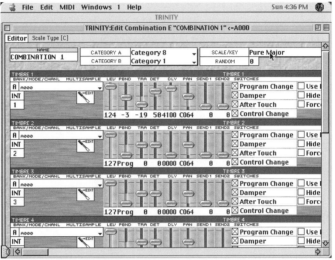

Templates can be a big help when the muse strikes you.
Nothing is more frustrating than searching through thousands
of patch names when you have an idea for a new sequence.
Most professional electronic musicians will create templates for
common ensemble groupings such as jazz or rock combo,
techno, or orchestral ensemble. With this type of approach, you
can start work on a new composition with only a few mouse
clicks. As the sequence progresses you can always take time to
select or edit new sounds.

SEQUENCER VIEWS

Most popular sequencing programs provide at least four ways of
viewing MIDI data:
• Event list
• Piano roll (matrix view)
• Notation
• Graphical (usually used for editing tempo, note velocity, or
  continuous controller data)

You should spend some time familiarizing yourself with the
various views provided by your software. If you are like me, you
will find that you rely on one view as your primary edit screen,
but keep in mind that each of the views facilitates specific types
of editing operations. If your software supports macros or key
assignments, you may wish to assign a keystroke for each of the
primary views. This will help you to quickly bring up a window
that is most relevant for the type of editing you need to do.

Figure 10.2 Event list

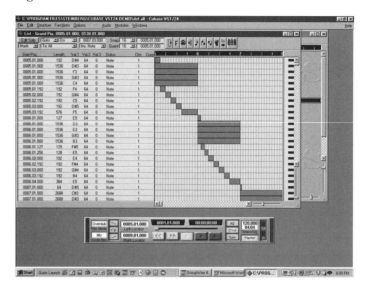

Event list. An event list is the heart of your sequencing environment. The event list simply displays a sequential list of MIDI data found in one or more tracks, or clips, as the case may be. The event list is most helpful when you need to edit MIDI data numerically, as is the case when inserting or deleting program changes, tweaking the timestamp of a note, or deleting extraneous controller messages such as a "stuck" damper pedal or pitch bend.

Most software sequencers allow you to set up a filter for the event list. By setting up a filter, you can filter out unnecessary data from the current view. Let's say you would like to find and delete a volume change message (continuous controller #7). By filtering note-on and note-off messages, you will be able to view only controller or system messages. This can be a godsend when you are searching through a complex event list or doing multiple edits such as deleting all continuous controller data. Note that most applications also allow you to "scrub" musical data in the event list. Scrubbing involves using the mouse to play a region of notes: the faster you move the mouse, the faster the playback. Scrubbing can help you to quickly find a wrong note in an event list.

Making Music with Your Computer

Figure 10.3 Event list filter

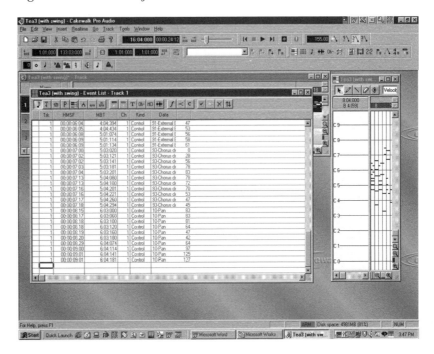

If your software supports it, a *find similar data* function can be very useful when manipulating data in an event list. With a find or search function you can quickly find all instances of one type of data in a sequence. I have found this function to be helpful in removing specific types of data such as pitch bend or panning.

Piano roll. The piano-roll view lets you view and manipulate data in a graphical fashion. The term *piano roll* suggests the similarity of a matrix screen to piano rolls from the early part of this century: pitch is represented in the *y* axis (i.e., higher notes will appear near the top of the screen, lower notes near the bottom). Time (both attack and release) are represented on the *x* axis. Although the piano-roll view can be helpful when transposing or quantifying notes, I find that the piano-roll view is perfectly suited to editing note durations. Music notation is notoriously inaccurate at representing durations of notes. It is very hard to tell if a staccato quarter note is really an eighth or sixteenth, for example. The piano-roll view is well suited for this type of editing. Most sequencers allow you to select a grouping of notes and edit the pitch or duration of the entire group with a single mouse drag.

Figure 10.4 Piano roll (changing the duration of a group of notes)

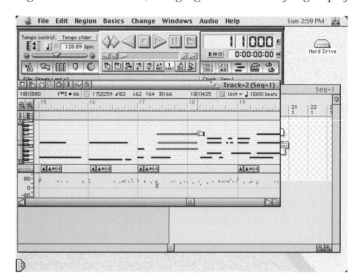

Another tip you may want to try is using the piano-roll view as an editing tool when you compose drum patterns. I often select a group of notes (such as a repeating hi-hat pattern) and drag this group to various pitches. This can be a wonderful way to come up with new and interesting drum grooves. A similar tip involves dragging notes vertically to create a more linear drum style. A simple hi-hat pattern when extracted over various percussive instruments can be a welcome change. Many programs even let you view and edit data while the sequence is playing back. Again, this can be a wonderful source of inspiration. Real-time experimentation: what a concept!

Figure 10.5 Using the piano-roll view to change a simple hi-hat pattern into an interesting linear pattern

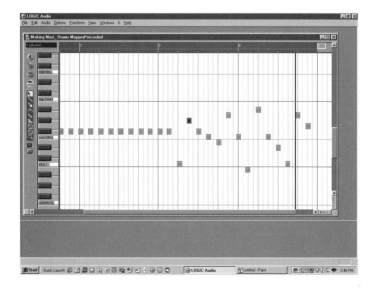

Making Music with Your Computer

Notation view. If you have a traditional music background, you may find that the notation view best serves your needs when editing a sequence. The primary advantage of this view is the familiarity of viewing MIDI data as a musical score. Though real-time transcription algorithms are steadily improving, most software applications only provide a rough approximation of a real transcription in the notation view. The reason for this is simple: the goal of any sequencer is to provide accurate and rock-steady playback of MIDI data. A program that spends too much time analyzing MIDI data for the purposes of accurate transcription might result in inaccurate playback. A notation view is most helpful when you need to find and edit a wrong note. Most programs allow you to simply drag a wrong note to the correct pitch.

Figure 10.6 Notation view (fixing a wrong note)

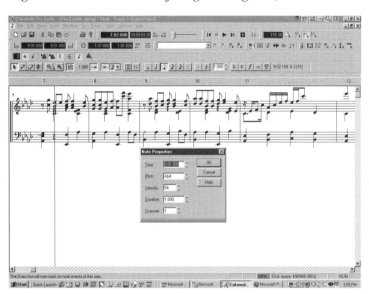

Some of the more sophisticated sequencers will allow you to edit and create complete scores using a notation view. If you plan to use sequencing software in this way, I would suggest spending some time evaluating the notation view before making a purchase. Many sequencers only provide minimal score editing and formatting capabilities in this view.

If your software supports it, a combination of notation and graphical editing views can be very helpful. With this type of setup, you can view notes in a familiar notation format while utilizing the benefits of graphical notation for drawing crescendi or tempo changes.

Figure 10.7 Combining notation and graphical editing

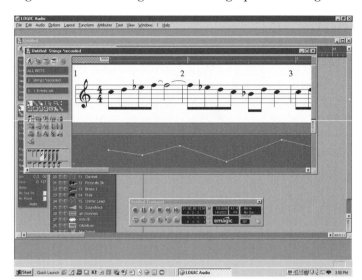

Graphical view. Many years ago I used sequencing software that was devoid of many of the bells and whistles found in a modern sequencing environment. I will never forget the frustration of trying to edit a ritardando using only a series of tempo changes in an event list. Graphical editing views have evolved to provide a comfortable means of manipulating MIDI data graphically. Graphical editing views are primarily used for editing data that fluctuates (e.g., tempo change and continuous controller data such as modulation or pitch bend).

Figure 10.8 Graphical editing view

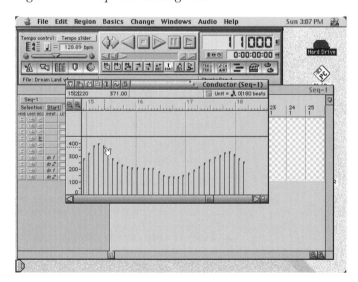

Most sequencers provide a virtual pencil or pen for drawing data changes directly to the screen. You will probably want to memorize the keystrokes for zooming in and out. I find it most helpful to zoom in for detailed editing and to zoom out to see how my edits relate to the surrounding musical context.

You may also want to consider setting up multiple graphic editing windows to view the relationship of several types of data. Pitch bend and modulation are often related in a musical context, so viewing and editing this data at the same time can be very helpful.

Figure 10.9 Multiple views of graphical data

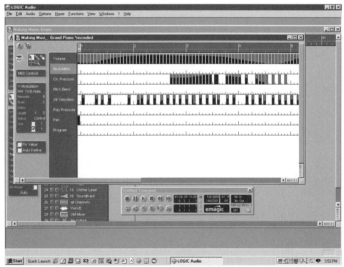

Although I didn't cover a few other types of views (such as drum matrix or pattern views), a familiarity with the primary views listed above will help you to function efficiently in almost any sequencing environment. Once again, you will want to use an editing view that is most suitable for the task at hand. If your software supports it, be sure to assign hot keys to the editing views you frequently use. This will allow you to view and manipulate data easily. If you find that you are using more than a few mouse clicks or keystrokes, you are probably using the wrong view for the task at hand.

In this section we will explore many of the common editing functions available in a modern sequencing environment. Along the way, I will also present a number of tips on manipulating and experimenting with musical data in new and interesting ways.

Quantization. One of the most helpful (and sometimes overused) editing functions is quantization. Quantization is used to "fix" rhythmic inaccuracies in a MIDI performance. In simple quantization, the user selects a note value for note attacks and/or durations. The software analyzes a selected region or tracks and adjusts the timing of notes to reflect the selected note value. Applying an eighth-note quantization to the following passage would result in a quantification of all sixteenth note (or shorter) note lengths.

Figure 10.10 Quantization using eighth note value. Note the absence of sixteenth notes in the post-quantified passage

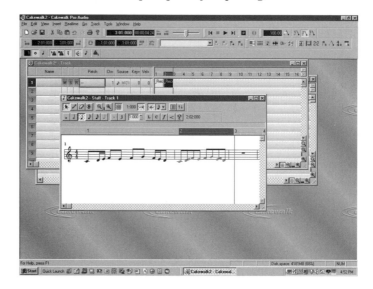

Use quantification judiciously: many programs destructively edit MIDI data and, unless multiple undo is available, your original performance may be lost forever! If you are using a "destructive" mode sequencer, be sure to listen back to the entire quantified region before continuing your work. A performance inaccuracy might result in notes being quantified in the wrong direction in a later region of the sequence, so be sure to check this out.

One of the problems with traditional quantization is that it may make your music sound mechanical. Although this is desirable for some styles of music such as dance or techno, sequencing vendors have developed several new forms of quantization that may be more suitable. Some programs allow you to select a *sensitivity value.* If a note is close to the quantification grid (i.e., a specified number of ticks before or after the quantization value), the software will not change its rhythmic position if you define a sensitivity or strength value.

Figure 10.11 Setting a sensitivity value when quantizing

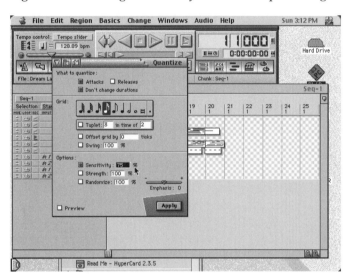

Groove quantization. Another problem with simple quantization is that only rhythmic values are quantified. Any mature performer will tell you that there is more to creating a good groove than simply using good time. Many successful grooves are the result of a combination of rhythmic values and dynamics or accents. Groove quantization provides a means of manipulating both of these characteristics. Although there are many ways of implementing groove quantization, most programs will provide a number of built-in "groove maps" that represent specific styles such as shuffle, laid back, or edgy. In general, design of groove maps involves analyzing digital audio performances (i.e., a groove recorded by a great drummer). Timing and velocity data are extracted and users of the software are able to apply these maps to their own sequenced data. If this topic interests you, you may wish to purchase a sequencing program that allows you to create your own groove quantization templates.

Figure 10.12 Selecting a quantization groove

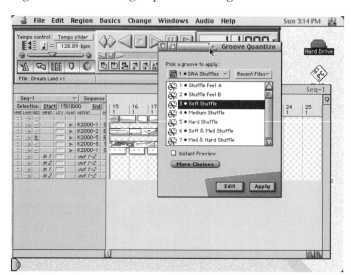

Humanize. A perversion of the quantize function is the so-called "humanize" function. Humanizing (sometimes included as a strength adjustment in a quantification dialog box) is used to add an element of imperfection or randomness to a passage of music. As I mentioned earlier, if a performance is quantified, it will tend to sound mechanical or rigid. Humanizing is used to add slight timing imperfections to a passage of music. The user can select an adjustment range of, say, a thirty-second note. The software will analyze a selected region and add some slight rhythmic inaccuracies (within the specified value range) to the performance. I have found humanizing functions to be less helpful than, say, traditional or groove quantization because the computer generated inaccuracies tend to sound, well, inaccurate. The performance inaccuracies that most musicians use tend to be slight variations that enhance the given style of music (e.g., natural rubato that might be the result of "laying back" during the climax of a melody).

Making Music with Your Computer

Figure 10.13 Humanize dialog box

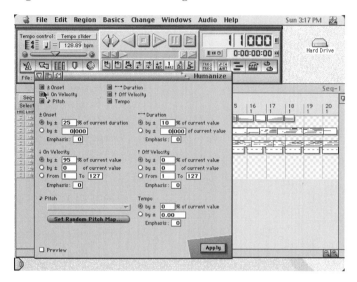

Swing quantization. Most software synthesizers allow you to adjust a *swing percentage* when applying quantization to a range of notes. Although it is certainly possible to have swing sixteenth notes, the most common scenario involves applying a swing percentage to a passage of eighth notes (e.g., for swing-jazz music). In general, you will want to select a large swing percentage for slower swing tunes and a small swing percentage for faster tunes. For example, the eighth notes for a fast bop tune are usually played very close to even notes (i.e., very little swing). The eighth notes in a slow swing blues will tend to be very "wide." One of the problems I have experienced with swing quantization is that, in most implementations, the swing feel is applied to *every* eighth note. In jazz, an eighth note that is combined with sixteenths or smaller rhythmic value is usually *not* swung. An alternative is to apply swing quantization selectively to sections of music that include eighth note (or higher) durations. Another option with some software is to create your own quantization routines. The Cakewalk Application Language (CAL) that is included with *Cakewalk Pro Audio* provides an elegant way to develop your own selective quantization routines. With this type of software, you can design context-sensitive quantization routines.

Figure 10.14 Adjusting swing quantization parameters

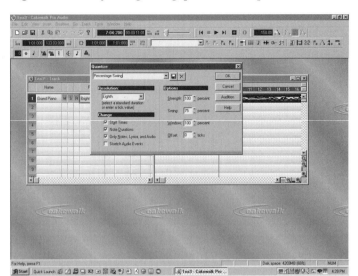

Duration. The duration of notes can also be quantified. Use duration to change a legato passage to staccato or vice versa. Note that many programs include options to adjust the duration of notes as a part of a quantification dialog box: there may not be a specific duration function provided. I almost always turn off the duration function when applying quantification to a passage of music. In most cases, quantifying the release of notes in a phrase will make it sound even more mechanical than simple quantification. Even if a musician has good time, he or she will probably use note durations that fluctuate widely. This variety of note lengths will be an important musical aspect of most MIDI performances.

Figure 10.15 Duration option in a quantization dialog box

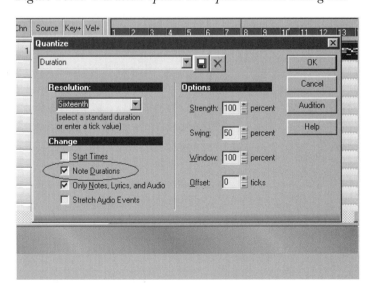

Making Music with Your Computer

Velocity scaling and adjustment. It is often helpful to adjust the velocities of a group of notes. Software sequencers employ a number of functions to adjust velocities. In most cases you can adjust velocity of a group of notes by a specified percentage or with a ratio. Ratios can be helpful for effecting a smooth crescendo or decrescendo. Percentage scaling is most helpful to adjust a phrase that is too loud or too soft. In this instance, the user may elect to scale a track (such as a bass track) by 80 percent. This has the effect of reducing all of the note velocities by 20 percent. It is also possible to specify a value for each of the notes in a selected region. Keep in mind that this type of adjustment will tend to make the phrase sound artificial; even the best musicians are unable to perform a passage with "perfect" attacks on every note. This method works best for techno and dance styles of music where you want the music to sound artificial or computer-generated.

Figure 10.16 Adjusting note velocities

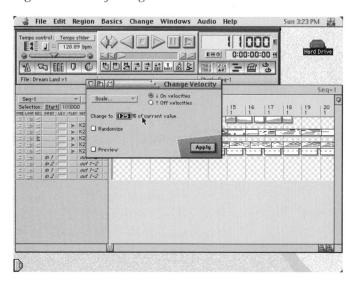

Track or clip shifting. Most sequencers will allow you to adjust a track or clip by a specified range of "ticks." This can be a great way to experiment with variations on a rhythm section groove. Some bass players, for example, tend to play a bit behind the beat. By offsetting a bass or other track by a few ticks, you may find some interesting variations to an existing groove. I sometimes find it helpful to adjust percussion tracks in this manner. A repetitive hi-hat pattern can sound very interesting when offset by a value of a sixteenth or thirty-second. One other way that track offsets are helpful is to fix problems with "slow"

patches. If your string pad responds too slowly but otherwise works well, applying a track offset may help make it sound more appropriate for the surrounding musical texture. If you experience problems with MIDI lag, track offsets may also help to alleviate timing problems.

Figure 10.17 Setting a track offset

Transposition. One of the more straightforward sequencing operations is transposition. Simply select a region of notes and transpose up or down by a specified amount. One caveat when using a transpose function: drum tracks can also be transposed. In most situations, transposing drum tracks will result in strange or unusual results. This is because, on most synthesizers, each key is mapped to a specific drum sound. Transposing a drum track has the effect of remapping the entire track. Because of this problem, I usually place drum tracks as the top few tracks in a sequence. By placing your drum tracks near the top of the screen it is easy to drag-select lower tracks for transposition and other types of editing functions. Of course, transposition can be combined with cut and paste operations to quickly create modulations in a last verse or chorus. Transposition can also be helpful when creating parts for transposing instruments. Though most sequencers do not support part extraction that includes transposition, it is easy to temporarily transpose a saxophone or other transposing instrument track before printing parts for your band.

Figure 10.18 Transposing notes

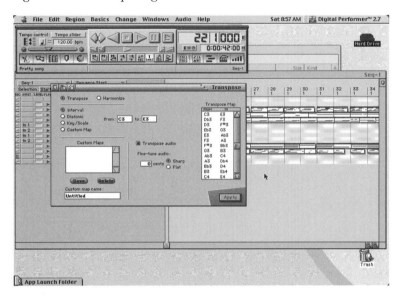

Search and replace (interpolate). Interpolation involves searching for and changing or inserting a specified element *en masse*. An interpolation or search-and-replace function is valuable when you need to change one type of MIDI data to another. You might, for example, decide that a sequence that utilizes a drum sound on C-4 would sound better using another drum sound that resides at D-4. By interpolating all of the C-4 notes in a selected region, it is easy to make this type of change. Some programs will even let you replace one type of MIDI data such as a note-on event with another.

Figure 10.19 Limiting note velocity in Logic Audio

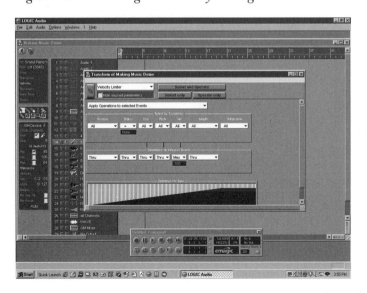

Time stretching and shrinking. Stretching and shrinking functions are most helpful when doing film and commercial work. You may decide that the first 15 seconds of a 30-second radio spot need to be 18 seconds to better complement a voiceover. Event stretching allows you to change the timing of your sequence without the need to rerecord to a different tempo. Some programs even let you specify a graph or ratio to effect a natural sounding accelerando or ritardando.

Figure 10.20 Scaling time in Performer

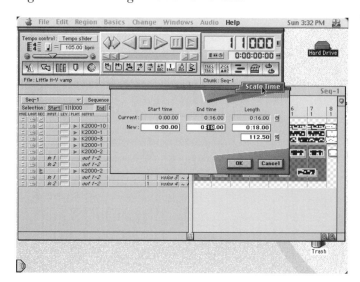

Retrograde. A retrograde function simply turns a phrase of music around (i.e., the notes play in reverse order). Why would you want to do this? This function is most helpful for some types of twentieth century music, such as twelve-tone music where the composer uses and manipulates a specific ordering of notes called a tone row. I have also found this function to be helpful as a way to manipulate and experiment with drum grooves.

Conductor tracks. As the name implies, a conductor track is used to "direct" a sequence. The conductor track is responsible for establishing and tracking tempo, key, and time signature changes. In other words, the conductor track is the road map for a sequence. You may not need to worry about editing a conductor track if your sequences generally consist of a single meter and tempo. One instance where conductor tracks are extremely useful is on film projects. In this situation, you can create a road map of tempos and meters that best complement visual images. If you plan to convert your sequence to traditional notation, it is also advisable to insert appropriate key and meter changes into the conductor track. Although most popular sequencing programs provide functions that make it easy to create ritards and diminuendos, a similar effect may be achieved by manually inserting tempo changes into a conductor track.

If you are sequencing a tune that includes many tempo or meter changes, you will find it helpful to take the time to create an accurate conductor track before you begin sequencing. Nothing is more frustrating than stopping the sequencing process every few bars to insert tempo or meter changes. By establishing an accurate conductor track, you can play each track naturally without stopping. Happily, the click track or metronome will even follow these tempo and meter changes.

Figure 10.21 Conductor track in Performer

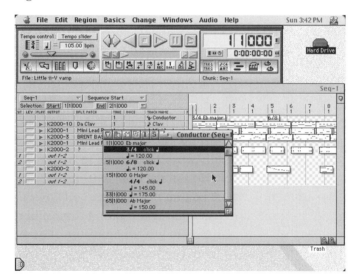

Fit improvisation. The *fit improvisation* function, sometimes called *extract timing,* relates very closely to the concept of a conductor track. This function is used to create an accurate conductor track for an existing sequence. For some styles of music such as a solo piano jazz ballad or classical performance, a tempo or click track would be obtrusive. Could you imagine Bill Evans or Arthur Rubinstein recording to a click track?! Many programs will allow you to establish a tempo map that follows an existing performance. The benefit of this approach is that you can turn off the metronome as you record. Once you have recorded a rhythmically "free" performance, you can then teach the software how to interpret the rhythmic pulse of the performance. The usual method is to record another track of *pulse* notes. These pulse notes represent the beats or tempo of the performance. The software then uses these pulse tones to create a tempo map that actually follows the original performance. It goes without saying that this process is essential if you plan to convert a free-style sequence into notation. Although it is possible for the software to transcribe such a performance, the resulting notation would be virtually useless to other musicians. An accurate tempo map will allow the software to determine where beats and measures occur and will help it to better transcribe the performance.

Continuous controller editing (graphical). Continuous controllers, as the name implies, provide a steady stream of performance data. Of the 127 possible continuous controllers, the most common controllers are volume, panning, modulation, and pitch bend. Although the damper pedal is considered a continuous controller, we will not talk about damper pedal messages in this section because it is a simple *switch* controller: a damper pedal is either on or off as far as MIDI is concerned.

Although it is possible (and sometimes desirable) to edit continuous controllers using an event list, most software sequencers allow you to make these edits visually using a graphical editor. This approach is much more intuitive: it is much easier to "draw" a smooth crescendo than it is to insert a number of volume change messages into an event list!

Panning. Panning is used to place a sound in the stereo field. Most modern sequencers provide a virtual mixing console approach to panning and volume. In most cases, a virtual console is used to represent relevant panning, volume, and patch information for each track in a sequence. If you have not yet experimented with panning, you are in for a real treat. Careful use of panning can help your sequences to sound much more professional. Use panning to create spatial imaging for your sequence (e.g., bass and drums in the middle, piano on one side, guitar on another). Once you get in the habit of using panning to enhance your sequences, you will wonder how you ever survived without this controller. If each of the instruments in a sequence is panned "straight up," the tracks will tend to fight one another. Panning provides a way to create a pleasing stereo image.

Although panning can be helpful as a mixing tool, MIDI musicians have the added benefit of using panning as a compositional tool. An interesting experiment involves inserting panning events at a specified rate in a sequence. Try panning a repetitive cymbal or synth pad every quarter or eighth note in a phrase. Though the results are not natural, many remarkable special effects can be achieved. Keep in mind that most sequencers will allow you to record changes made to a virtual panning button or slider to a track as MIDI data. For better control you may wish to assign this parameter to a knob or slider on a synthesizer. I usually record panning events to a separate track, one that outputs to the same channel as the sound you wish to pan. This approach makes it easier to edit (or delete) panning data without messing up your original track.

Figure 10.22 A typical MIDI mixing and panning console

Volume. Volume change messages are one of the more helpful continuous controllers, but they can also be tricky to handle. Unlike note velocity (which simply represents how loud or soft a given note is played), volume changes are used to affect the dynamic level of an entire channel. Unless your software resets continuous controller data at the start of a sequence as some do, a fadeout that you record at the end of a sequence effectively mutes the track when you try to play it back. To avoid this situation, I usually record volume changes at the start and end of each phrase. This will have the effect of "hard wiring" a specified volume level for each passage of a sequence. With this method, you will never worry about a volume change edit that you make near the end of a sequence effecting an earlier passage of music on playback.

As I mentioned previously, although a volume slider is always included in any "virtual console" to represent a general dynamic level for a track, you may wish to take a more proactive approach to using volume change messages. If you listen to a wind player such as a flutist, clarinetist, or saxophonist, you will hear that these players rarely play statically. Put another way, it is rare to hear a wind player play a whole note that does not subtly change in dynamic level. I find it most helpful to use a MIDI volume pedal or keyboard data slider to record volume changes as I record a passage of notes. This approach lets your music breathe and sounds much more natural. Even if you primarily use synthetic sounds, a melody that has a dynamic contour will sound much more accessible to the listener. As with panning data, you may want to insert volume changes into an event list to tweak a soft or loud note or to establish a general dynamic level for a passage of music.

Figure 10.23 Adjusting channel volume in Logic Audio

Modulation. Most keyboards provide modulation and pitch bend wheels or sliders. Although these wheels can usually be programmed for any number of functions, modulation is usually used for vibrato effects or control of a synthesizer parameter such as filter cutoff or resonance. As with panning, modulation can be applied using onscreen sliders, the modulation wheel, or an event list. To achieve a very expressive playing style, you may want to consider recording volume, panning, and pitch bend as you record a passage of notes. Most professionals will control volume changes using a foot pedal while the left hand is free to control the modulation wheel. You may even consider using a breath controller to control pitch or other parameters for a truly expressive style of playing. Most often, modulation is used to enhance a climactic point of a melody, but as with panning, modulation can be interesting as a compositional device (e.g., use it in a rhythmical fashion to control filter cutoff or resonance).

PITCH BEND

Real-time control of pitch can add an expressive dimension to a sequence (just listen to any good blues guitarist or saxophonist). Unfortunately, pitch bend can be very difficult to implement in a natural or musical way. Here are some tips that I have found to be helpful.

• Set your pitch wheel to a range of a major second. Most acoustic instruments can only bend pitch in a range of about a major second to major third. Although it is possible to set your pitch wheel to a larger interval such as an octave, such a large interval is very hard to control and will tend to make the music less natural.

• Use pitch bend in the same way acoustic instrumentalists do (e.g., to create a blue third in a blues sequence).

• Practice continuous controller etudes (e.g., arpeggiate a series of major triads and bend the top note of each triad up a half or whole step). Most sequences I hear where pitch bend is ineffective have more to do with the synthesists' limitations of pitch bend technique than inappropriate use of pitch bend. If you can get to the point where the pitch wheel is an extension of your body (as your hands are when you input notes), pitch bend can add a wonderful dimension to your sequences.

One word of warning when you use pitch bend. When sequencing, if you press stop before the pitch wheel has had a chance to reset to the unity position, you will find that your synthesizer sounds as if it has drifted out of tune. The reason for this is that pitch bend messages are similar to volume change messages. Your synthesizer will respond to these messages in a very direct way. If the synthesizer never receives the messages that reset pitch on a given channel, it will continue to play back at the wrong pitch. The solution is simple: record a pitch bend movement at the end of a phrase or start of the sequence to reset the synthesizer.

Data thinning. Keep in mind that continuous controllers (pitch bend in particular) produce a huge volume of MIDI messages. In a worst-case scenario, a high volume of continuous controller messages may clog up the MIDI stream creating a noticeable MIDI lag. In these situations it may be desirable to "thin" MIDI data. Thinning involves removing a proportion of the messages. In most cases, the thinned track will still sound the same as the original. Thinning pitch bend by 50 percent will not usually even be noticeable. You will want to consider data thinning if you plan to prepare sequences for the Web. In this case, it is best to provide MIDI files that are as small as possible. The following screen shot represents just two beats of pitch bend data in a typical MIDI file.

Figure 10.24 Two beats of pitch bend data in a typical MIDI file

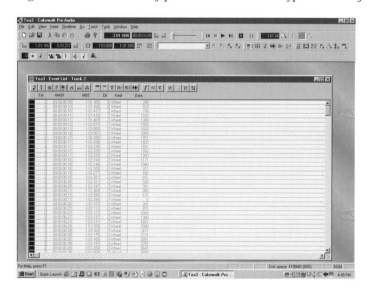

REAL-TIME MIDI EFFECTS

MIDI delay. A relatively new trend with software sequencers is the concept of virtual or real-time MIDI effects. Real-time MIDI effects are used in much the same way as outboard gear in a traditional recording studio: a MIDI track may be processed with a MIDI effect, and the resulting sounds are output from the MIDI Out port.

Making Music with Your Computer

MIDI delay is usually used to create repetitive or delay effects. Although MIDI delay can be used as a traditional delay effect, I find that delay can also be a wonderful composition tool. Unlike traditional delay effects that always fade out over time, many MIDI delay processors allow a group of notes to repeat for a specified amount of time with little or no fade. Real-time delay can be a great asset when composing minimalist sequences or other styles of music that rely on a great deal of repetition.

Arpeggiation. I remember salivating over an early arpeggiator in the 1970s. This unit allowed a person to arpeggiate up to sixteen notes! Electronic music seems to have come full circle, and arpeggiation is a big part of some styles of computer-based music. Note that the goal of using an arpeggiator is not usually to recreate "pianistic" arpeggios. An arpeggiator is a tool that is more along the lines of a synthesizer's low-frequency modulator. Arpeggiators are typically used as a compositional tool. Although there are a variety of implementations, most sequencers allow you to arpeggiate a group of notes in real time. The arpeggiation may be down, up, random, or some user-defined pattern. Most computer musicians will use arpeggiation to repeat the notes of a chord at a specified rate such as sixteenth notes at the same tempo as the sequence. Incidentally, arpeggiation can be fun when applied to drum tracks. For a mondo drum fill, hold down the snare, kick, and hi-hat keys as you apply virtual arpeggiation at a value of one twenty-fourth note or thirty second. Some sequencers will even allow you to toggle an arpeggiation on or off. This can be fun to use in a live setting. (For example, get a number of arpeggiated riffs going and interact with these rhythms in real-time.)

RECORDING MIDI DATA

To conclude this chapter, it might be helpful to discuss some of the methods of actually recording MIDI data into a sequencer. The three primary methods of data input are real time, step time, and input quantization. Real-time input is the most natural form of input. Of the three common methods of data entry, recording a real-time performance generally yields the most musical results. I find that, even if a passage is difficult to play in real time, it is better to record it slowly than resort to step-time entry, which is usually less musical.

Step-time entry is helpful if your keyboarding chops are not sufficient for the passage at hand, but I have found this method to be useful also when sequencing nonkeyboard parts such as drums. Step-time entry can be a useful way to input drum fills that might otherwise be difficult or impossible to play in real time. To experiment with this concept, try using step-time entry to insert a measure or two of thirty-second-note tom and snare sounds. If you vary note velocities and insert an occasional rest, you can easily come up with many interesting fills. Step-time entry can also be useful for recording drum rolls which are notoriously difficult to execute on a keyboard in real time.

Figure 10.25 Step time entry dialog

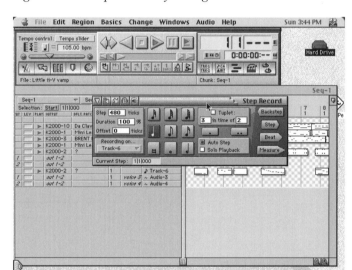

Although I don't personally use input quantization much, some MIDI musicians prefer to record some real-time tracks with input quantization on. The benefit of this method is that tracks such as drum tracks will be rhythmically fixed at the same time they are recorded. The problem with this method is that, unless you are sure to pick the correct quantization value, your performance may not be accurately recorded. Another problem with input quantization is that, if you forget to turn this feature off, you may find yourself inadvertently quantizing a real-time performance.

We have covered a great deal of ground in this chapter: entering MIDI performance data, using a variety of editing views, and real-time MIDI effects. I would like to reiterate a point that I made earlier in the chapter: Evaluate your sequencing style and use templates, key assignments, and a variety of editing views in order to become an efficient MIDI musician. I also encourage you to experiment. One of the great things about sequencing is the many tools that are available to record and manipulate MIDI data. These tools can be helpful to fix and tweak a sequence, but editing functions can also be a great source of inspiration. Explore and experiment with the tools, and you will find many new creative assistants.

Synthesist's Delight

As unbelievable as it sounds, the first electronic instruments were created in the early 1900s. By 1906, Thaddeus Cahill had completed one of the world's first electronic instruments called the telharmonium. This monstrosity weighed in at over 200 tons and was designed to produce music for delivery over a telephone network (sound familiar?). This instrument was particularly amazing when you consider that his invention predated the invention of the amplifier by 20 years! Though the telharmonium never caught on, Cahill had set a precedent for synthesizer design, including new ways of creating and manipulating sounds.

In the 1920s, Leon Theremin designed what was to be one of the first viable electronic instruments. The pitch and volume of the theremin was controlled by proximity of the performers' hands to an antenna and loop. The theremin proved to be one of the first electronic instruments to find favor with composers of the day. Composers who wrote for this instrument include Edgar Varése and Percy Grainger.

By the 1950s, many serious music composers were exploring exciting new sounds available on early synthesizers. Composers such as Stockhauzen and Babbitt were attracted to the synthesizer's many sonic possibilities. These composers were also interested in utilizing the synth's capabilities to realize compositions that were unplayable by human performers.

Early synthesizers were plagued by two major deficits: they were very large and very expensive to produce, so only a select few composers had the luxury of using them. The advent of the transistor changed all of this. By the 1960s, synthesizer pioneers Robert Moog and Donald Buchla had created the first voltage-controlled synths. The Minimoog was one of the first synthesizers to be designed and manufactured for a mass market. Though these first synths were monophonic (able to produce only a single note at a time), the relatively small size and low cost made synthesis available to a generation of musicians. The obvious result of this development was that the synthesizer came into vogue with many popular musicians of the day. Groups such as Pink Floyd and Emerson, Lake & Palmer utilized the sonic possibilities of the synthesizer in their music. Other musicians such as Wendy Carlos used these early synths to realize new orchestrations of traditional classical literature. If you have not yet listened to *Switched on Bach,* try to find a copy of the Carlos' version of J.S. Bach's *Brandenburg Concertos.* This milestone recording is a gem of synthesizer prowess: as you listen, keep in mind that the entire recording was produced, one phrase at a time, using *very* primitive synthesis and recording techniques.

We have learned a bit of the history of electronic music and synthesis, but what exactly is a synthesizer? A synthesizer is an instrument that produces and modifies sound entirely by electronic means. Although early analog synths provided just a few ways of generating sounds, modern synths are capable of producing complex waveforms including emulations of traditional acoustic instruments. If you have ever used or listened to an analog synthesizer, you probably noticed how synthetic the sounds were. The reason for this is that analog synthesizers could only produce simple waveforms such as sine, square, triangle, and sawtooth waves. As you will see later in this chapter, digital technology has provided the synthesist with a palette of many new and complex waveforms.

COMPONENTS OF A SYNTHESIZER

We will begin our discussion of synthesizer architecture with a look at a typical analog synth. Even though the newer digital synthesizers often provide more options for manipulation of sound than the early analog ones did, an introduction to analog synthesis will provide a solid foundation to understanding the components and signal path of even the most advanced digital synthesizers. Synthesis architecture and options for manipulation of sound have evolved over the past thirty years, yet most hardware and software-based synthesizers still use a modular design that is very similar to the first transistor-based synths developed in the mid-1960s.

Where digital synthesizers use numbers to represent sounds, analog synthesizers use electrical oscillators. These electrical oscillations are *analogous* to sound produced through a loud-speaker, hence the term analog. An analog synth consists of three primary components: sound source, modifiers, and control voltage. In the early days of synthesis, sounds were created by connecting with a patch cord various controller, sound source, and modifier modules. Though few modern synthesizers still require the use of patch cords, we still refer to a particular sound on a synthesizer as a patch. It is interesting to note that some synthesizers such as the Yamaha EX-5 and E-mu E-Synth still use a virtual patch cord architecture for routing controllers and modifiers.

SOUND SOURCE

The primary sound source of an analog synthesizer is the *voltage-controlled oscillator* (VCO). The output frequency (or pitch) of a VCO is controlled by application of control voltage. A control-voltage keyboard is typically used to control the frequency of an oscillator, but other types of control may be used, such as an envelope generator. Most analog oscillators provide several types of waveforms. We will not go into the math behind each type of waveform; what is important to understand is that the combination of fundamental frequency and the relative amplitude of overtones is what provides the unique timbral quality of each waveform. A sawtooth wave, for example, provides a brilliant or piercing timbre because the summative amplitude of the first three overtones is greater than the amplitude of the fundamental. In contrast, a sine wave has no overtones and provides a timbre that might be characterized as mellow. If you do not have access to a vintage analog synthesizer, you may wish to download one of the many software-based analog emulators. Note that some companies such as Big Briar still manufacture modular analog hardware.

The following graphs represent waveforms available on most analog synthesizers. Note that when viewing a waveform, amplitude is represented on the *y* axis and frequency is represented by the *x* axis.

Figure 11.1.1 Sine waveform

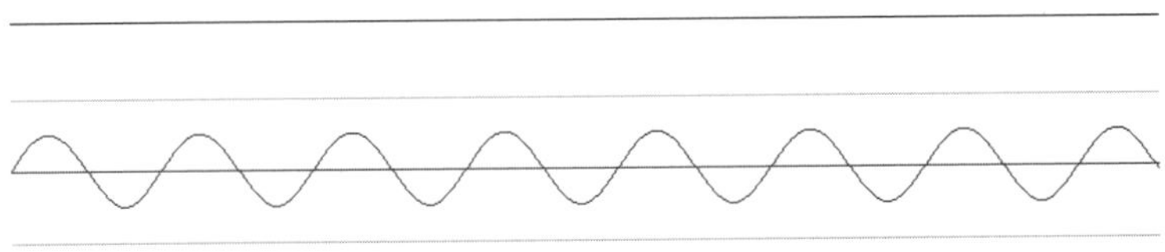

Figure 11.1.2 Triangle waveform

Figure 11.1.3 Sawtooth waveform

Figure 11.1.4 Square waveform

It might be helpful to visualize a guitar string as you view a waveform graph. On a stringed instrument such as a guitar, the thicker the string, the slower the rate or *frequency* of vibration. If more force is applied to the string, it is obvious that the volume or amplitude of sound produced is louder. Additional force applied to a string causes it to move in a bigger arc, but the frequency of vibration remains fairly constant. The following diagram may help to clarify this concept.

Figure 11.2 Waveform diagram: same pitch or frequency, two levels of amplitude or volume

One of the things I learned when first designing sounds using analog synthesizers is that it is important to start with an appropriate waveform. Attempting to create a bright sound such as an alto saxophone using a sine wave is beating the proverbial dead horse. This concept is still true today: select (or sample) an appropriate waveform before applying modifiers to a sound source.

Noise generator. Most analog synthesizers provide a noise generator to complement the traditional VCO. A noise generator typically generates pink or white noise. White noise consists of random frequencies and sounds much like radio static. A noise generator is usually modified by one or more filters and/or an amplifier. Noise works well as a sound source for designing many sounds that occur in nature, such as wind, ocean waves, or a waterfall. Noise can also be useful as a sound source for some types of percussive instruments such as a snare drum.

External sound source. Many early analog synthesizers provided an input for an external sound source. One such instrument, my trusty Korg MS-20, provides the ability to process a microphone, guitar, or other signal. By routing an external sound source through the various modules of the synth all sorts of interesting sounds may be created.

MODIFIERS

Though the quality and variety of sound sources available on a synthesizer (analog or digital) is the primary ingredient for good sound, modifiers provide a way to manipulate these sounds. If you are considering investing in a sound-design synthesizer, it is essential to evaluate the types of modifiers that are provided. You should also evaluate the ways these sound modifiers can be controlled. (For example, is it possible to control filter cutoff using note velocity, an envelope, and/or a data slider?) As with sound sources, a look at common analog modifiers will provide a good foundation for learning how to use modern-day digital, analog, and software synthesizers.

Filters. Filters are an important component of sound synthesis. As a vocalist uses the shape of the throat and oral cavity to affect timbre, filters provide the synthesist with a means of modifying the timbre of a sound. Though there are many types of filters available, we will focus on three of the most common filters: high-pass, low-pass, and band-pass.

Voltage-controlled filters (VCF) work by cutting or attenuating a range of frequencies while letting other frequencies pass through. Filters are fun to use in that they provide the ability to control or alter the timbre of a sound in real time. A common filter on most any analog synthesizer is the *high-pass filter.* As the name implies, a high-pass filter lets high frequencies pass while setting a cutoff for lower frequencies. It is important to note that frequency cutoff represents the frequency range where filtering is evident to the listener; it is not an abrupt boundary.

Figure 11.3 High-pass filter graph

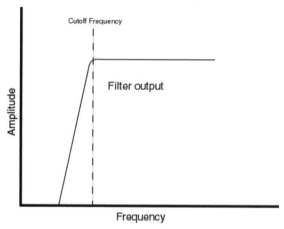

A *low-pass filter* provides a complement to the high-pass filter. Again, as the name implies, a low-pass filter lets lower frequencies pass unaffected while setting a cutoff point for higher frequencies.

Figure 11.4 Low-pass filter graph

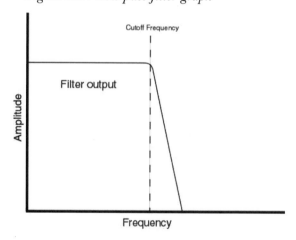

If you combine a high-pass and a low-pass filter you have a *band-pass filter*. A band-pass filter lets a range of frequencies pass while setting both an upper and lower cutoff boundary.

Figure 11.5 Band-pass filter

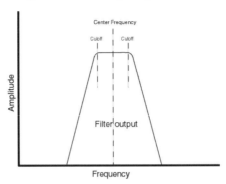

Filters can be used for all sorts of interesting effects such as wah-wah guitar sounds or more subtle timbral variations. As with our discussion of analog waveforms, the best way to get a sense of how filters work is to experiment with them. (You may want to consider purchasing one of the excellent analog emulation software synthesizers available in order to explore this type of synthesis.)

Resonance. An interesting option on many early analog synthesizers was a resonance or peak control. A resonant filter loops a portion of the output of the filter back to the input. The result of this loopback is that frequencies near the cutoff range are accentuated. Through careful control of the filter cutoff and the amount of resonance, many wonderful filter feedback effects can be achieved. A fun experiment to try is to resonate low-pass filtering of a sawtooth or triangle wave. By fine-tuning the amount of peak and adjusting the filter cutoff point, you can actually hear each of the partials as they are resonated.

Amplifier. As Samuel Pellman points out in his excellent book, *An Introduction to the Creation of Elecroacoustic Music,* most *voltage-controlled amplifiers (VCA)* do not amplify a signal, they attenuate it. In other words, as a signal passes through a VCA, it will either continue through at its highest level or the signal will be attenuated or lessened. As with the other modules of an analog synthesizer, more than one VCA may be used in the signal chain. A common use of the VCA is to control the attack and release of a sound. An envelope generator is often used in conjunction with a VCA to automate the attack and decay of a sound, but it is also common to control a VCA using a knob or foot pedal in real-time.

The concept of control voltage is the heart of analog synthesis. Control voltage is used to control a sound source or sound modifiers, but control voltage sources do not, by themselves, create any sound. By far the most common control-voltage source is a control-voltage keyboard. In the following example, control voltage from a keyboard is used to control the frequency of a voltage-controlled oscillator. The output of the oscillator module is then routed through a voltage-controlled amplifier (VCA) that finally sends the signal to a loudspeaker.

Figure 11.6 Keyboard control voltage, VCO, VCA, loudspeaker

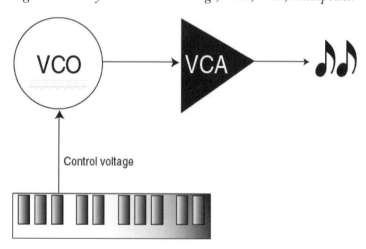

Although it is most common to use a control-voltage keyboard to control pitch, the voltage output of the keyboard may also be used to control a modifier such as a filter or VCA. *Keyboard tracking* is a term used to describe the tandem control of both an oscillator and filter cutoff by a control-voltage keyboard. As the performer plays the higher notes on the keyboard, the control voltage is used to increase the frequency cutoff of a low-pass filter so that the timbre of the higher notes remains unchanged.

Envelope generators were (and still are) an important tool to synthesists. An envelope generator provides a specific control-voltage shape or contour. This shape can then be used to control another module such as a VCO, VCF (voltage-controlled filter), or VCA. Most analog synthesizers provided a four-stage envelope generator that included attack, sustain, decay, and release (ADSR). During the attack stage, voltage rises from zero to a peak level. During decay, the voltage drops to the sustain level. During the release stage, voltage falls back to zero. The following example illustrates a typical ADSR contour.

Figure 11.7 Attack, decay, sustain, release stages

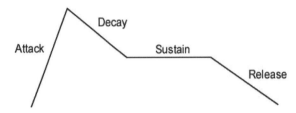

A common envelope generation (EG) function involves application of the output of the EG to a VCA. In this scenario, the envelope generator begins its operation when the user presses a key on the control-voltage keyboard. This initial trigger initiates the attack portion of the envelope. As the key is held down, the envelope continues through the initial decay portion until it reaches the sustain stage. When the key is released, the envelope generator continues with the release stage where, if the envelope generator is used to control a VCA, the sound will fade out.

Be careful when applying envelope contours to amplitude. A snare-drum sound (even a sampled snare) will not sound very drumlike with a slow attack. I have found that, in addition to realistic sound sources, amplitude envelopes are one of the most important considerations when attempting to emulate traditional instruments. The *Switched on Bach* recordings I mentioned earlier in this chapter are a fine example. Though the early analog synthesizers used on these recordings were horribly inept at reproducing sounds from the Baroque era, Carlos' masterful use of envelopes and other sound-design techniques makes these recordings much more natural and musical.

Figure 11.8 ADSR applied to VCA

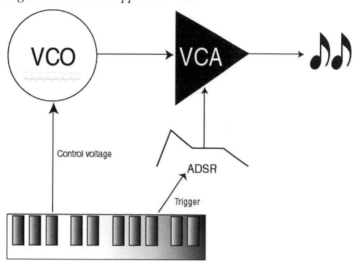

Many other options for sound design are available when you use an envelope to control a modifier such as a high- or low-pass filter. You should consider using an envelope generator whenever you want to automate a particular characteristic such as a changing filter cutoff or a scoop (a note that starts flat and "scoops" up to the proper pitch).

Figure ll.9 ADSR applied to a low-pass filter

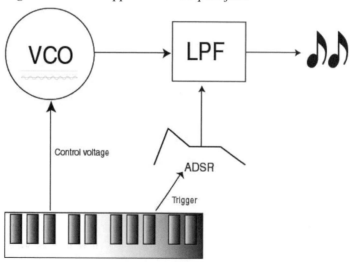

I remember when I purchased my first analog synthesizer many years ago. I spent many hours enjoying how to manipulate sounds using the *low-frequency oscillator* (LFO). An LFO can be used to create striking effects such as a siren or laser gun, or it may be used for subtle effects such as vibrato. Like an envelope generator, a low-frequency oscillator provides a source of voltage control that may be applied to a sound-source or modifier module. Where the envelope generator provides a voltage shape or contour, a low-frequency oscillator provides a series of slow-moving oscillations.

Though an LFO is similar to a traditional voltage-controlled oscillator, the frequency rate is generally slower than the range of hearing by humans (i.e., LFO is *only* used as a control-voltage source). Again, like a traditional oscillator, most LFOs provide several types of waveforms. These low-frequency waveforms can then be used to control another synthesizer module such as a VCO (to control pitch), VCF (to change the timbre of a sound), or VCA (for fading types of effects). In addition to a choice of waveforms, an LFO will also provide a frequency or rate control as well as an amplitude control. It is interesting to note that, when the output of an LFO is applied to a VCO, the frequency of the LFO determines the rate of pitch fluctuation. Similarly, the amplitude of the LFO affects the range of pitch fluctuation. The following diagram demonstrates a typical use of LFO. In this case, LFO is applied to a voltage-controlled oscillator to create a siren effect.

Figure 11.10 LFO applied to VCO to create a siren

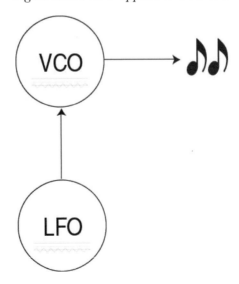

As with the other control-voltage sources we have talked about to this point, LFO may be applied to any other sound source or modifier (e.g.,you might use an LFO to control both pitch and filter cutoff frequency).

OTHER ANALOG TIDBITS

Most of us are familiar with the term *sample*. In a moment we will discuss the concept of digital sampling, but it is interesting to note that analog synthesizers also had a form of sampling. A *sample-and-hold* circuit was a component of many of the early synthesizers. This circuit would measure the voltage of a waveform at a given point in time and "hold" this sample as an output until another sample was taken. It was common in analog synthesizers to use a clock source to trigger the rate of sampling. The output of the sample-and-hold circuit was often used to control a voltage-controlled oscillator. In the next diagram, a sample-and-hold generator is used to sample white noise. The output of the sample-and-hold generator is used to control the pitch of an oscillator. The song "Karn Evil 9" on the Emerson, Lake & Palmer album *Brain Salad Surgery* demonstrates an effective use of sample and hold.

Figure 11.11 Sample and hold (sampling white noise, routed to a VCO)

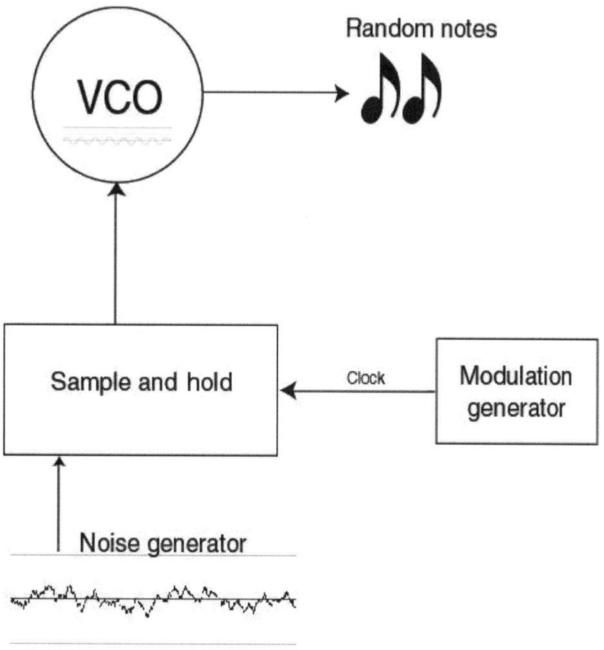

Another interesting circuit available on some analog synthesizers is a *ring modulator*. A ring modulator is a special form of amplitude modulation. The concept of amplitude modulation is as follows: when an oscillating voltage (above 30Hz) is used as the control-voltage of a VCO, and the VCA is passing an audio signal, new frequencies called sidebands will exist in the output of the VCA. A ring modulator multiplies the voltages of two input signals. The output of the ring modulator is the sum and difference frequencies. The original signals are not a part of its output. When complex waveforms are used as input to a ring modulator, interesting bell-like sounds result. Let's use some numbers to demonstrate the concept of a ring modulator. If a frequency of 500 is applied to one input and a frequency of 63 is applied to the other, the resulting output would be a combined signal of 563 (the sum) and 437 (the difference).

Let's review what we have learned so far regarding analog synthesis:
• An analog synthesizer consists of modules that may be connected in a variety of ways.
• The three types of modules available on an analog synthesizer are sound source, modifiers, and voltage-control sources.
• Voltage-control sources may be used to control a sound source or modifier, but voltage-control sources by themselves do not produce an audible signal.
• Filters such as high- and low-pass filters are used to affect the timbre of a sound source.
• Voltage-controlled amplifiers are used to modify or attenuate a given input source.
• The voltage shape or contour of an envelope generator (often ADSR) is typically used to control amplitude, frequency, or filter cutoff.
• Another control-voltage source, the low-frequency oscillator, may also be used to control an oscillator, filter, or amplifier.

This would be a good time to reiterate that, though synthesizers have grown in complexity since the days of analog synthesis, the basic concepts such as application of modifiers to a sound source and the use of various controllers to modify a module in real time or through automation is still at the heart of modern synthesis design. Modern synths may provide tens (if not hundreds) of modifiers, envelopes may include eight or more stages, and many new options such as sampled waveforms are available as sound sources. Still, the basic signal flow and modular approach of analog synthesis is still germane.

If you are new to synthesizers or perhaps you have relied on the default patches of a synth, it can be a daunting task to learn how to navigate the mass of menus common on most modern synths. Of course, nothing is quite as helpful as spending some time with the manuals because each synthesizer will provide a different architecture (and often different terms) for the various modules. With that said, the following suggestions may be helpful as you begin the process of exploring your synthesizer.

Modes. Most synthesizers will provide several modes of operation. The most common mode is *multi*[1] mode. In multi mode your synthesizer will be able to respond to several channels of MIDI data. This mode is typically used for mulitimbral operation in a sequencing environment. Some synths allow you to freely select sounds for each channel (e.g., the Kurzweil K2000/2500 series). Others, such as most Korg and Alesis synths and the newer Yamaha keyboards, require you to set up a multi that specifies which MIDI channels are enabled and make patch selections for these channels. A multi can be helpful when using complex layered sounds in a multitimbral environment. In this instance, a layered sound that responds on channel one might actually reserve channels 1 to 3 (i.e., a different sound and channel for each layer), the remaining channels might be enabled for single-channel sounds such as bass and drums. Many synthesizers also provide a *voice* mode. Generally, voice mode is used when using the synthesizer for a single sound (i.e., though the synthesizer will not respond as a multitimbral instrument, voice mode will use the entire processing power of the synthesizer for a single "mega" sound).

Global settings. Synthesizers will generally provide a global or master page to set transposition, tuning, intonation, local control, velocity sensitivity curves, and output settings. If your synth is not responding to MIDI data, the master page or MIDI page is a good place to start. You will generally need to set the keyboard to MIDI mode to respond to incoming MIDI messages.

MIDI settings. A MIDI settings page is often available. Here you can usually set the synthesizer to filter some types of MIDI data such as program change or pitch bend messages. Most newer synths also provide an option for setting the bank select method. If you are unable to select patches and banks from an external sequencer, a quick look at the MIDI settings page will usually provide the solution: the sequencing software and synthesizer need to agree on the bank select method.

Chapter Eleven **263**

Effects. Effects such as reverb, chorus, and delay are implemented in many different ways. Some synthesizers only provide effects on the global level (e.g., you can select a reverb and delay that is available on a global level for each sound). This is similar to how outboard effects are used in a recording studio: a piano and bass might be processed through the same reverb unit but one sound might be more dry than the other in the final mix. Note that some synths will allow you to set effects on the program level; that is to say, each sound might include its own effect processing. This can be helpful when you want to use delay and reverb to place sounds in specific locations in the stereo image.

Disk or store menu. Many synthesizers provide the means for storing and retrieving data. A disk menu might be used to access an internal floppy drive or allow you to mount an external SCSI device. Other synthesizers may provide a similar *store* button to save patch edits to a PCMCIA card or internal memory. Most synthesizers will also provide a store function that allows you to backup internal settings to an external source via MIDI. Usually this option will be described as a *system exclusive dump* or similar menu item.

Song mode. Many newer synthesizers also provide a minimal internal sequencer. This is usually accessed through a song or sequencer button. Though I have found software sequencers to be generally easier to use, an onboard sequencer can be very helpful when performing live. Simply save your sequences as *Standard MIDI Files* (SMF) and load them into the synthesizer before a performance. If you are like me, the thought of packing up and transporting my computer to a gig is a nightmare I would prefer to avoid.

Edit mode. Sound design synths will provide an edit mode for designing and manipulating sounds. In most cases, selecting a sound and then pressing an edit button will place the synthesizer in edit mode. While in edit mode, you will want to familiarize yourself with the relevant modules of the synthesizer.

Sound source. The sound source is usually labeled as OSC, DCO, voices, or the like. Be sure to experiment with how to select various waveforms and keymaps. A sampler may provide both a layer mode (i.e., layering two or more sounds) as well as a keymap option, which is used to assign samples to specific keys on the keyboard. Some synthesizers will provide a variety of sound sources that might include sampling, physical modeling, or digital signal processing (DSP) methods.

MODIFIERS

Filters. Most digital synthesizers will provide various forms of filters. On some instruments like the Kurzweil K2000/K2500, these filters are accessible from an algorithm page. Other synthesizers such as the E-mu E-Synth provide a dynamic processing page where you can route a signal through filters and other modifiers.

Tip: If your interests lie in sound design, be sure to evaluate the types of filters provided on an instrument you intend to purchase. Some sample-playback synthesizers do not provide any filters.

Envelopes. Synthesizers often provide one or more envelopes. On many synthesizers the envelopes are "hard wired" to a specific function such as amplitude or filtering. Other synthesizers may provide a separate multistage envelope page. With these systems it is necessary to implicitly set the envelope as a control source on the relevant modifier page (e.g., select the envelope as a control source in the filter or amplifier page).

Low-frequency oscillators. Low-frequency oscillators are another common option on digital synthesizers. Most LFOs provide several waveform options as well as several methods for controlling the rate of oscillation. The most common setting is to use the modulation wheel to control LFO rate within the minimum and maximum rates as determined by the LFO page. As with envelopes, the LFO may be "cabled" to an oscillator to control pitch or may be used to control filtering or amplitude.

Amplifier. As the name implies, an amplifier is used to attenuate a signal. Most synthesizers provide an amplifier page where you can set a control source such as an envelope generator, attack velocity, LFO, and the like. Low-frequency modulation of an amplifier can produce tremelo effects. Similarly, application of an envelope generator to an amplifier can produce interesting "soundscape" effects.

Tuning. In most cases, it is possible to set global tuning as well as intonation parameters for each patch. Both coarse- and fine-tuning options are provided. As with filters, you may want to evaluate the options for nontempered and user-defined tunings. One of the benefits of synthesis is the flexibility of experimenting with new (or old) tuning systems.

Common settings. Typically, a common or voice setup menu option is available to set the range of pitch bend for a specific patch as well as other parameters such as monophonic mode or portamento control. This page might even include toggle modes for an internal arpeggiator.

Cords or cables. Many synthesizers use a virtual cable paradigm for routing sliders, key data, control wheels, and other sources to the various modules of the synthesizer. A flexible cabling scheme would allow you, for example, to use a data slider to control both a filter cutoff and filter resonance.

CREATING SOUNDS FROM SCRATCH

One of the best methods of learning how to design and manipulate sounds is through experimentation. Before you dig in and start twisting knobs and sliders, it is a good idea to take a moment to back up the user banks of your synthesizer. Once this is done you will be able to enjoy the process of editing and creating new sounds without worrying about trashing existing sounds. If your experimentation goes awry, it is then a simple process of loading in your previous sounds. I would also caution you to keep your monitors or headphone volume at a low level while creating new sounds. This is particularly true if you experiment with signal algorithms[2]. Some synthesizers such as the Kurzweil K2000/K2500 provide various signal paths in the form of algorithms. Depending on the algorithm you use, it is very easy to overdrive your system and create a nasty wall of sound. Again, keep your monitors at a low level to avoid damaging your reference system or ears.

Although there are as many ways to design sounds as there are synthesists, I have found that the following steps can be helpful when creating sounds from scratch.

Start with the sound source. The goal here is to use a waveform that best matches your vision for the final sound. An obvious example would be to select white noise if your goal is to create the sound of wind, waves, or a waterfall. A less obvious example might be to select a square wave to best represent the nasal quality of an oboe or a sine wave to represent a flute. Many synthesizers allow you to select a sample or physical model as the sound source. Depending on the sound you wish to create, this can open up an exciting array of possibilities for sound sources.

Adjust the amplitude envelope. As I mentioned previously, one of the things I realized when first experimenting with analog synthesizers is that humans tend to be very perceptive when it comes to hearing an amplitude contour or envelope. For example, the difference between a 44 magnum handgun and the sound of a backfire of a car are distinctive. Though you could easily tell the difference between these sounds if you heard them back to back, it is the similarity of sudden attack and decay that might cause us to mistake one sound for another. Of course context is also important: white noise might be a perfectly acceptable substitution for a snare drum if the listener expects to hear a snare and the amplitude envelope closely matches that of a real snare drum. This type of substitution can be wonderfully effective when designing sounds. Why not use a sample of a slamming door or other effect as a percussive instrument in a sequence?

Apply filters to modify timbre. After completing the first two steps, you should have a sound that is beginning to take shape. I find that this is usually a good point to begin to tweak the filters. As with amplitude envelopes, filters can go a long way in creating a convincing sound (if your goal is to mimic a traditional instrument). Because of their effect on timbre, filters can also be wonderfully effective when designing nontraditional sounds. As an example, you might want to try routing your signal through a low-pass filter to create a convincing bass drum sound (turn down the cutoff point until you find a frequency range that works well to your ear). Conversely, you might consider using a high-pass filter to cut out low frequencies when designing a snare drum.

Apply real-time modifiers. To my ear, the most musical sounds are often those that change over time. Vocalists and woodwind players almost always use a touch of vibrato to add more expression to a musical passage. Real-time modifiers can be an equally expressive tool for synthesists. For me, tweaking a sound with real-time modifiers is the most creative part of the sound-design process. Some examples are as follows: a touch of low-frequency-oscillation (LFO) might be used to control pitch for a vibrato effect; use an envelope generator or data wheel to control a filter cutoff or resonance setting; or use LFO to sweep a filter cutoff and assign a slider or modulation wheel to control the rate of the low-frequency oscillator. Of course, we are only scratching the surface of sound-design concepts, but the important thing to remember is to experiment and have fun. I am the first to admit that some of my most successful designs were the result of haphazard experimentation.

Here is one last bit of advice regarding sound design: Pick out a few of your favorite patches on your synthesizer or sound module and take some time to study the design of these sounds. These sounds are usually created by professional designers who have a vast experience with getting the most out of any synthesizer. I often learn many new tricks when studying the sound designs of other musicians. It can also be fun to listen to a sound and ponder how you would create such a sound. Consider the probable sound sources, filters, modulators, and the like and then study the sound to see how it was actually created. Again, you will probably be surprised at the innovative methods used in many of these patches.

ANALOG VS. DIGITAL SYNTHESIS

Just as the transistor had a huge impact on the design and availability of synthesizers to the mass market, the introduction of inexpensive microprocessors set the stage for a revolution in the field of music synthesis. Although analog synthesizers provided many new sonic possibilities for composers and performers, analog synths were plagued by several deficits: a limited number of basic waveforms to choose from, a tendency of oscillators to drift out of tune, limited or no ability to store and retrieve patches, and limited polyphony (many of the synthesizers from this era were monophonic).

One of the first commercially available digital synthesizers was manufactured by Yamaha in 1983. The Yamaha DX7 was a huge success and set the stage for the decline of analog synths. The relatively inexpensive cost of this instrument combined with the mind-boggling array of sounds (by 1983 standards) ensured its success. It is interesting to note that analog synthesizers are making a comeback: several companies manufacture analog synthesizer hardware.

Before we delve into the details of digital synthesis, it will be helpful to discuss the concept of how a digital synthesizer works. Where an analog synthesizer uses voltages that are analogous to a soundwave, a digital instrument uses numbers to represent sounds. Though many methods of digital synthesis are available, each of these instruments uses numbers to represent the sounds we eventually hear through a set of headphones or speakers. Advanced digital synths provide many functions for manipulating or modifying a digital signal.

SAMPLERS

One of the most common forms of digital synthesis is the sampler. As with the sample-and-hold circuit common in analog synthesizers, digital samplers use an *analog-to-digital converter* (ADC) to take a periodic "snapshot" or sample of the amplitude of a given input signal. The resulting collection of *samples* provides a numeric representation of the input source. I should point out that the term sample is typically used to refer to both the individual snapshots as well as the collection of samples. For example, a one-second sample of a piano key would actually contain 44.1 thousand samples (providing it was recorded at the standard CD recording rate). Even though this recording contains thousands of tiny samples, we still refer to the collection of individual samples as a sample.

Keep in mind that the accuracy or quality of a sampler is primarily dependent on three factors: the quality of the analog to digital converters, sample rate, and bit depth. Figure 11.12 illustrates the concept of sampling. Notice how a sample must be taken at both the positive and negative portion of each cycle to accurately represent the vibration digitally.

Figure 11.12 A sample of positive and negative portions of a vibration

A truism in the digital domain is that the higher the sample rate, the more accurately a DAC will convert an analog signal to its digital representation. An important consideration here is that to accurately sample a given frequency component, two samples are required for each of the frequency cycles. If you combine this with the knowledge that the range of human hearing is roughly 20Hz to 20,000Hz, it is evident that a sample rate of at least 40,000 samples per second is required to accurately represent frequencies within the range of hearing. The Nyquist frequency (named for Harry Nyquist, a theorist who developed the theoretical basis for these concepts in the 1920s) is the frequency that is half that of the sample rate. The Nyquist frequency represents the highest frequency that may be accurately represented by a given sample rate.

One of the problems associated even with high sampling rates is that frequencies that are higher than the given Nyquist frequency will be quantified and may actually be audible as an *alias* (i.e., an overtone of a high note may become audible as a new and usually unwanted frequency). To deal with the problem of aliasing, many digital devices use a low-pass filter to remove frequencies from this range. Because a low-pass filter does not provide an abrupt boundary between filtered and unfiltered frequencies, the actual sample rate must be slightly higher to account for this discrepancy. As it so happens, the sample rate of a compact disc is 44.1kHz. This rate provides a "buffer" for the hardware to filter unwanted aliases while still providing a Nyquist frequency that is at the upper limits of the human hearing range.

The other important factor associated with analog-to-digital conversion is *bit depth*. In short, the greater the range of numbers that are used to represent a given amplitude, the more accurate the conversion will be. An 8-bit number (11111111 binary) provides a maximum of 255 levels of amplitude. In contrast, compact discs use 16-bit numbers to represent levels of amplitude. A 16-bit number (1111111111111111 binary) provides a whopping 65,536 levels of amplitude. If you ever wondered why your old 8-bit sound card sounds so terrible, it is evident that a 16-bit card is potentially 257 times more accurate! Even when converting with a 16-bit number, an undesirable process called *quantization* still occurs. Simply put, a given amplitude must be quantified to the closest numeric value in the range provided by the bit depth. In an 8-bit system, *quantization error* is very evident:

a numerical range of 0 to 255 is simply not accurate enough to provide a quality sample. The greater the numeric range, the more discreet quantization errors become. Though a 16-bit analog converter is very good, many feel that the resulting signal-to-noise ratio of 96dB is still not sufficient. As amazing as it seems, many studios are now moving to 32-bit numbers (0 to 4,294,967,295) and sampling rates of 96kHz and higher.

SAMPLING CONCEPTS

Before we delve into useful sampling concepts, I would like to take a moment to point out that, though extremely useful, samplers are not an end-all for synthesists. One of the inherent problems with samplers is that, while they provide useful snapshots of sound, the resulting sounds are just that: snapshots. An analogy would be to compare samplers to photography. A camera can be used to provide a useful and even artistic sample of a musical performance. The resulting photograph may conjure up emotions or even provide an insight into the human experience, but a photograph, as with a musical sample, lacks the perspective to change over time. A sample of a complex sound such as a piano only provides a snapshot of a given note at a given velocity. The sounds of a real piano, however, are constantly changing as vibrations from one string interact or cause sympathetic vibrations in another. Velocity also has an effect on the timbre of a note. As you work with sampling synthesizers you may want to consider this limited aspect of the technology. As with the photography analogy, a musical snapshot can either be a poor substitute for the real thing or a wonderful opportunity for creativity.

As I get off of my soapbox, let me also mention that, in practical terms, samplers can be very useful. Let's face it, most of us do not have the luxury of writing for a studio orchestra every day. The reality is that many commercial productions, for obvious financial considerations, utilize samplers to mimic the real thing. I would encourage the reader to explore sampling technology for both its ability to mimic as well as its potential for more creative pursuits.

Before you attempt to sample a traditional instrument such as a piano or guitar, it would be helpful to do a little preplanning. Your sample will only be as good as the gear you use, which is true of any type of recording. High-quality microphones and preamps are essential if you wish to accurately sample an acoustic instrument. As with any audio recording, the characteristics of the room are also an important consideration. Unwanted background noise or reverberations will end up in the recording if your sampling environment is less than pristine. You may also want to consider purchasing commercially produced sample libraries if your goal is to sample something as complex as a piano.

Consider the characteristics of the instrument you intend to sample. How does the timbre of the instrument change at various dynamic levels? Will it be necessary to capture special nuances such as fret or breath noise? Will the sample be static or should it change over time? (For example, asking a wind player to add some vibrato to the end of a note can add a wonderfully natural quality to an otherwise dry sounding sample.) You should also consider how you intend to sonically use the sample. A sample of a saxophone that includes room ambience may sound awkward when mixed with relatively dry or synthetic sounding backing tracks. A final consideration is memory. Keep in mind that a stereo sample at the standard rate of 44.1kHz will take up 10MB of memory per minute! If you consider that an accurate sampling of a grand piano will require a variety of samples (at varying velocities) for every couple of notes across the keyboard, it is evident that memory soon becomes a precious commodity. Once you have done your homework, it is time to record the samples and begin the editing process.

If you plan to record a sample from an analog source, be sure to take a minute to adjust the gain of the input source. As with any recording, the goal is to get the strongest possible input signal while still remaining under the 0 db threshold. Look at the level meter on the sampler and adjust your levels until you have optimized the signal. If you have not had much experience with recording, it might be helpful to point out that, though signal clipping will most certainly wreck your sample, recording at a volume that is too low will be equally problematic. When you sample a weak input source, the ratio of background noise to signal level is lessened and the resulting sample will be less than pristine. Also, be sure to select an appropriate sampling rate. Most samplers will let you set a rate of between 22.05 to

48kHz. It is important to remember that your sample rate must be at least twice as high as the highest frequency to be sampled. Though 48kHz provides a more accurate sample rate for some material, keep in mind that audio CDs run at a rate of 44.1kHz. I have found that, in most cases, it is best to sample at 44.1kHz as the downward quantization required to go from 48 to 44.1kHz may provide more problems than it is worth.

If you plan to sample a digital source such as a DAT, you will want to ensure that the sample rate matches the incoming source (44.1kHz, in most cases).

Most samplers allow you to begin the sampling process using one of three modes: threshold, key, or force mode. Generally, the threshold method will provide the best results and require minimal editing of the start of the sample. When using the threshold method, the sampler waits in an "armed" mode until the input signal reaches a user-defined threshold level. Most samplers presample a bit in order to record any attack transients that might occur just before the threshold level is reached. Force or key modes are helpful when you intend to record a sound that does not have a well-defined attack. (This would be the case if you wanted to record room ambience.)

After taking a sample, you will need to assign or place the sample on a specific key or range of keys. In most cases, if you sample a pitched instrument, you will want to place this sample at the same key represented by the pitch of the instrument. It is always a good idea to take the time to name your samples with a descriptive name (believe me, a complex collection of samples is a real pain to work with if they are not appropriately named). Most musicians will include the key name as a part of the sample name. For example, "My Piano C3" would clearly indicate that this sample represents middle C on the piano keyboard. You will also need to set a sample range. The sample range might be a single key for a percussive sample or two or more notes for a piano or other pitched instrument. As I mentioned before, you may need to sample every other note to get an accurate sample of some instruments. Some instruments such as an electric bass will sound passable by sampling in fourths.

Multisamples. Most effective sampled sounds are actually *multisamples*. A multisample is a collection of individual samples that are mapped across a range of notes. More than one set of multisamples is often used to account for a variety of timbres or effects. Typically, you will set up these groups of sounds to respond to changes in velocity or other controller data. Using samples in this way provides more expressive capability, that is, the timbre of your samples may change as a result of an increase or decrease in key velocity levels. Multisamples are also essential if the sound you intend to record changes over time e.g., a saxophone with vibrato. In this instance, the rate of vibrato will change as you play the sample at various pitches. For best results, you need to plan on sampling six or more notes for every octave.

Truncation. It is usually necessary to truncate both the beginning and end of a sample. Simply put, truncation cuts the unwanted portion of a sample from both ends of a sample. Some synthesizers will attempt to automatically truncate a sample, but you will probably need to make some manual adjustments.

Normalization. Normalization is often used to "equalize" the dynamic level of one sample to another. A normalization algorithm is actually quite simple. The highest peak of a given sample signal is raised to 0 dB. All of the other samples are raised by this same proportion. Note that some samplers allow you to set a level other than 0 dB (i.e., you may wish to normalize to some lesser level for contextual reasons).

Looping. Sample looping is used for a variety of reasons. A sample loop can provide the ability to sustain a note that would ordinarily decay (e.g., a sustained snare or other percussive sound). Sample looping is also used to conserve memory. A case in point: if you strike middle C on a piano at a dynamic level of forte, you will find that you would need about 20 seconds (or over 3MB for a stereo 44.1kHz recording) to capture the entire attack and decay of the note. If you consider that it would take at least 44 samples (sampling every other note) of at least two dynamic levels, the resulting 88 samples would require about 293MB of sample memory. With sample looping, you could save a great deal of memory by simply looping the first two to four seconds and adding a shortened decay of another several seconds. The resulting sample will not be entirely accurate, but the memory savings may be necessary depending on the gear you are using. Most samplers will allow you to set separate points for looping, attack, and decay. Another common application of sample looping is for sounds that typically sustain, such as an organ or bowed violin sound. With these types of instruments, it makes more sense to simply loop a short sample.

One of the tricky things you will need to consider when setting a loop point involves finding an appropriate boundary between the end of the loop and the start of the loop. Without editing, loops will generally emit an audible pop if the start and end amplitudes of the loop do not match. Many samplers provide tools to help you match the start and end of a loop.

Figure 11.13 Setting a loop point

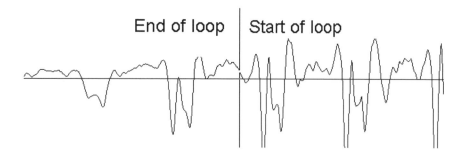

Crossfade. An effective sampling technique involves splicing two samples together. You might wish, for example, to splice the sound of an amplified guitar together with the sound of a guitar feeding back. Simply splicing the two samples together will usually result in a sudden change of timbre that may be too abrupt. Using a crossfade allows you to gracefully splice the samples together. Depending on the amount of time you allow for the crossfade, the transition from one sample to the next will be very subtle.

Pitch shifting. It is often necessary, for intonation purposes, to adjust the pitch of individual samples when creating a multisample. Keep in mind that gross adjustments in pitch will alter the quality or timbre of the sound. Avoid altering the pitch of individual samples more than a few cents in either direction. An almost comical version of this effect can be heard on some sample playback synthesizers that use a limited amount of RAM or inferior sampling methods: a sample of a flute sound that contains vibrato will sound very unnatural if the pitch is shifted more than a semitone or so. Wind players rarely (if ever) increase the rate of vibrato as they play an ascending scale, but this is an effect I have heard on more than one synthesizer! Pitch shifting can also be used for special effects. On one recent project, I sampled a recording of Adolph Hitler and adjusted the pitch down two octaves. The resulting devil-like sound was creepy, to say the least.

Gain. It is often necessary to change the level of one or more samples in a multisample. As with adjustments in pitch, gain can be used to equalize the levels of samples in a multisample so that key velocity, when applied equally across the keyboard, will result in the same output level.

Compressor. Compression is used to fix dynamic range problems with a sample. By carefully adjusting the threshold level and compression ratio, a signal that is dynamically extreme can be fixed to a more constant level. By setting a ratio of less than 1:1, this function may be used to expand the amount of dynamic range. A typical example is sampling a vocal performance that includes whispers. By compressing this type of sample, the dynamic level of the whispering portion of the performance becomes more prominent (i.e., the whisper will not be lost in the mix).

Limiter. A limiter is used to prevent a signal from exceeding a specified threshold level. This might be used to tame a sample of an electric guitar, thus providing a more manageable sample when used in a musical context.

Noise reduction. Similar to a compressor, noise reduction is used to reduce low-level noises. Generally, a threshold, ratio, and attack and release times are adjusted to reduce unwanted background noise. Keep in mind that this is not an end-all: it will be impossible to reduce serious noise problems because you may end up filtering out a musical component as well.

Equalization. EQ is used to fix or adjust a problem range of frequencies (i.e., too much high or low end). Most professional recordists advise that you avoid using EQ unless absolutely necessary. In any case, save EQ editing until you hear your sampled sound in context with other sounds. Unless the samples themselves are truly problematic with regard to equalization, it may be advisable to process the sound through an outboard equalizer in order to avoid destructively editing your original samples. Many synthesizers provide virtual send and return functions. With this type of gear, it is possible to apply equalization to a sound in real time. Again, this type of approach provides the flexibility of adjusting the EQ to fit a specific musical context.

Parametric equalization. A parametric equalizer allows you to boost or cut a specific band of frequencies. A typical example would be to roll off the low end to remove problems associated with sampling a piano on a hardwood floor. EQ might also be used to add some extra sizzle to cymbals. It is generally advisable to avoid using EQ unless it is absolutely necessary. Wanton adjustments to EQ can create many problems when a sample is used in a musical context. For example, using several samples that have been equalized to emphasize a specific range of frequencies may well result in a muddy mix.

Time compression or expansion. Time compression and expansion algorithms are notoriously difficult to develop. With that said, many of the current products offer the ability to speed up or slow down the speed of a sample without changing the pitch. Many of these compression routines are surprisingly good. As with pitch shifting, you will usually want to avoid gross changes unless you are striving for a special effect. Time compression might be used to make fifteen seconds of dialog fit into ten seconds without making the announcer sound like a chipmunk.

Pitch change. Pitch change is the complement to time compression. Where time compression retains the original pitch of a sample and alters the length, pitch change is used to alter the pitch of a sample while the time is retained. With pitch changing, a five-second A-2 could be transformed into a five-second D-3. Again, large changes of pitch will affect the quality of the sample. (An octave will probably be the maximum amount that you can effectively change the pitch.)

Aural exciter. An aural exciter is used to add brilliance to a sample. An exciter adds new harmonics to the source material and makes it stand out in a mix. Exciters are often used for vocal passages to make them more present in the mix.

Doppler. As the name implies, a doppler function mimics the well-known Doppler effect. Dopplerizing a sound shifts a sample from one side to another or from front to back while the gain is adjusted appropriately.

Other DSP options. We have covered many of the common digital editing options available on most samplers. Of course, many other functions are available depending on the synthesizer you use. If you are thinking of investing in a sampler, you should evaluate the types and quality of digital editing functions, because these functions can be a great asset for a serious sound designer. Although these functions are often used to enhance or perfect a sample, they can be a good source of inspiration for nontraditional applications as well. Consider experimenting with a Dopplerized drumset or crossfade a voice and a violin. An amazing array of opportunities is available to the creatively inclined synthesist.

ARCHIVING AND LOADING SAMPLES: THE SCSI CONNECTION

Depending on the sampling hardware you use, it will usually be necessary to archive or store your samples to some type of storage media such as a hard drive, floppy disk, or other removable media. Because samples require a great amount of memory, floppy disks are useful for storage of only the most minimal samples. Most professional samplers provide an interface to connect to an external storage device such as a Zip disk. By far the most common connection is a SCSI bus. SCSI is an acronym for *small computer system interface.* SCSI is a fast parallel interface that allows you to link together up to eight devices such as hard disks, optical disks, or other storage devices. Though SCSI is rather ubiquitous in the electronic music industry, the use of SCSI devices can be tricky. You will certainly want to take time to read your manual regarding the types of devices that may be connected to your SCSI chain and, more importantly, to learn about some of the dangers associated with connecting SCSI devices. In short, you can cause serious damage to your synthesizer or computer if you attempt to connect these devices with the power on: *Always turn off the power to your synth, computer, and any other SCSI devices before hooking up SCSI cables.*

SCSI uses ID numbers to differentiate between different devices on a SCSI network. Be sure to set each of your SCSI devices to a different ID number before powering up your system. Just remember that each device *must* have its own unique number. Some devices such as your synthesizer or computer may have a fixed ID number that cannot be changed. Again, it is important to read your manuals before connecting these devices. Before you purchase SCSI cables or devices, you need to find out what type of cable is required. Two types of SCSI cables are common:

DB25 and 50-pin Centronics. Depending on the equipment you intend to use, it may be necessary to purchase a special adapter.

When hooking up a SCSI chain remember that the total length of the chain should not exceed fifteen feet. If you can get by with shorter lengths, do it: the shorter the length of cables, the less likely you will have problems with transmission errors. You will also need to consider the issue of *termination*. Terminators are resistors that you add to both ends of the SCSI chain. Some devices include internal terminators, but these resistors may also be added in the form of a termination block that is plugged into the SCSI device.

It is sometimes helpful to connect your sampler directly to a computer using SCSI. The benefit here is that you can use your sampler to record the samples and special software such as *Sound Forge, Alchemy,* or *Recycle* can be used to edit and manipulate the samples. An added benefit is that you can use the storage devices on your computer to archive your samples.

If you experience problems getting your SCSI network to work properly (and most people do experience problems when first setting up a SCSI chain), it may be helpful to consider the following solutions:

- Use high quality, shielded SCSI cables.
- Ensure that your SCSI chain is as short as possible and that it does not exceed fifteen feet in total length.
- Ensure that each device is set to a unique ID number.
- Be sure to mount the drives. (You will find a menu option or button on the sampler to initiate the mounting procedure.) You may need to remount the drives after removing and inserting new media in a removable SCSI device.
- Check for termination on both ends of the SCSI chain.
- Find the problem: power down, disconnect a device, and power up again. Repeat this process until you find the offending device.
- Change the order of devices on the chain. You may need to experiment to find an order that works. Note that the device ID numbers *do not* need to reflect the order of the device in the chain. ID numbers are simply used to determine what data belongs to which device.

SAMPLE DUMP

The MIDI specification allows for transferring sample data over a MIDI network. Note that only sample loop data is retained: you will lose preset information when sending or receiving a MIDI sample dump. In most situations it is advisable to create a closed loop using two MIDI cables: In to Out and Out to In. Though a MIDI sample dump can be helpful to move data from one system to another, you will probably want to avoid this setup as your primary means of storing data. A MIDI sample dump is substantially slower than SCSI, and you will still need to consider how to store preset data. For most people, a dedicated hard drive or removable storage device is the best solution for archiving data from a sampler.

WHY PHYSICAL MODELING IS SO EXCITING

As I mentioned earlier, one of the problems with samplers is that they can sound very artificial because real-world sounds constantly change. The timbre of a saxophone, for example, is dependent on many factors such as the shape of the embouchure, speed of airflow, vibration, thickness and quality of the reed, and the like. Saxophonists constantly adjust these and many other parameters during a performance. As microprocessor technology continues to improve (and the technology continues to become less expensive), it has become practical for instrument manufacturers to look at new ways of creating and processing sounds. Physical modeling is one such technology. Instead of simply recording or sampling sounds, a physical modeling synthesizer attempts to use abstraction to describe some of the physical characteristics of a given instrument. Physical modeling involves developing algorithms that describe the physical properties of a given sound. A physical model for a woodwind instrument might include algorithms to describe type of material the instrument is made of (e.g., wood or metal), wind velocity, shape of the embouchure, length of the instrument, and many other parameters. These physical models are then used to "construct" a sound in real time.

The potential for physical modeling is very exciting in that it provides a natural way to control changes in timbre in real time just as a real instrumentalist would utilize these parameters in a performance. Another interesting potential of this technology is that physical models may be used to create virtual instruments that would not be possible in the real world (e.g., using bowing parameters to "play" a woodwind or percussive instrument). As you might imagine, physical modeling technology requires a

Making Music with Your Computer

tremendous amount of processing power. I suspect that, as microprocessors continue to improve, you will see many new synthesizers that utilize this type of synthesis. You might be interested to know that the electric guitar sound on the *Rhythm and Blues* example on the accompanying CD was a sound that was processed using several physical models of a guitar amplifier. Though we have a long way to go with this technology, I hope you will agree that the guitar tracks on this recording are fairly expressive.

SOFTWARE SYNTHESIZERS

A relatively new trend in synthesis involves using the processing power of modern-day personal computers to create a virtual or software-based form of synthesis. In their early days, personal computers were too slow to be viable as synthesis machines. Though sampling has been available even on the early computers, several software companies have taken this concept a step further and provide full-fledged software synthesizers. Many types of software synthesizers are available in the shareware and retail domains, but the two common paradigms are offline synthesizers and real-time synthesizers. Programs such as *Metasynth* or *CSound* offer unique ways of creating sounds but are not capable of interacting in real time within a sequencing environment. Real-time software synthesizers such as *Reality* by Seer Systems and *Gigasampler* by NemeSys provide the ability to playback notes in real time using a sequencer or other MIDI software. You may be interested to know that many options exist for General MIDI software synths. Microsoft provides a free General MIDI synthesizer as part of the DirectX 8 multimedia system. Apple provides a similar solution with Quicktime 4 (available for both Mac and PC).

The main problem with using software synthesizers is *latency,* which refers to the amount of time it takes for a synthesizer to respond to a MIDI event. Though many factors affect latency, the primary issues are processor speed of your computer, multitasking considerations such as simultaneous use of digital audio software, and the efficiency of the algorithms implemented by the manufacturers of your software synthesizer and audio card. The newer breed of software synthesizers run with very low latency levels, but timing problems may arise if you plan to run a software synthesizer along with a sequencer that is handling many channels of digital audio with DSP effects. My best advice here is to download demonstration software before you invest lots of money in a software synth.

You also should consider the type and quality of your soundcard hardware before you invest in a software synth. Though a consumer-model sound card may provide perfectly acceptable results for a hobbyist, you will probably need to invest in a professional audio card if you intend to use a software synthesizer for professional productions. A professional audio card will provide higher quality outputs and may also allow you to send the output from the synth directly to a DAT recorder via a SPDIF or AES/EBU connection. Again, you will need to check with the software manufacturer before investing in such a card—many of these programs require specific hardware to work properly. Also, note that some programs such as the *Reality* software synth allow you to record the output of the synthesizer directly to disk (i.e., as a .WAV file). If you plan to use a software synthesizer for this type of work, the quality of audio output only becomes an issue when referencing through a monitor. Such a system will keep the audio pristine as it never leaves the digital domain.

CHOOSING AND EVALUATING A SYNTHESIZER

Having been burned several times by the unfounded claims of synthesizer manufacturers, I humbly submit some suggestions for you to consider before investing a lot of money on a new synth. Of course, budget is probably the most important factor to consider. Once you have established a price range, you should spend some time researching the synthesizers available in your price range. The following are some suggestions on evaluating potential new gear.

• Sound quality: It matters little how many bells and whistles are available on a given synthesizer. If it doesn't sound great, you will soon regret spending money on the instrument. I usually only buy from dealers who offer a liberal return policy. This is essential because a dealer showroom is usually not a good place to make an informed decision on sound quality.

• How do you intend to use the synthesizer? You will want to evaluate your needs in terms of functionality. Are 88 keys essential or will a module suffice? Will the unit be used for basic General MIDI sequencing or do you plan to design and sample sounds? Will you need an internal sequencer and floppy drive for live performances? Will the weight of the instrument be an issue? If you need a synthesizer as well as a controller, you will want to evaluate the options for controlling external gear such as the flexible split points, data sliders, pitch and modulation wheels, breath control connection, and the like.

- Sound design: If your goal is to design and manipulate sounds, you will need to evaluate the quality and types of modifiers. What types of filters are provided? Are the filters resonant? How flexible is the synth regarding routings? How many envelope generators are provided and how many stages are included? What types of synthesis methods are provided? Many newer synthesizers will provide two or more modes of synthesis such as physical modeling, sampling, FDSP, frequency modulation, and the like.

- Sampling: If your interests lie in sampling you should evaluate the quality of the analog-to-digital and digital-to-analog converters. Does the sampler support common file formats such as WAV and AIFF? Are commercial sample libraries available for the instrument? Can the synth load sample libraries from other manufacturers? Does the instrument sport a SCSI port?

- Inputs and outputs: Professionals often require multiple outputs to enable them to process individual outputs through external processing gear. Many newer synths support digital output and input. As we move toward inexpensive digital mixers and digital recorders, a digital output and input becomes very important.

- Does the company have a good track record? Are problems resolved in a timely way? It may be helpful to visit some user-group Web sites to see how the instrument is being received in the trenches.

As you can see, evaluating a synthesizer is not an easy task. In the twenty years that I have been involved with electronic music, I have yet to see a synthesizer that truly addresses each of the previous concerns. My best advice to you is to not be swayed by salespeople. Take the time to do your homework and evaluate the gear in a thoughtful manner. You will most likely end up with the most appropriate product for your needs.

- Set an oscillator to produce a triangle or sawtooth waveform. Use the peak or resonance control to accentuate the cutoff point of a low-pass filter. Slowly change the filter cutoff and listen as each overtone is resonated.
- Apply an amplitude envelope to pink or white noise to create a snare drum. Apply filtering to change the timbre of the instrument.
- Set two oscillators to the same octave. Detune one oscillator slightly to create a natural chorusing effect.
- Use crossfading to combine two dissimilar sounds (e.g., a duck quack that turns into a vocal "ah" sound, or a violin that blends into an organ).
- Create a patch using several layers, such as an electric piano that is layered with the sound of a muted electric guitar and an organ.
- Use an envelope generator to control filter cutoff of a low- or high-pass filter. Use a low-frequency oscillator on the same filter and compare the results.
- Use an amplitude envelope to modify a nontraditional sound: for example, a stringed instrument with a sudden and percussive attack, or a drum with a gentle attack.
- Use a low-frequency oscillator to create a siren sound. Route a data slider or wheel to control the rate of oscillation.
- Use sample looping to loop a portion of a percussive sound (e.g., an infinitely decaying gong sound).
- Use velocity scaling to control a multilayered sound (e.g., an electric piano that sounds more percussive the harder you strike a key).
- Create an interesting drone texture. Drone or ambient sounds usually change over time such as with automated filter sweeping, amplitude modulation, or other real-time modifier.
- Create a new sound based on a sample in an unusual range such as a bass flute or soprano contrabass.
- Use dopplerization to create a "moving" voice. Try to emulate left-to-right as well as front-to-back movement.
- If your instrument supports it, create a sound that utilizes nontempered tunings such as Werkmeister or Indian raga.
- Use a filter envelope to create a wah-wah guitar sound.
- Design a sound using a new algorithm (e.g., pitch->low-pass filter->shaper->bandpass filter->amplifier).
- If you have access to a physical modeling synthesizer, create a sound that utilizes a traditional physical model for a nontraditional sound (e.g., breath and embouchure control of a stringed instrument).

- Create a groove patch by sequencing a bass and drum groove and sampling the output of the synthesizer.
- Edit the previous example to create a time-expanded groove.
- Edit the previous example to create a pitch-shifted groove.
- Create a snare drum map where snare samples are placed on consecutive keys at slightly different pitches (i.e., to create natural sounding rolls and fills).
- Assign the modulation wheel to crossfade between two multi-samples such as an electric guitar and electric guitar feedback.
- Use a low-frequency oscillator to control pitch and assign the modulation wheel to control LFO amplitude (e.g., for a vibrato effect).
- Create a keyboard split (e.g., bass in left hand, piano in the right hand).
- Use a data slider to control two or more modifiers at the same time (e.g., control filter cutoff frequency and filter resonance).

[1]For a complete discussion of MIDI modes see Chapter 9, "Introduction to MIDI."

[2]In computer vernacular, an algorithm refers to a sequence of instructions to solve a specific problem. In synthesis, the term algorithm generally refers to the specific routing of a signal through the various modules of the synth. For example, the simplest algorithm on a synthesizer would be pitch->amplifier. A more complex algorithm might be as follows: pitch->filter 1->filter 2->amplifier.

PART THREE: PUTTING IT ALL TOGETHER

12. Anatomy of Styles: Sounds and Scores

Anatomy of Styles: Sounds and Scores

We have covered much ground in this book: music theory, chords and scales, composition, keyboard techniques, drum and bass grooves, arranging, orchestration, computers, MIDI, sequencing and sound design. Now for the fun part. My goal for this chapter is to provide you with demonstrations, in a variety of styles, that may be helpful as you begin to create music with your computer. This chapter is not a "how to" chapter: the examples here are just that—examples. I hope that these pieces will provide some insights into how to create bass and drum grooves, develop harmonic progressions, arrange and orchestrate material, and utilize controllers for a more expressive form of MIDI performance.

When producing the music for this book, I felt that it was important to limit myself to equipment that would be available to the average reader. Although a $1,000 orchestral library might be useful in the production of more accurate symphonic sounds, most of us simply do not have the resources to spend this amount of money on a sequencing project. I also felt it was important to refrain from using alternate controllers in the production of these recordings. Although it would have been easy for me to ask one of my MIDI percussion friends to play the drum tracks on these cuts, I felt that this was contrary to the "do it yourself" spirit of this book. All of the music on the accompanying CD was sequenced using a keyboard controller and a fairly modest MIDI setup.

You might be interested to know what gear was used in the production of these demonstration recordings. The primary synthesizers I used were an E-mu E-Synth and a Yamaha EX-5 module. I used a Kurzweil K2000 for some sound design as well as on the orchestral piece. In addition to the synthesizers, I used a Kurzweil Micro Piano for some of the acoustic and electric piano tracks. I used *Logic Audio Gold 4* as my primary sequencer.

CD Architect (Sonic Foundry) was used to master the DAT recordings to CD. I used an Opcode SonicPort to transfer the DAT recordings to the computer. The mixing console was a Mackie 1604 (original model). The scores and musical excerpts were created with *Finale 2000*.

"FUSED SHUT"

"Fused Shut" represents a fusion of pop and jazz vocabulary. The percussion tracks are fairly thick—I used a variety of percussive instruments on several channels. I panned many of the percussion instruments across the stereo field in an attempt to create a "wide" or "open" quality in with mix. Most of the chords include extension tones (9, 11, 13). One problem I ran into with this piece involved the piano tracks: in the first master I utilized a stereo piano module. It soon became evident that this sound "fought" with the other instruments in the mix. I ended up running this module in mono and panned it slightly off-center. This helped to clarify the mix.

"ORCHESTRAL"

My goal with "Orchestral" was to demonstrate a variety of orchestral textures. Although this recording can't compete with the sound of a real orchestra, this piece could be suitable for a production that necessitates providing the illusion of the real thing. The composition and orchestration techniques are fairly traditional. I adhered to standard orchestral ranges and had some fun using a variety of instruments. The real challenge of sequencing this piece was to allow a more flexible approach to rhythm than might be common in popular music. It is interesting to note that I did not use a click track when recording this piece. I worked through the piece a phrase at a time and attempted to match each of the parts aurally (both rhythmically and dynamically).

"TECHNO TOYS"

Although this piece is not in a true techno style, it represents an approach to sequencing that is common in many styles of techno and dance music. The drum tracks are extremely thick and ultra-repetitive. I used two different drum kits (one of which was transposed). This doubling of the percussion tracks helps to provide the full percussive sound that is common to this genre of music. Of course, all of the tracks on this recording were heavily quantified. A techno-style piece would certainly last longer and would develop more slowly (perhaps over five or more minutes). For some styles of dance music it would be more common to implement a more pronounced bass. The selection of sounds is typical for this style of music: many synthesized patches and bright electric piano sounds.

"OLD TIMEY"

"Old Timey" demonstrates several techniques common to folk, country, and bluegrass music: simple chord progressions, active banjo and guitar accompaniment tracks, and a distinct "two" feel in the bass and drums. The orchestration is primarily acoustic, though I tweaked a guitar sound on the EX-5 in an attempt to create an almost corny "Telecaster" patch. The banjo track proved to be one of the most challenging components of this composition. One technique that helped with this track was to use a "cross hands" technique. I used my left hand to play a high "drone" note while the right hand arpeggiated the notes of the chords simulating a finger picking effect. It is interesting to note that the last phrase of the bridge is five bars in length. Unusual phrase lengths are common in folk and bluegrass music.

"HARD AND HEAVY"

As the name implies, "Hard and Heavy" is an attempt to use MIDI keyboards to mimic the sound of a rock band. I must confess that I cheated slightly on this recording. Although my EX-5 module provides some wonderful guitar sounds, it does not have the processing power to play more than one of these sounds at a time. My solution was to digitally record the rhythm guitar track into *Logic Audio*. This allowed me to utilize the full processing power of the EX-5 on the lead guitar sound. You will note that the tracks are heavily compressed—extreme dynamic changes are not common in this style of music. I had fun attempting to sequence some of the "mondo" drum fills that are common in this style of music: a lot of cymbal crashes and floor toms. I sequenced the fills in real time (but at a slow tempo). I find that this approach can be helpful when it is not feasible to record the fills in real time using a MIDI keyboard.

"POPOMATIC"

"Popomatic" illustrates several techniques associated with pop music. The orchestration is thick; several keyboard tracks and a variety of pad sounds helped to create this texture. The mix is very "wet," with the drums and bass in the middle and the pad and keyboard sounds panned across the stereo field. The harmony of this example is typical of pop music: many sus2 and sus4 structures and diatonic progressions. One problem that I ran into with this piece was that the orchestration was so thick, I had some problems with notes dropping out because I exceeded the polyphony limits of my synthesizer. Reassignment of some of the sounds to another synthesizer fixed the problem.

"FUNKY GROOVE"

I had two goals in mind when I started working on this composition: demonstrate a typical funk groove and utilize several of the keyboard sounds common in this style of music. A wah-wah clavichord plays a prominent role as do other typical funk instruments such as the Hammond organ and electric piano. Note that though the groove is fairly complex, each of the individual tracks are rather simple. Although it would be common to voice the horns in four or five parts, unison figures and riffs seemed to be most appropriate for this piece. The drum groove utilizes both the hi-hat and bell-ride sounds. The bell sound can be helpful in providing a change of texture in a bridge or "out chorus." Notice that the organ is used for fills and as a percussive instrument in the last section of the piece.

"SILICON DREAM"

I composed "Silicon Dream" with the thought of demonstrating some sound-design techniques. The melody consists of a simple pentatonic motive over a drone bass tone. For the drone, I used an envelope generator to control the cutoff of a resonant low-pass filter. The lead voice demonstrates physical modeling techniques. I used changes in embouchure to execute the "fall offs" at the end of some phrases. A low-frequency oscillator was used to control vibrato. Although this sound is not entirely natural, to my ear the physical modeling vibrato sounds more natural than LFO that is applied to a sampled sound.

"RHYTHM AND BLUES"

This was a fun piece to sequence. The progression of chords is a simple twelve-bar blues. The orchestration is common for this style: piano, bass, drums, organ, and guitar. I debated on the merits of using so much effects processing on the guitar sound because most R&B guitarists use a cleaner sound. After experimenting with a variety of settings I decided that, for this piece, I preferred the heavier sound. To my ear, the effects help to mask the fact that this is a keyboard, not a guitar. The guitar solo implements many techniques common to this style of music: many "bent" notes, pentatonic runs, and blues scale licks.

"SONG FOR JOBIM"

I originally wrote this song in honor of the great composer Antonio Carlos Jobim. This piece demonstrates several techniques associated with Latin and Latin-jazz music. A variety of percussive instruments are used to establish a bossa groove and the bass functions in a traditional way. The piano track implements several concepts from Chapter 4, "Contemporary Keyboard Techniques," such as a montuno pattern and repetitive comping style. Notice how a variety of cymbals are used to create variety and to mark the formal sections of the piece. Although the sequencing techniques are straightforward on this piece, it is interesting to note that the chord progression is very unusual. The last A section is a step higher than the first two A sections. In effect, this creates a sense of modulation between each chorus, though the modulation is always back to the tonic key.

"LITTLE BIT 'O COUNTRY"

I had a hard time deciding what type of piece to compose to demonstrate the country genre. As with the other styles, country is a vast topic and a single piece will necessarily be limited to a few techniques. Because the lines between pop and country have blurred somewhat in recent years, I elected to attempt a more traditional sound. Steel guitar is typically used in country, so I decided to use this instrument as the primary melodic sound. This piece was certainly a good exercise in pitch bend technique: follow the score as you listen to the recording and you will see that the majority of melody notes are bent. I found that it was most helpful to sing this melody as I sequenced because it was disconcerting to perform this track. In order to achieve the slide sound, most of the notes were played either a step above or below the arrival tone.

"PEE WEE'S BIG ADVENTURE"

I wanted to write one piece to demonstrate common Hammond organ techniques such as repetitive riffs and melodic pedal tones. "Pee Wee" is a jazz shuffle that provides a vehicle for these techniques. The rhythmic unison between the snare and ride cymbal is common in jazz shuffles, as is the walking bass line. The form of the tune is a simple AABA form—the A sections are a variation of the twelve-bar blues and the bridge provides a contrast (both harmonically and melodically). I re-recorded the tracks several times: as I solidified the solo tracks, it was necessary to re-record the accompaniment tracks in order to "respond" to the solo tracks in a natural way. I avoided using quantization on this cut in order to achieve a more natural swing feel.

"SOUNDSCAPE"

I wrote "Soundscape" to demonstrate a more textural approach to sequencing: layers of sounds are used to create this sonic setting. Note that a score is not appropriate as the piece does not utilize traditional tonal resources. I must give credit to the wonderful sound designers at E-mu because many of the sounds on this recording are presets. Although I enjoy designing my own sounds, I had many wonderful preset textures to choose from. After experimenting with several of these pads, the piece almost wrote itself. I sometimes find that an interesting sound can be inspiring as the impetus for creating a new composition. Notice that filters were used to implement a climax in the "development" section of this piece. I also used some real-time panning in an attempt to simulate movement of the audio environment.

FUSED SHUT

FUSED SHUT - 2 -

FUSED SHUT - 3 -

FUSED SHUT - 4 -

Making Music with Your Computer

FUSED SHUT - 6 -

FUSED SHUT - 7 -

FUSED SHUT - 8 -

ORCHESTRAL

ORCHESTRAL - 8 -

ORCHESTRAL - 4 -

ORCHESTRAL - 5 -

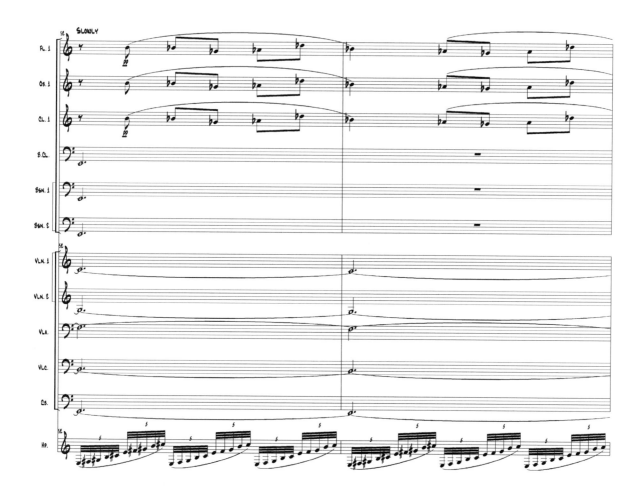

Chapter Twelve   **311**

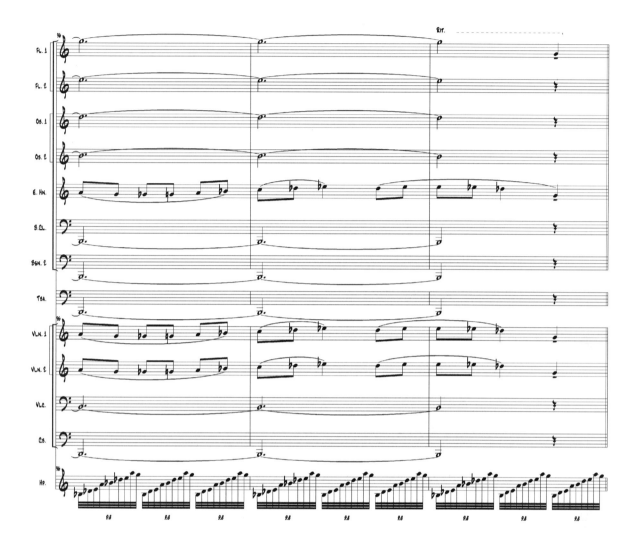

Chapter Twelve

ORCHESTRAL - 13 -

Chapter Twelve

Making Music with Your Computer

TECHNO TOYS

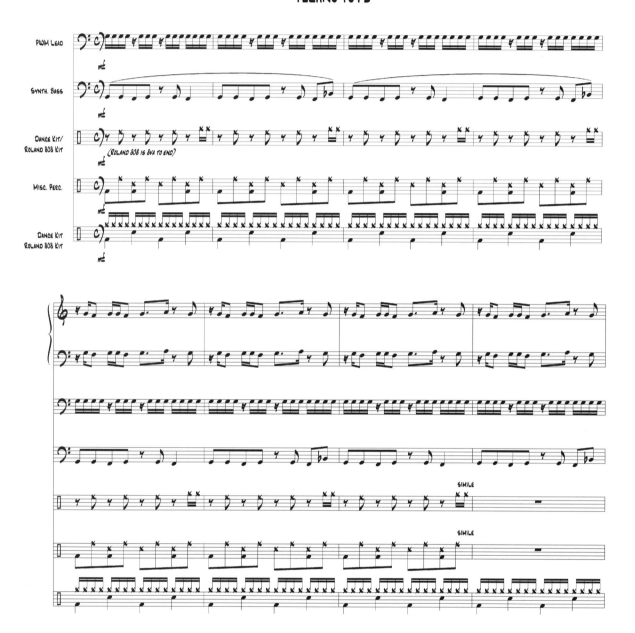

TECHNO TOYS - 2 -

Making Music with Your Computer

TECHNO TOYS - 3 -

TECHNO TOYS - 4 -

Making Music with Your Computer

TECHNO TOYS - 5 -

OLD TIMEY

*Note: Banjo and guitar are always written in treble clef. The grand staff is used to illustrate MIDI playing technique.

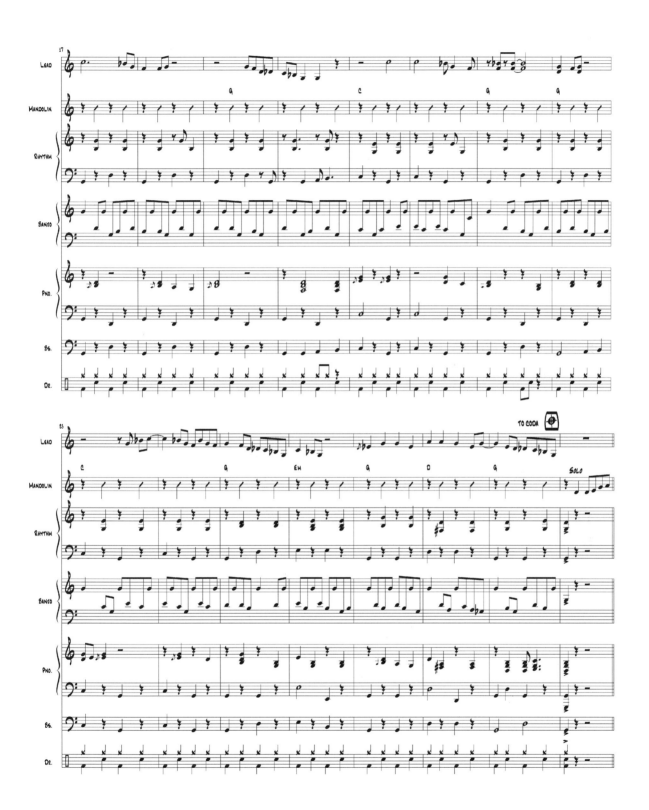

OLD TIMEY - 2 -

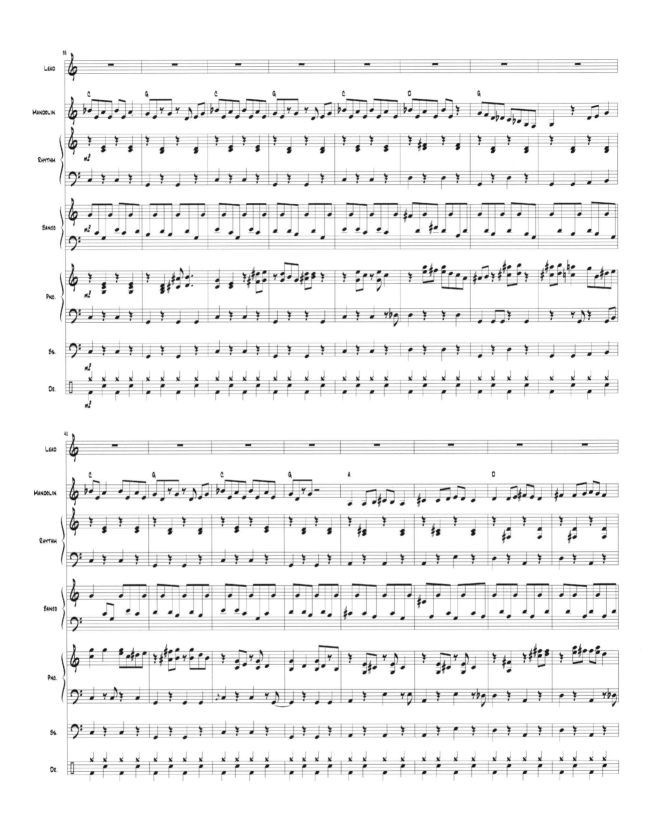

OLD TIMEY - 3 -

Making Music with Your Computer

OLD TIMEY - 4 -

HARD AND HEAVY

* OUT OF RANGE ON SOME BASS INSTRUMENTS

HARD AND HEAVY - 2 -

HARD AND HEAVY - 3 -

POPOMATIC

FUNKY GROOVE

Making Music with Your Computer

FUNKY GROOVE -2-

FUNKY GROOVE -3-

FUNKY GROOVE -4-

FUNKY GROOVE -5-

Making Music with Your Computer

FUNKY GROOVE -6-

FUNKY GROOVE -7-

Making Music with Your Computer

Silicon Dream

Performance notes:

Melody: Pan flute and echo strings

Bass: Slow Low Pass resonant filter sweep

Making Music with Your Computer

SILICON DREAM - 2 -

SILICON DREAM - 3 -

SILICON DREAM – 4 –

Rhythm and Blues

RHYTHM AND BLUES - 4 -

Making Music with Your Computer

RHYTHM AND BLUES - 6 -

RHYTHM AND BLUES - 7 -

RHYTHM AND BLUES - 8 -

352   *Making Music with Your Computer*

Chapter Twelve

353

SONG FOR JOBIM

SONG FOR JOBIM - 3 -

Chapter Twelve

Little Bit 'O Country

LITTLE BIT 'O COUNTRY -2-

LITTLE BIT 'O COUNTRY -3-

LITTLE BIT 'O COUNTRY -4-

LITTLE BIT 'O COUNTRY -5-

Pee Wee's Big Adventure

PEE WEE'S BIG ADVENTURE -3-

Pee Wee's Big Adventure -4-

Chapter Twelve

PART FOUR: APPENDICES

Electronic Euphoria

by Jeff Casey

The evolution of electronic musical instruments is undoubtedly the most important advance in music-technology in the past thirty years. The computer revolution has certainly been groundbreaking, but the rise of synthesizers in fact helped initiate the early use of computers in the personal studio. When synths hit the streets, the industry was introduced not only to a new kind of instrument but to an entirely new process of creating sounds.

We were no longer limited to the acoustic and electric instruments we and our friends could play; with practice, we could emulate a wide range of instruments using synths and samplers controlled with our favorite keyboard (and later, a variety of MIDI controllers). Our dependence on hired guns, although not eliminated, was reduced. Best of all, we could even create sounds that didn't exist in the natural world. It took a while for mainstream studios to get the idea, but eventually synths and samplers became essential tools for many types of music production.

Working with electronic sounds has become an art form all its own. Combining synths and samplers to create a mix can be quite different from mixing acoustic instruments, and it can be just as tricky. Let's take a look at some of the things you can do to create a successful mix of electronic musical instruments.

SOME REMAIN THE SAME

Whether you're working with acoustic or electronic tracks (or a combination of both), some principles of mixing apply across the board. There are six essential rules that I adhere to in any mixing situation. No matter how great a mixmaster you think you are, if you ignore these basic principles, your end product will suffer. So, let's run them down quickly.

1. Be mentally prepared to tackle the mix. Get yourself in the right frame of mind. Make sure that you're properly rested. This also means taking breaks from the mix periodically; I've found that a breather every two to three hours is sufficient. Avoid interruptions: mixing requires just as much concentration from the engineer as laying down a solo does from the musician, so turn off the phone. Finally, make sure the mood is right. Get a comfortable chair, dim the lights, and fire up the lava lamp. (Okay, the lava lamp is optional.)

2. Know your client. What kind of music are you working on? If it's a band project, has the band previously released a record that you can listen to? What are the producer's goals? You can completely alter the sound of a record in the mix, so you need to know what direction to go before you start working.

3. Be familiar with the monitors. If you're not working in your own studio, or if the producer brings unfamiliar speakers, give yourself a crash course in monitoring on the equipment. Pop in a CD that you are thoroughly familiar with; listen for exaggerated or muffled frequencies, paying particular attention to the low- and high-end content. Make mental (or even written) notes. Once you feel that you know the speakers' response, start working on the mix immediately.

4. Monitor at low levels. There are three reasons for keeping the monitors low while you mix. First of all, you'll avoid a case of listening fatigue (not to mention other health-related problems associated with loud music). Second, just about any mix sounds good when it's cranked up; the stellar mixes are the ones that sound good both loud and soft. Third, with the speakers at loud volumes, you won't catch level problems. I was mixing a radio promo recently and thought I had a great mix going, but I was completely crushed when I lowered the monitors to a normal level—I couldn't even hear the announcer's voice.

5. Reference your mix to similar commercial mixes. Listen to mixes that are similar in style to what you're working on. Again, if the band has other material you can use, great. If your console has a 2-track input for a CD player, use it. This way you can A/B between your own mix and the one you're striving to emulate. This step obviously isn't appropriate for those projects you have no intention of patterning after someone else's work, but it's often useful when producing commercial music, especially when you have to please a record label executive.

6. Reference the mix on a variety of systems. This is the most important point to remember: a well-balanced mix will sound good on poor monitors and great on good monitors. Check what you're mixing through several systems of varying size and quality. Before I complete a mix, I've listened to it on my studio monitors, a pair of headphones, a boom box, and my car stereo. If I really want to go crazy, I'll burn a CD and check it out on whatever system I can find. (I've actually done referencing in the electronics department at Sears.)

If you keep these six points in mind while you work, your mixes will improve 100 percent—I guarantee it. (For more information on basic mix principles, particularly with acoustic instruments, refer to "In Your Face Mixing," *Electronic Musician*, May 1998.)

ROUGH AND READY

If you're mixing on a computer, you have the advantage of building your mix during the recording process so that when it finally comes time to print to 2-track, only minor adjustments will be needed. I once produced a project when we didn't even have a dedicated mix day; instead, I took an hour to automate the vocal track and then printed the song to DAT.

Even if you're not working with a computer-based system, start getting some ideas together as you record. One of the best bits of advice I can impart is to periodically record rough mixes during tracking. All too often, after listening to the same song for weeks or months, you lose the fresh perspective that you had at the beginning of a project. Rough mixes are the perfect way to recall that lost perspective. Check in with them often to find out what your ideas were weeks ago.

WHAT GOES WHERE?

When working entirely with sequenced MIDI parts, you have the option of mixing tracks virtually without ever recording them to a multitrack. The benefits of mixing directly from the sound modules are obvious. For one thing, your signal path is shorter, so your chances of collecting sonic garbage drop substantially. In addition, sticking with MIDI tracks leaves more audio tracks available. But most important, it means you're not committed to anything—you can edit and automate synth sounds and sequences in ways that would be difficult to do with audio tracks, and you can do it at the last minute if necessary. (If you're performing virtual mixing with a digital audio workstation, make sure your system has the ability to mix live inputs and that you have enough I/O available.)

However, many professional engineers like to print MIDI sequences to multitrack audio media (especially analog 2-inch tape). Sometimes it's unrealistic for the personal studio owner to go this route, but it has several advantages. In a small studio with limited resources, for example, recording to audio multitrack allows you to apply outboard effects to individual tracks and submixes, freeing up your limited supply of effects processors for reuse at mixdown. In addition, submixing to tape or disk can simplify your final mixdown process. If you print to analog tape, of course, the tape recorder operates as a signal processor in the sense that it can add a desirable sonic quality.

Whether you mix virtually or print your sequencer parts to tape, it's generally better to clean up the signals at the sound modules rather than at the mixer. Selective filtering and compression can be used to remove unwanted frequencies or dynamics before a sound leaves the module. However, I usually try to save elaborate effects processing for the mixing environment, where I can employ dedicated units (unless I'm mixing on a digital audio workstation (DAW), where DSP is a precious commodity—in which case I might do some processing at the modules and some at the mixer). It's a balancing act, but it's better to have too many options than too few.

If your mixer doesn't offer dynamic automation, you can use MIDI Control Change 7 (Volume) and 10 (Pan) messages to automate your sequenced tracks. The drawback to this is that a mixer channel will remain open even when no signal is present, which is not the case when you manually ride the faders. With an analog mixer, you'll get some hiss; to fix this, you can use noise gates or expanders at the channel inserts.

In general, it's good practice to maintain as many dedicated instrument channels as possible. Granted, sometimes you may have no choice but to submix several parts to a stereo output, for instance. Just avoid unnecessary submixing; the more signals you have to work with at mixdown, the better.

There are three basic kinds of electronic sounds: emulations or samples of acoustic or electric instruments; completely artificial sounds; and emulations or samples of real-world, nonmusical sounds (a dog barking, for example). The mix engineer needs to approach each type differently.

When working with acoustic and electric instrument sounds, the goal is usually to replicate an accurate image of each instrument, positioning it in a realistic place on a virtual soundstage and making sure its frequency content is similar to what it would be in the real world. You'll then give the recorded instrument a volume and depth on that stage by using level control, reverb, and sometimes other processing, such as delay. (This is not a hard-and-fast rule, obviously; there are no rules in the creative arts.)

The same philosophy usually holds true if the "acoustic" or "electric" instrument happens to be a sample or synth patch. For example, even though the Roland JV-1080's grand piano patches are electronic samples, I'd probably still EQ them like real pianos and put them in realistic positions in the stereo image, unless I was trying to achieve a weird result. However, the methods you use ultimately depend on the style of music you're producing: for alternative and urban styles, perhaps the piano would need to be equalized like a guitar and spread across the entire stage.

When working with completely synthetic sounds, a different set of rules applies. Trying to place these instruments in a realistic spot on a "stage"—an acoustic environment where they wouldn't normally be heard—is pointless. In addition, there are no real-world templates of synthetic sounds on which to base EQ settings; I mean, what is a Telefunken or a Space Warp Pad supposed to sound like, anyway? The same is true of nonmusical samples (unless, of course, one of your band members is really a barking dog). The only exception here is when you are creating music for picture and want to position the effects to match the action.

Working with synthetic sounds essentially gives you carte blanche to create exciting mixes with sounds coming from all over the stereo image and frequency spectrum. And using creative dynamics control and multieffects processing, you can mold those sounds into practically anything you want.

Figure A.1: By conceptualizing the mix as a three-dimensional stage where the vertical axis represents frequency response, you can graph the soundstage from the front or above and see the frequency/pan position or volume/pan position, respectively. Make sure no two components are in the exact same place in either axis.

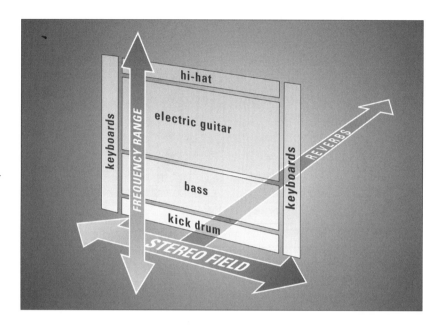

SPATIAL PLACEMENT

You have much more creative liberty with a mix of electronic instruments than you do with a mix of acoustic ones. I like to create a natural-sounding blend of all the elements. Artists such as Beck, Nine Inch Nails, Jane's Addiction, and Alanis Morrisette often employ contrasting timbres that don't blend smoothly—but for a lot of music, a smooth blend is preferable.

In most cases, instruments and sounds should not compete with one another either spatially or spectrally. You should be able to hear every part of a mix and immediately identify which instrument is which. To do this, I try to conceptualize the mix as a three-dimensional stage (see Figure A.1). Panning instruments moves them across the width of the stage; altering their level and adding reverb or other delay effects determines how far back they are. The vertical axis represents frequency response (for example, cymbals would be toward the top of the stage, with the kick drum sitting near the bottom). This way you can graph the stage from either the front or above and see the two most important relationships of a mix: frequency/pan position and volume/pan position.

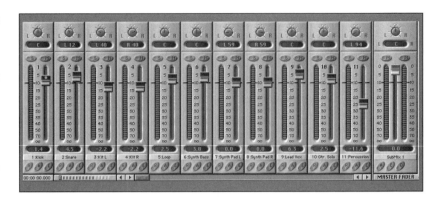

Figure A.2: In this example, the kick drum and one drum loop are right in the center of the mix, as in a live band. Because the synth bass has a heavy low-frequency content, I have panned it in the center, which also helps lock it in with the kick. The lead vocal and guitar solo are in the center and set hot. They don't occur at the same time, and they have different spectral content than the kick drum, drum loop, and bass, so each instrument will be distinct.

The goal is to make sure that no two components are centered at the exact same place in either graph. I don't mean that things can't overlap—the lower keys of a piano will inevitably be situated in the same area of the frequency spectrum as the bass—but elements shouldn't blatantly sit on top of each other. This is what causes a mix to become cluttered and muddy sounding. A clear mix is achieved through careful planning and adjustment of level, pan, and EQ.

PANNING AND PLACEMENT

Many people don't realize just how much EQ and level can affect the placement of an instrument in the stereo field. To check this out yourself, try the following experiment. Put the faders of your bass and kick drum tracks up with both channels panned to center. Boost them both by 15dB at 200Hz and turn up your monitors. You'll notice that it becomes difficult to distinguish the hit of the kick drum. Now pan the bass to nine o'clock and the kick drum to three o'clock. When you do, the kick drum hit returns. Finally, pan them both back to center and pull down the level of the bass track; you can again hear the kick drum better when the bass is lower.

This experiment illustrates how instruments can occupy the same frequency ranges, provided they aren't at the same spatial position in a mix (and vice versa). I'll discuss specific EQ applications below, but this is important to keep in mind when panning tracks.

In general, instruments that comprise the rhythm section are kept toward the center of the mix (see Figure A.2). Specifically, drum parts, bass parts, certain pianos, and loops should be spread no further than ten and two o'clock. In fact, try putting monotonous loops in mono; this opens up the horizontal axis for the supporting characters (guitars, piano, strings, and so on). Whatever you do, don't pan your drum tracks across the entire stereo image: have you ever seen an acoustic drum kit with toms that run from stage left to stage right? Keep the kit in the middle.

As a rule of thumb, any part that has a heavy low-frequency content should be situated toward the center of the mix. Simply panning the two signals is a prescription for trouble. True, Beatles engineer Geoff Emerick split the drums and bass to opposite channels on certain Beatles tunes. However, his drum and bass panning was almost certainly done out of necessity for bouncing tracks to overcome track limitations.

Slightly outside the rhythm section lie the supporting instruments: pianos, strings, guitars, and horns. This is also where you might want to place certain background vocals and percussion.

Lead vocals are generally put right up the middle; anywhere else just makes them distracting to listen to. Although instrument solos are usually panned dead-center, I prefer to spread them slightly to either side. Often, a solo will be played along with the lead vocal, and if both are in the center they will be competing with each other. (Many solo instruments have a frequency range similar to that of the human voice.)

Finally, the outside edges of the mix are usually reserved for effects returns (particularly reverb), certain types of percussion, and high-frequency background vocals (à la the Bee Gees). Be careful when placing sounds completely in one channel or the other, especially if you're also processing them with multieffects; in these instances, delays and reverbs that are panned opposite the source sound can cause phase cancellation.

Auto-panning synth patches should be addressed with caution. At what spectral position do these sounds start their journey, and where do they end up? This path must be clear of other sounds in the same frequency range; otherwise, dropouts will occur. Once you have a clear idea of where you want to place everything, it's time to make sure that instruments sitting in similar places aren't competing for room in the frequency spectrum.

Proper EQ means more than just getting a great sound from a track; it's about eliminating congestion in the mix. I want to stress the importance of subtractive EQ. In general, your mix will benefit more from cutting than from boosting. To tweak a sound with a parametric EQ, I usually start by doing the opposite of what I was taught in school: I turn the EQ gain down all the way and sweep the frequency knob, so I don't even think about boosting anything unless I really have to. However, if you cut enough frequencies, you'll probably need to make up gain at some point. Fortunately, many digital mixing consoles and DAWs provide a "gain makeup" capability as part of the EQ section.

With electronic replications of acoustic instruments, your best bet is probably to retain the authenticity of that instrument's natural sound. This does not mean that the samples don't need equalizing: although they are supposed to be accurate, pristine recordings of acoustic instruments, many are flawed. Basically, you want to eliminate frequencies that aren't needed. What is the instrument's primary range? In other words, which frequencies are needed to get it to cut through a mix, when that is desired, or to keep it back in the mix when it is supposed to be part of a pad? Once you determine the range, you can whittle it down to the necessary frequencies.

Two of the most important sounds in a mix are the kick drum and the bass part, and there should be a synergy to their relationship. These two tracks constitute most of the low-frequency energy in a mix. You need to decide which of these tracks will be the primary source of low end. For a traditional mix, I usually opt for bass, simply because there is more motion to it, and spot-lighting it makes the low end more interesting.

On a bass part, I find that rolling off frequencies below 50Hz is a good start. Boosting frequencies in the 300Hz to 1.5kHz range (admittedly a large range) will increase the track's clarity, and pulling them out will round out the low end. Once I have the bass sound, I work the kick drum in as support, accenting mid frequencies (1kHz) and boosting a little around 80Hz (3 to 6dB, with a narrow bandwidth).

On the other hand, if you're producing urban music, the kick drum sample or synth patch should be the more pronounced low-frequency element. Because many hip-hop beats are derived from premixed loops, you'll want to boost the track by about 3dB at 120Hz. Loops also have little high-end clarity, so you may have to roll off upper frequencies with a shelving filter (usually above 7kHz). A midrange boost might also be in order. Most other electronic percussion instruments are fine with little or no EQ; if EQ is needed, it's usually a boost at 7kHz or higher.

Certain synth pads—especially organ sounds—tend to be heavy on the low-end content. You'll probably find that, although they sound really fat by themselves, they just don't sit well with the rhythm instruments. Try rolling off frequencies below 300Hz or boosting the track in the 2 to 3kHz band and lowering the fader level.

Digital pianos can often present the same problem in a mix, especially when the lower half of the keyboard is being used. As long as the piano isn't the only instrument playing, my advice is to roll off the low end. I recently used snapshots to automate the EQ of a piano track in a rock song. The piano started the song out and needed to sound full, but when the rest of the band came in, it totally clashed with the bass. So I simply set up two snapshots—the second one with a high-pass filter engaged—and performed the change on the fly.

Electronic strings should accent the high-mid and upper frequency ranges, so a little boost might be needed somewhere above 5kHz. Try rolling the low frequencies off below 500Hz.

One very useful application of EQ is reducing hiss from sound modules. Although expanders and gates are an option, you'll find that rolling off frequencies above 10kHz is sometimes a better approach. Keep in mind that this will work only on synth outputs handling signals that have no frequency content above 10kHz (such as drum tracks, bass parts, and guitar parts).

Remember, every change you make to one track—no matter how small—will affect the other tracks as well. A tweak to the piano will change its relationship to the bass, which may alter the way the bass sounds. So if you make major changes on soloed tracks, be sure to check the sound in the mix immediately.

When used on acoustic instruments, compressors work to smooth the dynamics of a performance. Contrary to what many people think, electronic instruments have a good deal of dynamic range. You probably won't have to squeeze anything to death as you would with an electric bass guitar track, but slight compression of certain sounds can tighten up your mix. Synthesized strings generally sound good compressed at a light ratio (2:1 at -6dB). If you have a live piano track, you may also want to process it with a little compression (-6dB threshold, 3:1 to 4:1 ratio), especially if the musician performed with a lot of dynamic feeling.

Compression is often used in an electronic instrument mix to blend several synth outputs together by performing a submix of the desired tracks, busing them to a stereo pair, and patching a compressor across the two channels. Many people use this method to combine sampled sounds, particularly if the samples were derived from a variety of musical styles. I often do it with drum sequences if the samples didn't all come from the same kit. This achieves two things: first, it ensures that the kit will sound cohesive; and if I want, it lets me generate an intentionally overcompressed pumping sound across the drums (a typical hip-hop sound).

Gates are commonly used on synth outputs to quiet or eliminate noise if no mixdown automation is available. Getting rid of extraneous noise is a priority; I have heard some really nasty sounds come out of certain inexpensive sound modules. You don't need to gate the outputs if the modules are active throughout the entire song, only if there are extended periods of inactivity.

Although you could use an expander for this purpose, a gate doesn't affect the dynamics of the performance the way an expander does. Make sure that the gate's attack and release times are set properly; otherwise you may cut off part of the performance.

Finally, for those folks producing urban music, it's not a bad idea to patch a limiter across the stereo bus—just enough to catch peaks from the kick drum. After all, you don't want people getting mad at you because your mix blew their woofers out. (For a more detailed look at using dynamics processors, see "Conquering Peaks," *Electronic Musician,* December 1998.)

A TOUCH OF 'VERB?

In general, electronic sounds designed to emulate acoustic instruments should receive the same multieffects treatment as their acoustic counterparts. A piano should be processed like a piano, regardless of from where the sound originates. (A little room reverb is a nice touch on a piano, incidentally.)

Now, you can really have some fun with original sounds. Nobody is going to criticize you for processing a Kosmic Kazoo with too much chorus! But watch the spatial placement of the effects. Just because you have the returns panned hard left and right doesn't mean that the effect itself is located on the outer edges of the mix; it might be located somewhere in between, which could cause a conflict with one or more of the other mix elements.

FROM THE GROUND UP

When approaching a mix, I suggest you start by determining where you want to place everything on the stereo field and then pan the tracks accordingly. Push all the faders up and get a rough mix going. Next, use EQ to tweak the sounds in context with the rest of the tracks so that nothing is clashing. If you hear something funny with any of the tracks, solo that track, isolate the problem, and fix it. When you're done, pull all the faders back down.

Next, determine which track (or tracks) to mix the song around. Most people agree that you should build a mix around the most important element—whatever will sell the song. Doing this ensures that you won't be caught with a great mix that has absolutely no room for the prized track. So generally, pop music (especially ballads) should be mixed around the vocal; jazz around the soloist; and rock, urban, and alternative around the rhythm instruments (drums, loops, and bass).

Bring the volume fader of your focal-point track up to about 80 percent. (If you decided to mix around the rhythm section, start with the kick drum and bass guitar.) Apply whichever multi-effects processing you want, but don't obsess over the levels of the effects returns; they'll need to be readjusted anyway once you start adding more tracks to the mix. Then start bringing in the rest of the components, adding effects where needed.

If you're building around the rhythm instruments, follow the kick drum and bass with the snare and other drum tracks. Then bring in supporting instruments (piano, guitars, strings, and so on), followed by percussion, lead instruments, and solo instruments. Finish up by adding background vocals, samples, and sound effects.

When building around a solo instrument or vocal, I find it best to bring in some sort of accompaniment first, such as acoustic guitar or piano. Follow that with the rhythm instruments, as outlined above, and finish with the supporting cast. If all your levels are good, you should still feel the energy of the first track you put up even after you've added all the other instruments. Don't forget to check the mix in mono, especially if you think your recording could be broadcast; many radio and TV stations do not broadcast in stereo.

Next, address the tracks with dynamics processors where needed, make any necessary EQ changes, and adjust the levels of the effects returns. Finally, automate your tracks and print to tape. It looks easy on paper, doesn't it?

A LITTLE MASTERING

Once you're reasonably happy with what you hear, you'll want to establish the mix's overall frequency parameters. How much high end do you want? How much low end? True, the mastering engineer usually takes care of these things, but most professional mix engineers will use a parametric or graphic EQ across the stereo bus before printing the mix to 2-track. This allows them to set high and low boundaries for the mix—a particularly smart move when working with electronic instruments, where the frequency responses of the tracks can run the gamut. (It will also help you EQ and set the levels of the extremely high- and low-frequency instruments.)

Again, find a CD with similar content and audio quality to the project you're working on. Listen to the overall volume of the upper and lower frequencies. Then compare that CD with the mix you have going and make minor adjustments to the stereo EQ where needed. A graphic EQ—I prefer the dbx 2231—is an excellent tool for this application.

A lot of hip-hop, dance, and R&B music has extremely heavy low-end content. This contributes to these genres' distinctive sounds, but loud low end doesn't equal good low end. In other words, don't boost 9dB at 120Hz during mastering to get the kick drum to stand out more; go back and fix it in the mix. A good mix should require very little tweaking at the stereo bus.

Finally, a little compression (-3dB, 1.5:1 ratio) across the stereo bus can compensate for subtle level changes that you may not have caught in the mix. Alternatively, as I mentioned earlier, limiting may be in order. (Be sure to set your threshold just below the peaks you want to eliminate.)

BOOGIE DOWN

The most important thing you can do for any mix is put it to rest once you're done. Let it sit for a few days, allow your head to clear, and then listen to it with fresh ears. At that point, you'll probably want to make a few thousand adjustments, but that's fine. What's essential is that you take a break from the project.

When all is said and done, a mix of electronic instruments employs many of the same techniques as a mix of acoustic instruments. In fact, an electronic mix actually allows you to be more creative. If you keep in mind the basic principles I've outlined here, you should be able to construct a solid, three-dimensional mix that jumps right out of the speakers.

Mastering on a Budget

by Philip De Lancie

You spent every spare moment for the last two months polishing your mixes to perfection. You finally put all your songs on one tape, and you're ready for the moment of truth: your first listen to the material all the way through.

You press Play and the first song sounds pretty good. But at the very end of the fadeout, the sound seems to drop off abruptly, and you think, "I never noticed that before." Just then, the second song comes slamming in, quite a bit louder than the first. You turn down your monitors, but by now you've also noticed that this song, which was mixed a few months ago, sounds a bit duller than the first, which you mixed just the other day.

And so it goes, with each successive song seemingly crying out for its own little adjustments. Is it time for despair, time to chuck these mixes and start from scratch? No! It's time for mastering, a critical step that every professional project goes through.

WHAT IS MASTERING?

Mastering serves as a link between production (recording and mixing) and product manufacturing (CD replication, cassette duplication, etc.). The goal of this process is to compile the individual mixes into a smoothly flowing album, so that the listener, having adjusted the volume and tone on the first few bars of the first song, can listen to the entire program without having to readjust those playback settings.

Mastering is a three-step process. In a professional facility, a DAT copy of the final mixes is presented to the mastering engineer, who first edits the tracks into the desired sequence and adjusts the spacing between the songs. Once this is done, the engineer processes the audio, coaxing the best possible sound out of each mix, unifying the sonic characteristics of the individual selections, and creating a consistent listening level.

Finally, the material is transferred onto a "production master," which is presented to the manufacturing facility in an appropriate format. (For CD replication, this master can be delivered on a Sony PCM-1630 tape, an Exabyte 8mm tape, or a CD-R; for cassette duplication, a DAT is the most common format; and for vinyl record pressing, a master lacquer is required.) The production master embodies the record exactly as it will be heard by the consumer.

While practically anyone can sequence their mixes and transfer the material to the proper format, the skills needed to perform the sonic unification of an album are very specialized. Even those artists who are fortunate enough to work with the industry's best mix engineers rely on professional mastering engineers to put the final blessing on their work.

However, not everyone is in a position to take advantage of professional mastering. If you're a personal studio owner working on a limited budget, spending a few thousand dollars to "touch up" your project is probably not the most practical plan. But there is an alternative—mastering in-house.

Inspired by the wealth of software editing programs and DSP plug-ins on the market, many small studio owners have begun mastering their own material. While in-house mastering certainly won't generate the same results as what you'd expect from a professional facility, it is a decent, cost-effective solution. If you are adding the role of mastering engineer to a list that already includes artist, producer, recordist, and mixing engineer, knowing as much as possible about how and why professional engineers do what they do will help you make more informed mastering decisions and consequently turn out a better-sounding product.

WHAT YOU'LL NEED

Before you can think about mastering a record, you'll need to make sure that you have all the essentials. While you may already own the required gear, some of the other necessities may be a bit more difficult to acquire.

Figure B.1: The Multiband Dynamics Tool (MDT) from AnTares Systems offers real-time dynamics processing and features an intuitive graphic interface.

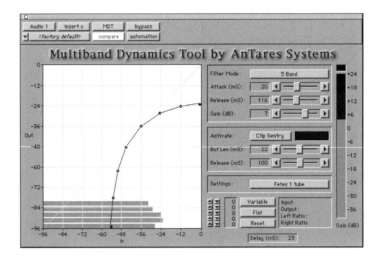

The tools. The tools commonly used in mastering are: a console or DAW (to make level adjustments), an editing medium (e.g., editing software, DAT machine, or analog 2-track), a 2-channel parametric EQ, and a 2-channel dynamics processor (usually a compressor).

Major mastering houses typically employ expensive digital mixing consoles (with onboard digital EQ and compressors) to process audio and rely on computers mainly for editing. However, for the personal studio owner, working in a self-contained desktop environment is a much more practical approach; every necessary tool resides within the computer, eliminating the need to transfer audio from one device to another. This doesn't mean that you can't master a project with a Mackie console, dbx 160A, and a Rane EQ. Of course, analog processors have the inherent tendency to introduce some amount of noise into the signal path, and since mastering is all about audio quality, this is something you should be aware of. If you own a digital console and feel comfortable with its onboard processors, you might explore that route, too.

Should you wind up mastering with analog processors, it's extremely important that all the equipment be free of hum and buzz (i.e., properly grounded), low in hiss (i.e., high signal-to-noise ratio), and operated at levels that won't introduce distortion into the signal. If you're using an analog mixing console to route signals and correct levels, make sure you maintain proper gain staging at the mixer's inputs and outputs.

Figure B.2: Offering up to ten bands of stereo parametric EQ, the Waves Q10 plug-in provides five filter types (bell, low shelf, high shelf, low-pass, and high-pass), in addition to 200 preset curves.

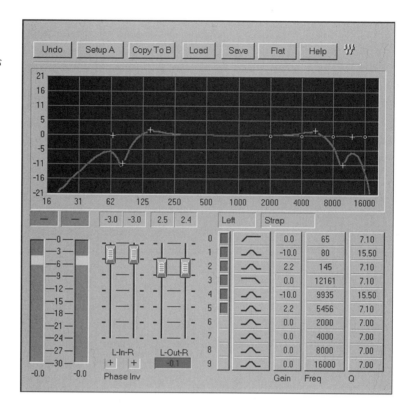

For those mastering on the desktop, there is a variety of high-quality DSP plug-ins available, and you probably already know what's out there for your particular DAW. One of my favorites for general compression applications is AnTares MDT (see Figure B.1), available for SDII and TDM, because I find its user interface to be very intuitive. For EQ, full parametric control is essential for mastering. I happen to like Waves' Q10 (see Figure B.2), available for a number of different PC and Mac formats.

When adjusting the various plug-in parameters during mastering, you'll have to be monitoring in real time, so you might need to increase your DAW's RAM allocation to get a decent preview length. (A 4-second loop doesn't cut it for setting EQ.) Depending on your setup, you may also want to look into utilities that let you use plug-ins in a live play-through mode, such as Waves' MultiRack, or HyperEngine from Arboretum.

If you plan on delivering your production master on a CD-R, you'll also need to have dedicated CD recording software capable of producing a Red Book standard disc (see Figure B.3). (For an in-depth look at CD-R programs for both Mac and PC, check out "The CD-R Software Cook-Off," *Electronic Musician* March 1998)

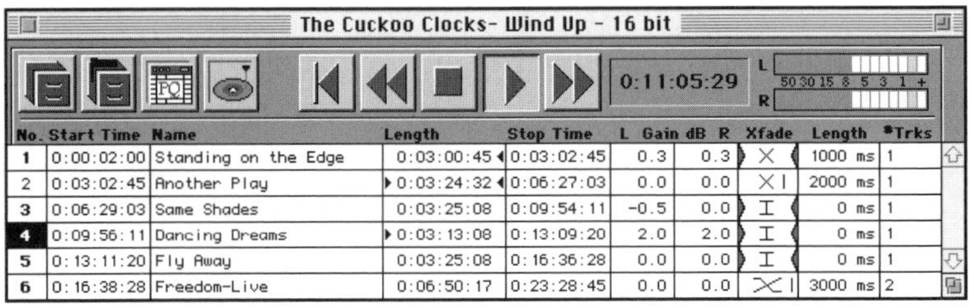

Figure B.3: One of the more popular CD-R programs, Digidesign's MasterList CD is capable of creating Red Book standard CDs or one-off reference discs. A comprehensive level adjustment feature displays the peak audio level within a selection and allows you to make amplitude adjustments in 0.1dB increments.

The Cuckoo Clocks- Wind Up - 16 bit

0:11:05:29

No.	Start Time	Name	Length	Stop Time	L Gain dB R	Xfade	Length	#Trks
1	0:00:02:00	Standing on the Edge	0:03:00:45	0:03:02:45	0.3 0.3	X	1000 ms	1
2	0:03:02:45	Another Play	0:03:24:32	0:06:27:03	0.0 0.0	X	2000 ms	1
3	0:06:29:03	Same Shades	0:03:25:08	0:09:54:11	-0.5 0.0	I	0 ms	1
4	0:09:56:11	Dancing Dreams	0:03:13:08	0:13:09:20	2.0 2.0	I	0 ms	1
5	0:13:11:20	Fly Away	0:03:25:08	0:16:36:28	0.0 0.0	I	0 ms	1
6	0:16:38:28	Freedom-Live	0:06:50:17	0:23:28:45	0.0 0.0	X	3000 ms	2

Decent monitoring. It goes without saying that you need to have a decent monitoring environment to master a project. You can't make informed judgments about how to improve a song's sonic quality if you are basing those judgments on a misleading representation of the material's actual sound.

A full exploration of studio monitoring is beyond the scope of this appendix. However, it should be noted that proper monitoring is not just a matter of buying a good pair of speakers. It also involves the correct placement of those speakers in relation to the listening position and the walls of the room, as well as the proper acoustic treatment of the room itself and, in some cases, the EQ of the monitor signal path.

A frame of reference. One of the invaluable traits that mastering engineers bring to the table is a frame of reference—in other words, they know how the sound of any given material compares to the sound of other material they've worked on. They also know how their studio environment sounds compared to the typical listening environments where their work is heard. (Unlike recordists and mixers, mastering engineers almost always do all their work in the same room.) These skills are developed only through experience.

However, you can give yourself a crash course on referencing. Pick a CD of material that you think is similar to the music you will be mastering in terms of style, instrumentation, and dynamics. Listen analytically and get familiar with the way it sounds in your studio. Are the lows full, or are they light? The midrange thick, or edgy? The highs dark, or airy?

Listen to the same CD in as many listening situations as you can (living room system, boom box, car, etc.), and keep mental notes about how the sound differs from what you heard in your studio. For instance, if you learn that the low end tends to sound boomier in the "real world" than it does in your studio, you can factor that in as you work, try not to overcompensate when you don't hear enough bass, and thereby avoid making your music too muddy. If you have a CD-R of your mixes (cassettes are not accurate enough for this purpose), you can go through the same comparative listening process with your own material to get a feel for how it will sound in the world outside your studio walls.

A good mix. Let us pay homage to the wisdom of a couple of timeworn proverbs: "garbage in, garbage out," and "an ounce of prevention is worth a pound of cure." The point of these aphorisms for mastering is that the foundation of a good mastering job must be laid in the mix, and the foundation of a good mix must be laid in recording. Because most problems are much easier to deal with before individual tracks are combined in a mix, the most important thing you can do to make your mastering job a success is to steer clear of trouble earlier in the production chain. The "fix it later" attitude is a prescription for regret—not only postponing problems but compounding them.

Some common problems carried over from the recording process include loud hums or buzzes on guitar tracks and harshness or distortion on vocals. If it's not practical to re-record these tracks, or the performance is too priceless, tools such as tunable de-essers can be used on an individual track to selectively downplay the frequency range most affected by the problem. At that point, you'll have to remix the song—it's much harder (sometimes impossible) to use such tools effectively when you are dealing with a complete mix, because every instrument with content in that frequency range will be affected by your fix.

Remember that mastering does not afford you control over the sound of individual instruments; instead, you are working primarily with frequency ranges. So, any EQ applied to address one instrument's issues at a given frequency will affect all instruments in that range. Let's say, for instance, that you end up with a mix in which the snare sounds somewhat dull or masked, but the vocals sound harsh and edgy. If it weren't for the vocals, adding snap to the snare would be, well, a snap! But you've mixed yourself into a situation where fixing the snare would make the vocals sound worse. While you are mixing, to avoid tying your hands in mastering, think about whether the characteristics of instruments in similar frequency ranges are consistent or pulling in opposite directions.

Also, keep an eye on the overall level while you're mixing. The sound enhancements used in mastering are much more likely to add to the level rather than subtract from it. Don't try to mix so that your peaks are at digital zero; a target for peaks of -2 or -3 will keep your mix plenty hot, while allowing some headroom for mastering.

PUTTING IT ALL TOGETHER

Before getting down to processing the audio, you'll need to edit and assemble your track sequence (see Figure B.4). It is possible, of course, to do this after you've processed the tracks. But because a big part of mastering concerns the flow of material from the end of one song to the beginning of the next, it's a much better idea to assemble a master of finished mixes first, then do a rundown (decide what you are going to do to each song), process it, and transfer everything to a production master. Hearing the transitions from song to song will help you make better mastering decisions.

The specifics of putting together your master will vary, depending on whether you have mixed to a hard drive, DAT, or analog 2-track. Obviously, there are several advantages to working in a random-access environment when editing, but a compilation sequence can be assembled with linear tape decks as well.

Figure B.4: Featuring drag-and-drop playlist assembly, Adaptec's Jam supports all major file types, including SDII, AIFF, and WAV. The product comes bundled with the BIAS Peak LE audio editor.

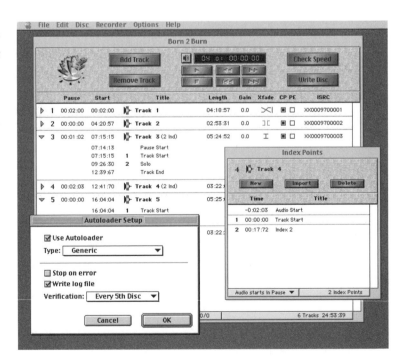

Making Music with Your Computer

Regardless, there are a few basic standards to uphold in creating a professional master. The space between songs may vary from zero to about four seconds; the mood and tempo of the material will determine the most effective pacing. However long they are, the spaces should be silent, with no extraneous noises (ticks, buzz, hiss, etc.). Hiss immediately before a song starts is distracting and should be removed by editing or noise gating. This is also a good time to assess whether your fades are gradual and smooth or too abrupt. (Unfortunately, the fix for a too-short fade usually is remixing the song.)

If you are making a master by assembly editing to a DAT machine, keep in mind that every time you put the machine in Pause or Stop mode, you create a break in the control track. On playback, these breaks will be interpreted by the machine as uncorrectable errors, possibly causing either a mute or a noise where there should be silence. Since different machines handle errors differently, you can't really predict how long it will take the deck to recover from the mute. So if your edit point is too close to the start of the incoming tune, the beginning of the music may be cut off.

Even if the tape plays fine on the machine it was recorded on, it is still a good idea to avoid problems down the road by taking the time to digitally transfer the assembled DAT in one continuous pass to another DAT machine or to a hard drive, listening carefully for errors the whole time. Assuming the program plays without problems during this transfer, you now have a more reliable assembled master, with no control track interruptions.

SPICING IT UP

With a clean, professionally assembled master in hand, it's time to enhance and unify the sound. Don't start this process at the end of a long mixing or editing session; you need to be able to approach the project with fresh ears and an objective attitude, just like a professional mastering engineer would.

Compression. Compression changes the relationship between a program's peak and average levels, boosting apparent loudness by bringing up lower-level signals without increasing peaks. Too much compression, of course, can destroy dynamics, squashing the sound and leaving it flat and lifeless. But if used properly, compression can make a song more lively, present, and full, bringing out subtleties in the backing tracks and filling out the foundation on which the lead tracks rest.

Compression settings for such applications vary quite a bit, depending on the type of music and the desired effect. In mastering, the compression employed is generally quite a bit subtler than what you would apply to individual tracks during mixdown. Typical parameter settings are a ratio between 1.1:1 and 1.25:1 at a threshold of around -20dB (below digital zero), with an attack of 1ms and a release between 10ms and 100ms.

EQ. Like compression, EQ settings vary a lot depending on the needs of the material—there is no typical setting. There are, however, frequency ranges within which different types of equalization needs are addressed (though they are very subjective, based on the ear and experience of the individual mastering engineer). These ranges can give you a starting point, but finding a setting that achieves what you're after comes from slowly sweeping frequencies in that range, with the bandwidth control narrow and the amplitude high. When you find the frequency you want to bring out or cut back, adjust the amplitude accordingly and broaden the bandwidth.

There's generally not that much done with the frequencies below 50Hz, except perhaps to roll them off with a low-cut filter if they are excessive. The area from about 60 to 120Hz gets a lot more attention. If your music sounds thin, this is the range to boost to bring out the richness and fullness of instruments like the kick drum and the bass guitar. Likewise, if the bass instruments sound boomy, you may be able to clear things up by cutting frequencies somewhere in this range. In particular, if the bass guitar sounds muddled and ill-defined, you can often bring it out by cutting frequencies in this range (to eliminate its boominess), while boosting frequencies in the next range up, somewhere between 120 and 200Hz. This can add definition to the bass line and keep it audible, even on small speakers that don't reproduce low bass.

In the low mids, cuts in the 200 to 400Hz range may be useful for clearing out thickness or muck that gives the overall sound a masked quality. Boosts in this area, meanwhile, can bring out the lower foundation of a guitar or piano, provided it's a solo instrument (i.e., there are no bass instruments in the mix). Slightly higher, from 400 to 700Hz, is an area you can boost to bring out the richness, or "meat," of midtone instruments— particularly vocals—that sound too thin or tinny.

The frequencies from about 700Hz to 2kHz are commonly boosted to add definition and presence to all kinds of midrange instruments. A lead vocal that is already a bit edgy, but still needs to be brought out somewhat, can often be helped in the 900 to 1200Hz area. Between 1.4 and 2kHz is the range that can add or subtract the crunchiness of a rock guitar. In jazz, the same range can subtly bring out comping instruments, such as piano or guitar, unless harshness in horns or vocals is a problem. If that is the case, you'd be safer bringing the piano out a little lower down (around 700 to 800Hz).

Higher in the midrange, from 2 to 5kHz, is where you can find the snap in percussive sounds, like a snare drum. As mentioned above, it's also where you will find the harshness that comes from distorted or poorly EQed vocal or sax tracks (you'll feel the pain, particularly between 3 and 4.5kHz). If you have to compromise the snap at 3.5 or 4kHz to minimize unpleasant edginess, you may still be able to avoid an overall impression of dullness by compensating with a little boost around 1.5kHz or in the "sizzle" range (hi-hat territory) of 5 to 9kHz. Above 9kHz, you're into the high frequencies, where a gentle nudge can often add brilliance or "air" to tired-sounding cymbals.

All these tips are both subjective and situational—what works one day on a given instrument with a given type of music won't necessarily work the next time. And with all these uses for EQ, it's easy to forget your better judgment and go overboard, so it's always a good idea to continually A/B your EQ settings against the flat material.

Also, remember that adding EQ increases the overall volume of the song, which could potentially drive you into an overload situation. Depending on your headroom, you may need to pull back the level to make room for your EQ. In some cases, your EQed version may sound better to you simply because you have added level. To avoid this, check your meters when you A/B, and pull back the fader to compensate when listening to the processed signal.

Levels. It's extremely important that you listen to the last part of each track going into the beginning of the next to ensure that the levels match. If you find yourself reaching for your volume knob when the incoming tune starts, your listeners probably will too. Your job is to make those adjustments for them, on the master.

If you were careful to record your mixes at comparable levels, the compression used in mastering should compensate for any level discrepancies, and you may not need to make any further adjustments. Otherwise, you'll have to add or subtract a little gain here and there. Software editors usually provide an amplitude adjustment feature, and several CD-R programs offer track-by-track level adjustment for quickly creating a consistent listening level.

TAKE A LISTEN!

If, when all is said and done, you are reasonably happy with the sound (perfectly happy would be too much to ask!), you are ready to transfer your material to the production master that will be sent to the plant. Hopefully, by this time, you will have checked with the manufacturing facility regarding specific requirements they may have for the layout of the master, as well as any information—such as a timing log—that should accompany it. However, before you send anything off, try to listen to the production master in several different environments to be sure the sound still comes across as you intended.

If you are not happy with the results, you may need to ask yourself whether the sources of your dissatisfaction could be addressed by remixing any of the tunes. That may not be an appealing prospect, but at least you have the option of trying to make things better, which wouldn't be the case if you had paid for a professional mastering session. It may wind up being one of the few times in life when you'll get to say "let's fix it in the mix"—and it actually turns out to be a sensible strategy!

A P P E N D I X   C

The Sound Design Studio

by Dennis Miller

So you want to be a sound designer and create sounds for games or theatrical productions, or maybe even produce a sample CD-ROM for sale? Sound design is a burgeoning business, and it doesn't take much to get into the game. I'll describe some of the tools you'll need to build a basic sound-design studio, and I'll provide some details on a more advanced setup. We'll look at the Macintosh and Windows platforms.

Sound design means many things to many people, but in nearly all cases (except perhaps creating instruments for use in music production), your job is to construct unique and interesting sounds to enhance some other type of medium. Often, you'll have to generate a sound from scratch, in which case a good knowledge of synthesis and some efficient synthesis tools will help you reach your goal. On the other hand, sometimes you can start with a preexisting sound and modify it until it suits your requirements. For this approach, you'll want a good recording device, some sound effects CDs, and a large number of sound processing tools. Fortunately, you have plenty of options.

Let's say, for example, that you were called upon to create sound effects for an alien-invasion game. Given that you can't sample all the sounds you'd need (unless, of course, you live in Roswell, New Mexico), you'd have to find creative ways to come up with sounds that would be convincing to the producer of the project. You need to consider which tools would be useful to have on hand and what approaches you could take to reach your goals.

Unlike some tasks that you're likely to perform in a home studio, sound design is not inherently a real-time endeavor. That means you don't need the fastest computer or hottest new controller to get your work done. Therefore, I won't discuss specific CPU speeds or minimum RAM requirements; I will simply assume that you have a functioning computer. Nor will I cover particular sequencers, mics, or studio monitors. For our purposes, you could use virtually any sequencer, or even no sequencer at all. Remember, you are creating sounds, not music. As for monitors and mics, there are many good options.

Instead, I'll deal with the tools you should add to your system in order to begin accepting sound-design jobs. For the basic, entry-level Mac and Windows studios, I'll fix the budget at approximately $2,000. That's all you'll need to build a well-equipped setup suitable for many types of projects.

Of course, if you're expecting to get calls from major clients, such as top television, movie, or game producers, you'll need a lot more than the basics. Therefore, I'll discuss numerous additional resources that you'll need for setting up an advanced Mac or Windows studio. Using these options, you will have enough gear to tackle even the most demanding assignments.

CAPTURING THE ELUSIVE SAMPLE

Regardless of your budget, having a good recording device is a must; it will allow you to bring home material that can serve as the basis for many of your sounds. For example, to recreate that perfect spaceship engine effect, you might want to spend some time at a construction site recording various engine and machine noises. You can probably survive with nothing more than a cassette recorder, a decent mic, and some sound-processing software to clean up and tweak your samples. In fact, before I got my first DAT machine, I did numerous jobs using a Marantz professional portable cassette recorder that is no longer in production (though newer models are still available).

Today, you are better off buying a MiniDisc recorder than a cassette deck, if you're just starting out. Most MiniDisc players have digital inputs—typically optical, for connecting to consumer model CD players or DATs—which give them added connectivity in your studio. (Of course, a digital output would be more suitable for the job at hand.) For just a few hundred dollars, you can get a top-of-the-line MiniDisc recorder such as the Sony MZ-R55 ($350). The MZ-R55 gives you more than two hours of record time, and at less than eight ounces, it's light enough to carry for long stretches. (Remember, Area 51 is a long way from the nearest highway.)

A good portable DAT deck will provide the best quality source material, but you should expect to pay double or many times the price of a MiniDisc recorder. The Tascam DA-P1 portable DAT recorder is my top choice for the advanced studio, though it's not inexpensive at $2,060. The DA-P1 has balanced and unbalanced analog I/O and S/PDIF ins and outs, and it's SCMS-free. It's also a rugged unit and a real workhorse. If the price tag is too high for you, then I suggest the Sony TCD-D8 ($899) as a second choice; I've used one for several years. But keep in mind that the Sony model requires an optional connector for many standard I/O functions, and that will add to the cost.

With your portable recorder in hand, your next purchase should be a good pair of microphones. I'd start with a pair of cardioid condensers and later expand the mic collection to include a broad variety of mics from different manufacturers and with an assortment of polar patterns (perhaps omni, M-S, PZM, and multipattern). There are advantages to using ribbon and dynamic mics, as well as condensers, and you might want both tube and solid-state mics. A shotgun mic can be handy for some kinds of field recording. You'll need to pick up a phantom power supply for some condenser mics, and if you plan to record acoustic sounds directly to a computer in the studio, you'll need a mic preamp.

SOUND EFFECTS LIBRARIES

If you can't capture the right sound out in the field, you might find good raw material among the hundreds of sample CDs on the market. Libraries range from collections of exotic, non-Western instruments, such as Spectrasonics' *Heart of Africa, Volume 1* ($129 for the two-CD audio set), to high-quality orchestral collections, such as the renowned *Miroslav Vitous Symphonic Orchestra* library ($3,899 for five CDs, which are also available separately). Another type of collection, generic sound effects, is particularly useful for the sound designer. In fact, in many cases, a good sound effects CD might be the only one you need to get the job done.

The advanced sound-design studios, both Mac and Windows, should include the Hollywood Edge *Premiere Edition* ($895 for the 20-disc set), which I've used for a number of projects. Hollywood Edge also produces one of my favorite special effects collections, the five-CD *Cartoon Trax* library ($395). It has more boinks and splats than you'll ever need, but the short, sharp attacks in many of these samples can be grafted onto longer, sustaining sounds to make some very unusual effects.

Our basic studios will be limited to just a few CDs at first, so I'll opt for the four-CD Hollywood Edge *Edge Edition* ($295), which has a wide range of high quality material. I'll also add a copy of Rarefaction's *Poke in the Ear III* ($149) to both the basic and advanced studios. This is the latest volume from folks who gave new meaning to the word twisted. These CDs will get you off to a good start, and once you land a few paychecks, you can look into adding more discs to your collection.

Another way to get good, quality sound effects is to download them from the Internet. Several companies offer this type of service; Sound Dogs (www.sounddogs.com), which has a huge library of material available, is a good place to start. Once you have a password, you can search by category or enter a keyword to limit your search. You can then preview the sounds in AU format before making your purchase. (Sound Dogs' site has no support for RealAudio at this point, but MP3 will be available soon.) Prices are based on the format you select, from just under $1 for 8-bit, 11kHz quality to several dollars for CD quality. If you choose the direct-download option, you'll immediately get an e-mail message with the URL where you'll find your purchased sounds. Alternatively, you can have Sound Dogs burn your selections onto a CD in any of the standard audio file formats and mail it to you.

AUDIO EDITORS

Even with good samples in hand, there's always a need to tweak and twist your sounds. One of the best places to begin the search for processing tools is on your desktop. You can find a good collection of tools in most audio editors (see "Shaping Better Waveforms," *Electronic Musician,* March 1999 for a roundup of stereo audio editors), and you might be surprised at the audio processing capabilities of your digital audio sequencer. There are also a number of dedicated processing applications, some of which run as plug-ins.

Most audio editors offer sound manipulation tools that go well beyond cut, copy, and paste. You might opt for a stereo editor initially and then add a multitrack program later for more flexibility.

Our entry level studios won't include a top professional editor, because you need to save your resources for other purchases. Therefore, my choice for the basic Mac studio is MicroMat's inexpensive SoundMaker ($30) 2-track editor. SoundMaker has a huge number of unusual sound-processing tools; the Robotize and Doppler effects are especially suitable for that alien game. The program also supports proprietary plug-ins, which adds considerably to its value.

Figure C.1: MicroMat's Sound-Maker offers an extraordinary variety of processing tools, a proprietary plug-in format, and numerous QuickTime features, including easy audio-offset adjustments and video scrubbing—all for an amazingly low price.

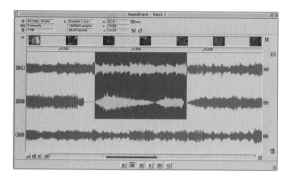

For the advanced Mac studio, I suggest the Peak 2-track audio editor ($499) from BIAS, recently upgraded to version 2.0 (although I'm basing this choice mostly on Peak 1.6 because we haven't finished testing the new version). The program's Convolution feature has great potential for the sound designer. (Convolution is a process that applies the sonic characteristics of one sound to another). Peak also includes a number of batch-processing features, and version 2 supports Premiere, AudioSuite, and TDM plug-ins.

For some kinds of sound design work, our advanced Mac studio will need a professional multitrack editor. Here I choose Digidesign's *Pro Tools* PowerMix ($795). PowerMix is identical to the software that comes with a full-blown Pro Tools 24/MIX system, except that it uses the Apple Sound Manager and the Mac's onboard I/O instead of Digidesign's high-end hardware. The software is deep, it has good file management tools, and it lets you create a variety of custom fades. PowerMix supports AudioSuite plug-ins, which means you can use some of the same plug-ins you use with Peak. *Pro Tools* is the de facto standard for pro multitrack recording; if you get gigs designing sounds for film or TV, for example, you will probably be expected to know this program. Finally, if you start with PowerMix, you can upgrade to a full-blown *Pro Tools* 24/MIX system later, if the gigs justify it.

On the Windows side, you'll get a lot of work done for a bargain basement price with Syntrillium's *Cool Edit* 96 2-track audio editor ($50), which has one of the most unusual effects you'll find anywhere. Syntrillium claims that by applying interaural time delays to a stereo sample, the Brainwave Synchronizer feature produces a state of serenity in listeners. I used the process in a Sound Health project, and the producer seemed happy with the results. The effect works only with headphones, but it might be just what your project needs. Of course, *Cool Edit* 96 has numerous other effects, and in nearly all cases, the user definable parameters are quite extensive.

For multitrack projects, you can't pass up the deal F.A. Soft offers on its *n-Track Studio* shareware, so I'm adding it to the basic Windows studio. For only $35, you'll get as many audio tracks as the computer hardware can handle, DirectX support, and integrated MIDI playback. The program's effects, though not extensive, sound very good, and the ability to view data in waveform mode and as a text-based tracklist is a handy option. You'll also have no trouble preparing files for the Internet, because a WAV-to-MP3 encoder is built into the editor.

Figure C.2 F.A. Soft's n-Track Studio offers Windows users multiple tracks of audio and MIDI file playback from a single screen. (MIDI data is shown in green.) The program supports DirectX plug-ins and can export audio in MP3 format.

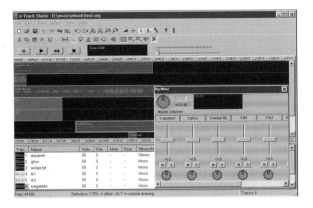

For a more advanced Windows-based studio, Sonic Foundry's *Sound Forge* 4.5 2-track editor ($499) has a massive feature set that offers traditional as well as outrageous options. You can perform unusual sound-altering feats with functions like the Gapper/Snipper and Pitch Bend, and you can use the Playlist

Making Music with Your Computer

feature to create pseudogranular effects if you splice and dice numerous short chunks of audio. In addition, you get batch-conversion features that can be very useful when doing some types of sound design.

Figure C.3: SEK'D's Samplitude Studio multitrack audio editor has many invaluable sound designing features. Its CD burning capability is an added bonus for musicians who need to deliver their work on a reliable medium.

On the other hand, for advanced work you'll probably opt for a multitrack audio editor, and you'll find great features in SEK'D's *Samplitude Studio* ($399). *Samplitude* has numerous functions that are optional in other programs, such as the ability to burn CDs directly from within the program. Its Live Input mode allows you to pass a stereo audio signal "through" the program without having to record the sound to disk. This turns Samplitude into a giant real-time effects processor. You also get a versatile filter designer, multiband compressor, and convolution effects, all of which offer great resources for fine-tuning your sounds. The ability to upgrade to SEK'D's *Samplitude* 2496 is another reason to make *Samplitude* your editor of choice in a high-end Windows studio.

DSP PLUG-IN EFFECTS

Now that you're set with your audio editing software, it's time to look into the numerous plug-ins that will enhance your resources. Alex Yermakov's SoundFront FX/SM ($15) is a choice plug-in for the basic Mac studio. It will operate under your basic Mac audio editor, SoundMaker, and its incredibly low price gives you lots of headroom for purchasing other handy tools.

I recommend one of my favorite plug-in effects programs for the advanced Mac studio: BIAS's SFX Machine ($299). This Premiere-format plug-in is a tweaker's delight and includes more than 300 preset effects, as well as a complete toolkit for building your own. You can use the presets to generate a massive range of sonic material, or you can employ the Edit screen's eight stereo modules to create extremely complex modulation routings. There's even a random effects generator that can quickly build entirely new effects automatically.

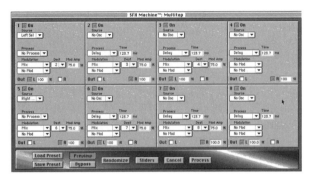

Figure C.4: SFX Machine, from BIAS, includes hundreds of presets for manipulating sounds. You can also build effects using the Editor screen or have the program generate them for you automatically.

Arboretum's Hyperprism effects plug-ins ($349 for the basic version), for both the Mac and Windows, is another powerful set of effects that extends well beyond your simple reverb and delay. Hyperprism's famous "blue screen" interface allows you to preview real-time changes to multiple effects parameters simultaneously. In addition to a great-sounding pitch shifter and numerous spatial effects, the program offers dozens of other features for fine-tuning or totally altering your sounds. The best way to run Hyperprism is using the included Hyper-Engine host program, available for the Mac only, which adds even more functions to the plug-in set. I recommend that you buy both Hyperprism and SFX Machine for the advanced Mac studio, to be sure that you'll always have the right tool for the job. The advanced Windows system will also have Hyperprism on hand.

In addition to Hyperprism, let's include Opcode's Fusion:Vocode ($149) in the advanced Windows and Mac setups. Fusion:Vocode takes an unusual approach to crossing two sounds, and it has an intuitive interface. You can use its onboard synthesis capabilities to generate source waveforms, and its real-time preview makes fine-tuning parameters an easy affair. On the Mac side, you can use the Premiere version with Peak.

Figure C.5 Arboretum Hyper-prism's blue screen provides access to multiple effects para-meters simultaneously. Using the HyperEngine host program on the Mac, you can draw control data or use the mouse in real time.

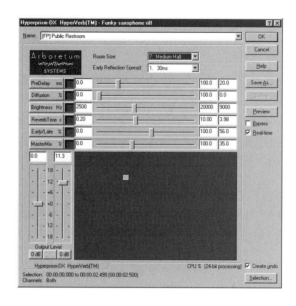

On the Windows platform, the DirectX format is nearly universal. This ensures that the DirectX software you buy will work with nearly all of the most common audio applications, including digital audio sequencers. My favorite DirectX plug-in for sound design is Sonic Foundry's Acoustic Mirror ($249). Though the software is intended primarily to apply different room ambiences to your material—which it does exceptionally well—it can also be used to convolve two sound files. I've spent hours crossing different types of material and have created some of my most interesting and unique sounds almost by accident. Acoustic Mirror is a bit of a splurge for a low-budget system, but nonetheless I'm going to include it on the must-have list for both the high- and low-end Windows studios because it has so much potential.

MAC STAND-ALONE PROCESSORS

Some digital audio processing software runs as independent, stand-alone applications. The Mac has a clear edge over Windows in this area, but powerful programs exist on both platforms.

Sadly, one of the oldest and best-known Mac programs is no longer being developed, though it is still available. Digidesign's Turbosynth SC ($349), surely the granddaddy of user-friendly, modular sound design software, is still available from the company, but it is not guaranteed to work with newer Mac models. It's too bad Turbosynth won't be updated for the next generation of sound designers. I'm not going to formally include it in our Mac studios, but I do recommend it as one of the most unique and versatile music programs ever made.

There are many sound processing tools on the Mac, and I'd need to write a separate article just to mention them all. But one valuable tool that should be included in a Mac studio of any level is Prosoniq's sonicWorx Artist ($199). Artist is a stand-alone application that offers 60 processing algorithms and some of the most unusual presets you're likely to find. The interface is not very intuitive, but the developer is addressing that in a new version scheduled for release later this year. The quality and scope of the effects you can create are amazing, though, so don't pass this one by.

No Mac-based sound designer should be without Tom Erbe's excellent SoundHack (available for $30 as shareware) and Kelly Fitz's Lemur (free). Both programs analyze existing files and allow you to perform mind boggling alterations before resynthesizing them. SoundHack excels at esoteric processing functions, such as its Spectral Extractor and Phase Vocoder. There are also several convolution and morphing options. Lemur is similar in function and works by tracking frequency and amplitude components of a sound independently. You can manipulate the analysis data in numerous ways before resynthesizing. The best part about these programs is that fully functional copies are readily available for download. Both of the programs belong in our basic and advanced Mac studios.

U&I Software's MetaSynth ($299), a truly unique sound design application, also belongs in both Mac studios. There is simply no end to the interesting, arresting, and provocative sounds you can make with it. If you haven't seen MetaSynth in action, it's a tough program to describe. What would "painting with sound" do for you? Or how about "scoring with pictures"? These are just two ways to conceptualize MetaSynth's approach to making music, and you'll simply have to trust me on this one. Still need proof of my sincerity? I bought my first Mac just so I could run this program!

Finally, MSP ($295) from Cycling '74 has some of the most advanced sound design and processing functions you'll find anywhere, and it would definitely be an asset to the advanced Mac-based studio. If you own Opcode's Max, you can create your own MSP patches as well as edit existing ones, but even without Max, you can use the numerous example patches, as well as others that you can find on the Internet. MSP offers a huge number of processing algorithms, and the excellent tutorial makes it easy to get a handle on how they function. (MSP patches can also be used inside Cubase VST via the Pluggo utility from Cycling '74.) If you like to tweak audio in real time, you'll appreciate the tremendous power MSP has to offer.

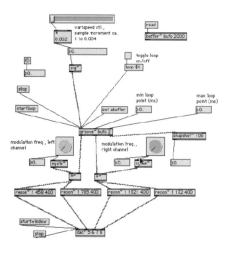

Figure C.6 Cycling '74 MSP is a set of extensions for Opcode's Max that allow you to develop your own audio processing programs. In this example patch, the playback rate can be altered using the slider at the top and ring modulation occurs as the signal is multiplied by two sine waves (labeled 'cycle ~').

If you don't mind using software that is a bit rough around the edges, consider joining IRCAM's Sound Design forum ($298), which gives you access to very advanced Power Mac–based tools. The French research center offers an annual membership to the forum and supplies you with a CD full of software that is under continuous development. Of the three main programs, my favorite is Modalys, which uses physical modeling to design "virtual instruments." Both of the other major programs, AudioSculpt and Diphone, provide exotic ways to modify the spectrum of a sound. The IRCAM CD also includes contributions from members, and a very active newsgroup is available to answer many support questions.

A number of Windows programs are available to help you build custom sounds using a modular approach. Rather than working primarily in real time—as software synthesizers such as Seer Systems' Reality and Native Instruments' Generator do—these programs "compile" the sounds that you design into WAV files on your hard drive. All of the programs I mention below use a graphic interface to build sounds, and each requires a split second to half a minute or more to generate the WAV files you design.

My favorite Windows sound design software is Virtual Waves ($199) from Synoptic. This professional application offers numerous sound-generating and processing tools that can be "wired" together to form complex synthesis patches. You can pick from a wide range of synthesis techniques, including such advanced methods as formant-wave function synthesis and physical modeling, and even use MIDI data extracted from a file to control a number of the processing parameters. Virtual Waves' Sound Assistant, a wizard-style feature, will even automate the process of sound design for you. Simply tell the Assistant what category of sound you want, and the design will appear on the screen instantly. You can then edit the design and, of course, save it to disk for future use. Add Virtual Waves to either the basic or advanced Windows studio, and you'll turn to it often.

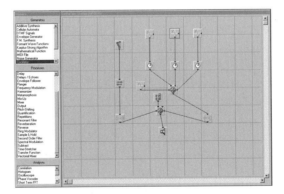

Figure C.7 Synoptic's Virtual Waves offers dozens of sound-processing modules you wire together to create complex synth networks. The Windows program also provides a number of modern synthesis tools.

Although not included in our recommended list, some other options in the same category are Rave Technologies' Audio Architect ($149) and WaveCraft from Last Unicorn (free). These Windows programs work much like Virtual Waves, but Audio Architect offers significantly more real-time features (though not nearly as many synthesis options). WaveCraft was a fully commercial application before its developer released it to the public, and its many synthesis tools can be used to serve up some strange and unusual sounds. Also take a look at Jim Bumgardner's Syd, which has excellent physical modeling modules and can read or write a Csound score file. (More on Csound in a moment.) Syd is a free program and runs on both Mac and Windows.

A final option for the Windows studios is a newcomer from Sounds Logical. The company's WaveWarp ($595) modular effects processor is a huge toolkit of functions that you'll use to create or manipulate sound files. The numerous effects, which include delays, filters, reverbs, and spectral enhancers, are of exceptionally high quality, and unlike the programs mentioned earlier, WaveWarp works in real time.

SOUND CODES

If you're willing to step outside the familiar interfaces that most programs offer, you'll find some amazing territory to explore in the world of sound-programming languages. The public domain synthesis programming language Csound, written by Barry Vercoe of MIT, is an excellent choice for synthesizing and processing sounds and is available for nearly all modern computer platforms. Csound is a powerful tool for building sounds from scratch, and you'll find hundreds of examples online that you can use as starting points. Csound requires two source files: an "orchestra," in which you design the sounds you want using the hundreds of algorithms, or "unit generators," that the language offers; and a "score," in which you specify how and when the sounds are to be played. You can build your sounds using plain text editors or with any number of graphic "helper" applications that make the task more intuitive.

In addition to synthesizing new sounds, you can use Csound to manipulate preexisting audio files. For example, using the "soundin" and "diskin" functions, you can load sound files from disk into the program's function tables. Then using an oscillator, for example, you can read the tables and employ the sounds in any of your designs. Csound is not for the fainthearted, but it's a free resource, so why not take the plunge? Watch for an authoritative new text, edited by Dr. Richard Boulanger, that will help you get the most out of this powerful language.

Another excellent choice for coding sound is James McCartney's SuperCollider 2 ($250) for the Macintosh. Like Csound, SuperCollider is a waveform compiler; it creates audio files on your drive based on the specifications you determine in your source files. SuperCollider is less "C-like" in its syntax but has numerous hooks for sending sound parameters in real time—for instance, from a MIDI controller, onscreen slider, or external audio source. The numerous included examples are ready to run, and by making even minor modifications to those files, you can generate dozens of new sounds.

Finally, for advanced sound design, Windows users should take advantage of the CDP (Composition, Development, Performing) system (about $541, payable in British pounds), a library of several hundred processing algorithms that fall into two main categories. First is a set of routines that are intended to transform data extracted by phase-vocoder analysis of preexisting sound files. You can perform a dizzying array of transformations on the analysis data before you resynthesize it: for example, morphing two analysis files or stretching a sound's spectrum like the bellows of an accordion.

The second set of processes runs directly on audio files. Here you chop, grind, twist, blend, or mutilate your data, all by entering a few parameter values on the command line. The range of processes is amazing, and the documentation and tutorials are superb. CDP will go into our advanced Windows studio, and it's guaranteed to get a real workout.

SOFTWARE SAMPLERS

Sound designers often need to deliver original music to clients, so sampling capabilities are essential to both basic and advanced studios. Good hardware- and software-based sampling options exist right inside the computer, so that's where we're going to have a look.

In the software-sampler category, we can use BitHeadz's new, cross-platform Unity DS-1 ($449), which works well either as a stand-alone module that you can play from a MIDI controller or as a companion to a sequencer that is running on the same computer. The numerous filters, effects, and modulation routings will be especially useful for designing custom sounds, and you can incorporate samples and map them automatically in several formats, including SoundFont 2.0, Akai S1000, and

SampleCell II. Unity DS-1 is especially suitable for Mac studios because it works particularly well with Steinberg's ReWire technology and Mark of the Unicorn's MAS audio format. Because the program is RAM-based, you'll want some extra RAM to get the most out of it.

Both of the Windows studios will have a copy of Seer Systems' Reality ($495), which doubles as a powerful synth engine and sampler. Though it doesn't have the range of sampling features that Unity has, it can load, map, and trigger up to four sound files from disk at once. And with all the synthesis methods available in Reality, you'll be able to create an enormous number of interesting and unique sounds suitable for many different projects. No doubt you'll surprise more than a few clients when you deliver sounds combining FM, AM, subtractive, and modal synthesis with physical modeling and samples.

Keep a close eye on the newest release from Native Instruments, which is called Transformator ($298). This modular software sampler runs on both Mac and Windows and offers some of the most interesting DSP effects available today. From everything I've seen, Transformator should be a worthy companion to Native Instruments' Generator, the 1999 *Electronic Musician* Editors' Choice winner for best software synth. The two programs are available separately and will also be combined into a single application called Reaktor ($469).

AUDIO I/O

For the basic Mac system, you can stick with the computer's built-in audio I/O. The software I've chosen supports it, and given that you can deliver your final product as WAV or AIFF files, you don't need more high-end outputs. You will need some type of small outboard mixer to provide separate monitor and headphone outputs. Any clean mixer can do that job, though, so I won't specify a particular product. (I will note, however, that Midiman makes several small, simple, inexpensive line mixers that would fit the bill nicely.)

For the advanced Mac system, you would do well to have digital inputs in order to bring your DAT field recordings into the computer in pristine condition. Digital outputs are less critical if you are going to deliver computer files, but they're nice to have. Fortunately, you can probably easily afford Emagic's new Audiowerk2 card ($299), which is based on the

Audiowerk8 technology. The new card has two analog ins, two analog outs, and stereo S/PDIF I/O. The Audiowerk2 analog ports are far better than the Mac's onboard audio ports, and the S/PDIF outputs can carry a separate signal from the analog outs, so you get 2-channel recording and 4-channel playback.

Bundled with the Audiowerk2 is Emagic's WaveBurner CD-R software, MicroLogic AV digital audio sequencer, and ZAP lossless audio file compressor, which will be handy for archiving your files. As you may recall, I wasn't going to specify a digital audio sequencer, but because Emagic has been nice enough to give you a good one, you might as well use it.

For the basic Windows studio, stick with the sound card currently in your computer, and if that happens to be a SoundBlaster or an E-mu product, take advantage of the support for SoundFonts that it probably offers. You can find numerous SoundFont banks on the Internet for little or no money, but I suggest you spring for all five of the Module Mania CDs from E-mu ($99 for the Penta-Pack; $30 per CD), which will give you a huge number of sounds.

If you're planning to upgrade anyway, maybe because you have a sound card that is not up to par, several new cards offer extensive sampling capabilities. I like the E-mu APS system ($699), which supports up to 32MB of sampling RAM and provides S/PDIF digital I/O as well as four analog inputs and two analog outputs. The APS ships with the Vienna SoundFont Studio 2.2 editor, which is the program you'll use to build keymaps and multisamples from your source material. This new version is more intuitive than previous ones and makes creating samples less of a chore. You'll also get hundreds of megabytes of SoundFonts to use right out of the box. By the way, E-mu plans to release its Mac APS driver by the time you read this, and assuming it works as promised, it would make a nice enhancement to your basic Mac system. However, we'll assume that your stock sound card is sufficient for now.

Other sound cards also have sampling capabilities, but before you buy anything, be sure to look at the software you'll be using to edit your samples. Some cards, such as the TerraTec EWS64 and Voyetra's Pinnacle Studio, offer full-blown editing options, but others have very limited capabilities. Suffice it to say that an onboard sampler is not of much use if the tools it provides aren't intuitive.

I've covered everything you'll need for a basic system, but there's one more major item for both Mac and Windows advanced setups: the Kyma System from Symbolic Sound ($3,300 for base unit). Now in its fifth generation, the Kyma System is a massively powerful "black box" full of Motorola 56309 DSP chips that you program using an intuitive graphic interface. The system has just had a significant upgrade and a substantial drop in price. Equally important, Kyma now includes four I/O channels as standard and is easier than ever to use.

Figure C.8 The Kyma System from Symbolic Sound is a hardware-accelerated sound-design workstation. The cross-platform system provides nearly unlimited resources for synthe-sizing and processing audio and has a powerful spectrum editor (right).

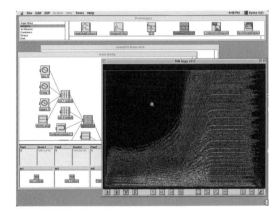

You can do just about anything with Kyma. Start with true stereo effects processing; add in a multimegabyte, disk-based sampler; stir in every synthesis method known to humanity; season with spectacular spectral-processing tools that should give you a good 20 percent of the picture. Extensive new tutorials will help get you up and running quickly, and an active newsgroup is also available to answer any technical questions you might have. Kyma will give any sound designer an edge, so plan on using it in your advanced studio for many types of applications.

FINAL DECAY

I hope that the ideas and suggestions here will assist your entry into the sound design world. Keep in mind that no matter how many tools you have on hand, you'll still need to master many basic skills.

Most important, familiarize yourself thoroughly with synthesis techniques and, of course, sound processing methodology. The more you know about methods such as FM, subtractive, and granular synthesis, and processes such as convolution and phase vocoding, the better you will be able to accomplish specific goals. Sound designers are fortunate to have such a massive array of hardware and software tools available, but it's up to you to learn how to use them.

The Music for Picture Studio

by David Rubin

Now that personal computers have thoroughly invaded the world of film scoring, the process of adding music to picture has undergone a technological sea change. By combining a computer and a video player with time code, composers can now add music to picture in real time. This has opened up many creative possibilities and new opportunities for otherwise disenfranchised musicians. Even composers who prefer to write away from the picture now have the option to try out musical cues against picture before making a commitment to a particular cue. Indeed, the use of synth/sampler mock-ups of scores has become widespread as a form of "insurance" for all involved in the project to guarantee that everything works musically and dramatically before spending big bucks on an expensive studio recording session.

Even so, low-budget features, educational films, industrial videos, TV commercials, and other audio-visual formats are often served well by scores that are created and recorded entirely on a desktop music system. In fact, the frenzied pace of today's TV and movie post-production schedules often relies on the speed and flexibility of desktop systems to get the work done on time and under budget.

What do you need to get started scoring to picture? That depends on what kind of "picture" you have in mind; the audio-visual universe has expanded a lot in the past couple of decades. Aside from films and TV, media such as computer games, Web sites, and desktop multimedia offer new points of entry into the picture scoring field.

To simplify the process of assembling a good desktop scoring system, I've divided the arena into two categories: the more basic system will be designed for multimedia music production, and the higher end system will focus on film/video scoring. In each category, I'll assemble a cost-effective, computer-based system for Mac and for Windows that will enable you to produce high-quality music with the option of future expandability. To heighten the challenge, these are to be true desktop systems: as many of the core components as possible will be computer hardware and software, avoiding unnecessary external hardware devices such as mixers, sound modules, and effects units. This approach will simplify various aspects of studio design and help you keep costs down. Of course, if you already have external hardware devices, you can add them to any of the systems described here as long as you get an audio interface with the appropriate inputs and outputs.

For our purposes, a film scoring system is one that can deliver quality, 16-bit, 44.1kHz (or better) digital audio in one or more tape formats, such as DAT, ADAT, or DA-88. SMPTE time-code support is essential. Such a system can handle almost any music-for-picture job, including fully synchronized film or video scoring.

The less expensive multimedia system may lack extensive synchronization capabilities, but it lets you try your hand at scoring to picture by working in the field of desktop multi-media. Instead of tape, these soundtracks are typically delivered as audio files (or MIDI files), so the ability to read and write a variety of file formats is important, as is the ability to suitably compress, edit, and process the audio. Let's begin by looking at basic, entry-level desktop multimedia systems for Mac and for Windows.

Unless you have connections in the film industry, a good way to gain experience combining music with picture is by creating soundtracks for multimedia. Apple's QuickTime architecture supports a wide array of file formats, such as digital audio and MIDI, as well as several audio compression schemes. You simply import a QuickTime movie onto your hard drive and add a soundtrack to it, or replace an existing soundtrack with one of your own. If you have a video-capture card, you can create your own movies and score them with your own desktop workstation.

QuickTime movies can be cross-platform compatible and are often used as elements within multimedia authoring programs, such as Macromedia's Director, or as design elements to enhance Web sites. Game developers can also use QuickTime movies at places where the flow of action allows for proper playback. In addition, countless CD-ROMs and Enhanced CDs rely on QuickTime to add a multimedia component to the rest of the content.

Although there are more than 26 million QuickTime users running Windows, Microsoft's AVI format is still the preferred digital video format for many Windows users. Both QuickTime 3 and Adobe Premiere 5.1 support AVI.

Speaking of Premiere, if you're interested in exploring QuickTime-based multimedia in depth, consider purchasing Adobe Premiere 5.1 ($895), a powerful, yet largely intuitive, multimedia authoring program for Mac and Windows. (For more on Premiere's audio capabilities, see "Desktop Musician: World Premiere," *Electronic Musician,* July 1997.)

But you don't need Premiere simply to add soundtracks to QuickTime. Most mid- to high-level sequencers and audio editors now support QuickTime (or AVI for Windows) and allow you to view movies frame by frame and position your music at specific places. That means you can often create, edit, and align a soundtrack in a single program. Which program you use depends on the nature of the soundtrack and of the particular project.

For that reason, a well-designed multimedia workstation must include an audio editor and an audio/MIDI sequencer for music production. It should also include a large palette of musical and nonmusical sounds. To avoid using external gear as much as possible, these sounds will be supplied by a software synth and sampler in our system. Of course, you'll need an input device for creating your music, and a MIDI keyboard is a logical choice. That, in turn, necessitates a MIDI interface, which completes the essential elements in a desktop studio. Now let's look at some specific setups.

THE MULTIMEDIA STUDIO

A good desktop music production studio should be centered on a solid and versatile audio/MIDI sequencer. Because multimedia is still predominantly a 16-bit, 44.1kHz (or lower) medium, you don't need to have high-resolution (24-bit, 96kHz) audio capability, although leaving the door open with upgrade options is a good strategy.

The Mac is especially well positioned as a platform for multimedia music production because of its onboard 16-bit stereo audio hardware and robust QuickTime authoring capabilities. I'll take advantage of the Mac's native audio to keep costs manageable in this entry-level system. You can always add a multichannel, high-resolution audio card later.

On the Windows side of the aisle, there are hordes of sound cards to choose from, and CD-quality (or better) output is now commonplace. For our system, I'm choosing Creative Labs' SoundBlaster Live ($200); it's relatively inexpensive and widely compatible. Moreover, SoundBlaster Live's S/PDIF I/O and support for E-mu's SoundFonts and Microsoft's DirectSound makes it highly compatible with the BitHeadz products that I'll be covering shortly.

Choosing a sequencer is difficult; personal tastes and work style preferences tend to muddy the picture. In general, however, you'll need a user-friendly sequencer with a well-designed interface, plenty of editing tools, good audio mixing and processing capabilities, and above all, excellent QuickTime or AVI support. High-end programs cost too much for this budget system; low-end programs typically lack the necessary tools for professional-quality work. That leaves a handful of midlevel sequencers in the under-$400 range.

Two other characteristics further narrow the field: plug-in support (for extensibility and versatility) and effective audio/video scrubbing (to help pinpoint cues and transitions). Emagic's MicroLogic AV ($99) supports QuickTime (or AVI for Windows) nicely, but the program provides only 16 audio tracks and doesn't support plug-ins. Emagic's Logic Audio Silver ($299) is a better choice, with its VST plug-in support, but it offers only 24 audio tracks, which might still be too limiting for some projects.

Cakewalk's Metro for the Mac ($249) also works with Quick-Time, and it supports VST and Premiere plug-ins. But Metro's scrubbing tool is awkward to use and not as well integrated as similar tools in competing products—a major drawback. Cakewalk Professional 8 for Windows ($269) provides excellent AVI and QuickTime support and works with DirectX plug-ins, but it has only eight audio tracks. Steinberg's Cubasis AV ($99) lacks plug-in support and also offers merely eight tracks of audio.

In spite of its higher cost, therefore, I've settled on Steinberg's Cubase VST ($399) as the best all-around choice for our Mac and Windows budget music-for-picture studios. Cubase VST has a vast number of editing windows, and its 64 audio tracks and support for VST plug-ins make it powerful enough for any job. Moreover, Cubase VST has an impressive mixer section with four inserts and eight effects sends per channel, and the program comes with several high-quality effects to get you started. That saves you money on an external reverb unit and other external processors.

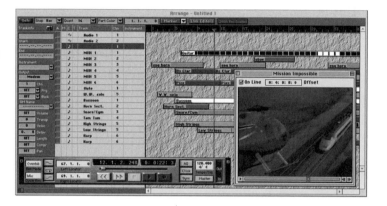

Figure D.1 You can scrub through a video clip frame by frame in Steinberg Cubase VST's dedicated QuickTime window. As you drag the scrollbar slider, the Song Position Pointer line moves with you to show where you are in the sequence.

Cubase provides an excellent environment for working with QuickTime or AVI movies. You can import a movie without its original soundtrack, or you can import the soundtrack and have it appear in the Tracks window, so you can build on it with more tracks. A separate MovieTracks window (Mac version only) lets you audition a movie and adjust the audio offset, panning, and volume with sliders.

The dedicated QuickTime window provides a scrollbar and playback controls (Mac only), and you can also play the video using Cubase VST's transport controls. To scan through the video frame by frame, grab the QuickTime scrollbar slider (or the Cubase transport slider in the Windows version) and drag left or right. In the Tracks window, the Song Position Pointer line moves along with you in real time (live scrolling) as the transport's location display provides a readout of elapsed time.

Let's say you want to add a harp glissando to an important transition in the video. The first step is to record and edit the harp part; you can record the part as you watch the movie, or you can record without the picture. Next, scrub through the video using the scrollbar until you find the frame where you want the gliss to begin. The Song Position Pointer line will appear at the corresponding place in the sequence. Simply drag the harp part to the line and that's it. Adding sound effects and clips of dialog is just as easy. When you're finished creating your sound-track, you can mix it, process it, and lay it back to the AVI or QuickTime video, thereby producing a finished digital video file.

Sometimes, of course, audio tracks need close-up editing, so a well-equipped desktop studio also needs a good audio editing program. Although Cubase can handle most editing tasks, a dedicated audio editor is sometimes essential. Most high-end editing programs support QuickTime on the Mac or AVI in Windows, which is a nice feature to have. In this case, however, we're trying to save money, so we'll let Cubase VST handle the QuickTime or AVI chores and choose an inexpensive editor to serve as an adjunct to the sequencer.

At less than $100, BIAS Peak LE 2.0 ($99) stands out as a particularly good buy. The program gives you the same well-designed user interface as Peak 2.0 and has many of the same editing capabilities. What's more, Peak LE supports Premiere plug-ins, which further broadens your plug-in options for processing audio files.

Peak LE lets you zoom in on a recording and view the waveform at the sample level. A Pencil tool enables you to smooth over clicks and mismatched loop points by redrawing the waveform. The program provides unlimited undo and sophisticated scrubbing features. You can create playlists in Peak LE (although without the crossfade and DSP options found in the higher-end version of Peak) and export them to Adaptec Toast, which is bundled with the program, so you can burn CD-Rs. That adds versatility to our system, as do Peak LE's abilities to import and export a wide variety of file formats and to encode MP3, Shockwave, and RealAudio 5.0 files.

For Mac users, Peak LE's lack of QuickTime support is adequately covered by Cubase VST, but if you want to work with QuickTime from within your audio-editing program, consider MicroMat's SoundMaker ($30). It handles QuickTime in an intuitive manner, with video scrubbing and easy audio-offset adjustments. In SoundMaker, you can view individual movie frames above the waveform display, and you can import, view, and edit multiple audio tracks simultaneously. This program is hard to beat for the price. However, SoundMaker sacrifices sample-level waveform editing, audio scrubbing, playlist editing, and, perhaps most importantly, support for third-party plug-in formats.

On the Windows side, Sonic Foundry's Sound Forge XP 4.5 ($50) gives you a lot of flexibility for a bargain price. It supports AVI files and several audio formats, including RealNetworks' G2 format. Sound Forge XP comes with lots of built-in effects, and you can expand its processing options by adding dedicated ExpressX plug-ins. The program includes unlimited undo capability and plenty of editing tools for most tasks.

Figure D.2 Sonic Foundry's Sound Forge XP packs lots of editing tools—along with support for AVI and RealNetworks G2—into an easy-to-use program.

Together, Cubase VST and Peak LE make a powerful yet cost-effective team, and they complement each other well. The same is true of Cubase VST and Sound Forge XP. In fact, you can set up Cubase VST to export audio files to either audio editor when you select the Launch External Wave Editor command in the Audio Functions menu. You can then make the necessary changes in the audio editor and shoot the file back to Cubase VST.

These programs also share another trait: they offer upgrades to more advanced versions (Cubase VST/24, Peak 2.0, and Sound Forge 4.5). One other option worth noting for Mac users is BIAS's Deck ($399) multitrack digital audio recording program. It comes bundled with Peak LE; although it's not a sequencer, it can import and play MIDI files along with audio files, and it supports QuickTime.

THE INSTRUMENTS

Now that we have the heart of our desktop system, let's assemble some musical colors to paint our scores. As mentioned earlier, I'll eschew the usual options of external sound modules and samplers in favor of internal solutions.

Software synths and samplers have been grabbing a lot of attention lately. The latency issue has been diminishing, and new products offer exciting potential. Two recent cross-platform programs from BitHeadz, Unity DS-1 ($449) and Retro AS-1 ($259), have made quite a splash. Unity is a software sampler that can import Sound Designer I and II, AIFF, CD audio, and WAV files; read DLS and SoundFont 2.0 formats; and read SampleCell I and II and Akai S1000 and S3000 discs with proper mapping of multisamples. That gives you access to an enormous library of sample CDs, in addition to hundreds of sounds (250 MB including a GM set) that come with the program. Unity outputs 24-bit, 96kHz sound (depending on your hardware, of course) with up to 64-note polyphony and 16-channel multitimbral capability. It has a full MIDI implementation and is extensively programmable.

Moreover, the Mac version can output its files directly to disk in 8-, 16-, and 24-bit format. Currently, the Windows version supports only 8- and 16-bit audio up to 48kHz, but support for 24-bit, 96kHz audio is in the works and should be available soon.

Figure D.3 BitHeadz's Unity DS-1 is an excellent cross-platform software sampler. Its ability to connect to other Mac programs makes it especially suitable for use on that platform.

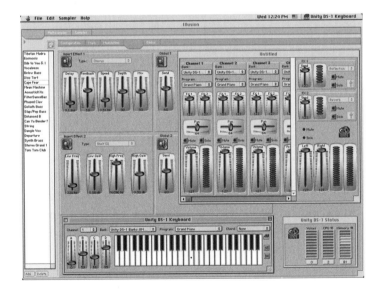

For the Mac system, we'll use some of the money we saved by not buying a sound card to expand our Unity instrument library. (The SoundBlaster Live adds lots of new sounds to the Windows system, so it seems only fair.) I'll choose E-mu's new Module Mania library ($99). It comes on five cross-platform CD-ROMs and consists of the sound sets, in SoundFont format, of E-mu's most popular sound modules: Proteus/1, Proteus/2, Proteus/3, Vintage Keys, and Planet Phatt.

Making Music with Your Computer

Retro AS-1 rounds out our instrument set nicely by adding the sounds of analog synthesizers from days gone by. Retro outputs 16-bit, 44.1kHz stereo sound (96kHz on the Mac), with up to 32-note polyphony; it reads and writes AIFF and WAV formats. With Retro you can create a wide array of sounds from scratch, and the program includes about 1,000 classic sounds to get you started. Retro and Unity pack an irresistible one-two punch and provide a solid foundation for building an open-ended palette of instrument sounds. Be aware that these programs can chew up a lot of CPU cycles; your computer will bog down if you try to run them simultaneously with other CPU-intensive programs, such as a digital audio sequencer with plug-ins.

Windows users also have two powerful options for expanding their sonic palettes: Seer Systems' Reality ($495) and NemeSys Music Technology's GigaSampler ($795). Unlike the RAM-based Unity, GigaSampler reads its samples directly from the hard disk, so you can have truly gigantic samples. Reality includes sample-playback capability, but the program really shines when it comes to synthesis: it offers several types with extensive control over parameters. If you have some extra room in your budget, it's worth exploring these exciting programs.

THE INTERFACE

To complete this desktop puzzle, you need a MIDI interface so that your MIDI keyboard can send messages to the computer. Because there are no external sound modules in our system at this time, an inexpensive, 1-In/1-Out unit can work fine. In the long run, however, you'll be much better off with a midlevel, multiport, multichannel interface.

One of my favorites in the under-$300 price range is Mark of the Unicorn's Micro Express ($295). This 4-In/6-Out interface supports up to 96 MIDI channels and can merge, filter, and rechannelize MIDI data. It also supports SMPTE time code and converts clicks to MIDI. That's a lot of power in a half-rackspace unit, and it provides an opportunity for easy expandability as your desktop studio grows (especially as you add external gear). In fact, because Cubase VST and the Micro Express both support SMPTE time code, your studio can easily evolve into an intermediate-level studio so that you can try out video scoring and time-code-related applications as well as desktop multimedia and game scoring.

That completes the core of our Mac and Windows systems for multimedia music production. As you might expect, however, there are always a few more things to consider.

ADDITIONS AND EXTRAS

Most computers—especially Windows PCs—come with a set of desktop speakers, and some multimedia monitors house small speakers next to the video display. In some cases, these desktop speakers work fine for mixing and editing music for games and multimedia. After all, most end users will likely be listening to your work on similar speakers. But many computer speakers provide such poor audio quality that they may adversely affect your mixing decisions and ruin the final soundtracks.

It pays to invest in a decent pair of modestly priced, self-powered, magnetically shielded reference monitors. They'll give a clearer picture of your musical output. You have lots of choices here, but I won't make any specific recommendations.

Don't throw away those cheap desktop speakers, though. You can use them to verify that your final mix will sound balanced on any system. Listening to your music on a variety of setups is always a good practice because you never know where the music will be playing next. Along those same lines, I always keep a set of high-quality headphones close at hand for carefully scrutinizing my music. Headphones make excellent diagnostic tools—and they let you work at night without disturbing your neighbors.

As I mentioned earlier, most multimedia soundtracks end up as audio files of some sort, even though you may be asked to submit your music in another format. An inexpensive DAT machine, therefore, makes a good investment. Mastering to DAT is easier and less expensive than keeping all of your music on removable hard-disk cartridges. And DATs are easy to mail across the country. Be sure to choose a DAT recorder with S/PDIF ins and outs so that you can digitally transfer your masters to and from the computer for further editing if needed. (For the Mac system, you'll need to purchase a sound card with digital I/O to stay in the digital domain when transferring audio files to DAT.)

The other obvious extra that you'll want is a MIDI input device, and that means a MIDI keyboard controller for most people. Preferences in keyboard action vary widely based on musical style and playing technique, so no single make or model will satisfy everyone. A number of suitable keyboard controllers are on the market, however, so you shouldn't have trouble finding one that suits your needs.

THE FILM SCORING STUDIO

Several important characteristics distinguish our professional-level, desktop film-scoring studio from the entry-level multimedia system. First and foremost, an advanced system must offer extensive synchronization capabilities, which include full support for SMPTE time code (all frame rates), video blackburst, and digital word clock. Because an advanced system must interface with outside film, video, and audio-recording facilities, it must also be compatible with more kinds of external gear than the desktop multimedia studio has to accommodate. In addition, it must offer better-than-CD-quality multichannel audio so that you can tackle the most demanding jobs.

Pro-level desktop systems range in price from a few thousand dollars to tens of thousands or—if you add high-end external hardware—even hundreds of thousands of dollars. For our purposes, I'll assemble a modestly priced desktop system that provides high-quality audio and supplies all the essential tools without permanently destroying your credit rating.

FROM HERE TO THERE

Although the process of scoring films varies from place to place and from job to job, it typically involves several common steps. After principal photography is complete and the film goes through several edits, a final edited version is transferred to video. Theoretically, this "locked" work print is to remain unchanged so that the composer has a reference for matching the music to picture. (In reality, however, things always seem to change.)

Ideally, the work print includes most of the dialog and a few temporary sound effects as references so you can avoid unpleasant collisions in the soundtrack. The tape will also include SMPTE time code (in the form of Longitudinal Time Code, or LTC) on one of the audio tracks. The work print should also include a time-code window onscreen so you can watch the SMPTE numbers flash by as the video plays. (For a thorough introduction to the topic of synchronization, see "That Synching Feeling," *Electronic Musician,* October 1996.)

Larger studios often use ¾-inch videotape for work prints, because ¾-inch decks are rugged, offer greater control over tape shuttling, and often provide a dedicated address track for time code. However, ½-inch (VHS) decks are common for midlevel desktop studios and are frequently used for independent, low-budget productions, even though they're a bit more trouble to work with.

Once a work print with a time-code window is available, the composer, director, and music editor (if there is one) get together for what is called a spotting session. They view the movie scene by scene and determine where the music should start and stop and how the music should sound. Notes taken at this session form the cue sheet, which the composer uses as a reference. The cue sheet shows SMPTE times, fragments of dialog, and descriptions for each musical cue. At this point, the composer retires to the dungeon and desperately tries to kick-start the creative process.

PICKIN' THE PIECES

As with our multimedia system, I'll rely on the Unity DS-1 and Retro AS-1 software sampler and synth from BitHeadz as the primary sources for instrumental sounds. That keeps the core system inside the computer and—for now, anyway—avoids the need for an external mixing board.

Your audio editing programs must be top-notch so that you are prepared to handle any music, dialog, or sound effects editing jobs that might come your way. Therefore, we'll step up from Peak LE to Peak 2.0 ($499) on the Mac and from Sound Forge XP to Sound Forge 4.5 ($499) for Windows. These programs offer lots of powerful editing tools—especially for close-up editing—and support for a wide range of file formats and plug-ins

Making Music with Your Computer

(Premiere, AudioSuite, and TDM in Peak and DirectX in Sound Forge). Peak 2.0 also has a QuickTime movie window (which the LE version lacks), and it lets you burn CDs directly from its playlist. It can record up to 32-bit files, if your hardware can support that resolution.

Perhaps most important, however, is that both programs offer sophisticated playlists that can be synched to incoming time code. That enables you to create a list of music cues, sections of dialog, or sound effects, for example, and have them trigger at specific SMPTE times—a highly useful postproduction tool.

THE SEQUENCER

With the sound sources and audio editors in place, it's time to confront the difficult task of choosing a high-end audio/MIDI sequencer. Emagic's Logic Audio Platinum ($799) is attracting a growing number of pro-level users, as is Cakewalk Pro Audio 8.0 ($429) for Windows. For our Mac system, however, I prefer MOTU's Digital Performer 2.5 ($795). Digital Performer integrates extremely well with the other components in our particular system.

Figure D.4 MOTU's Digital Performer 2.5 integrates well with Unity DS-1, Retro AS-1, the MIDI Timepiece AV, and the 2408 audio interface. The program's sophisticated editing features, high-quality audio effects, and sample-accurate sync capability make it well suited for our advanced studio.

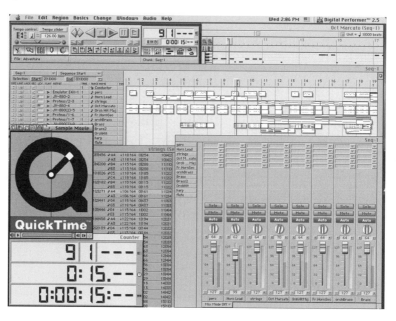

BitHeadz and MOTU have been working together closely in several areas, and their programs communicate with each other quite well. For example, Unity and Retro appear in FreeMIDI just like other sound modules, and inside Digital Performer, you can select their numerous patches by name from pop-up palettes, which eliminates a lot of hassle. What's more, MOTU will soon be offering a free version 2.6 upgrade, which will allow you to route Unity's outputs directly into Digital Performer's mixer for full audio integration. You can then mix Unity's outputs with Digital Performer's other audio tracks and apply any of Performer's plug-in effects to any or all of the audio tracks.

For the Windows studio, I'll stick with Cubase VST, but I'll step up to Cubase VST/24. It lets you record as many as 96 tracks of 24-bit, 96kHz audio if the need should arise. The program's full-featured music notation section lets you replace bar numbers with SMPTE times. You also get an impressive internal resolution of 15,360 ppqn (for more accuracy when positioning and editing audio segments) and a mighty powerful mixer with lots of good effects.

THE INTERFACE

For a MIDI interface, I'll step up from the Micro Express to the MIDI Timepiece AV ($595). MOTU's top-of-the-line, networkable interface gives you eight MIDI Ins, eight Outs, and 128 channels. It supports all the essential sync options, including SMPTE time code (all frame rates with variable freewheeling), MTC, video blackburst, word clock, Digidesign Superclock, and ADAT sync. The MTP AV also has a front-panel LCD window, which shows incoming time code and other useful information.

The cross-platform MTP AV can be hooked up to a Mac or a Windows PC, or to both at the same time; a USB version is due out soon. The MIDI Timepiece AV adds another element of integration by allowing you to select sound modules and other sound sources by name from pop-up palettes within Digital Performer. As your studio expands, this will become increasingly important.

THE AUDIO HARDWARE

Choosing a hard-disk recording system is another difficult task. The computer-music world is awash in excellent multichannel audio cards and digital-audio recording setups. In the film, TV, commercial, and recording industries, Digidesign's Pro Tools systems have become standards due to their powerful feature set (enhanced by TDM plug-ins), high-quality audio output, and well-established user base. But Pro Tools systems are not for the financially delicate. A complete Pro Tools/24 system (with necessary I/O and SMPTE support), for example, will set you back more than $9,000. That puts it off-limits for a "modestly" priced pro-level studio like the one I'm constructing here.

In spite of a long and deserving list of nominees from other companies, such as Korg, E-mu–Ensoniq, Event, Lucid, Frontier, Sonorus, Creamware, and others, I'm choosing MOTU's cross-platform 2408 hard-disk recording system ($995) for our desktop studio. The 2408's great bang for the buck and exceptional level of connectivity with the outside world make it hard to beat.

This PCI-card and rack-mount–I/O combo has eight analog ins and outs with 20-bit converters, 24 channels of ADAT optical I/O, 24 channels of TDIF I/O, and two channels of S/PDIF in and four channels out. That means you can connect three Alesis ADATs, three Tascam DA-88s, a DAT recorder, and eight analog devices simultaneously. The 2408 also offers ADAT sync input and word-clock in and out. Moreover, the 2408 can transfer files to and from Pro Tools systems, and with all those digital I/O ports, you can upgrade to 24-bit audio by adding a 24-bit A/D converter, such as Apogee's AD-8000. That helps you sidestep future obsolescence.

Most important, however, the 2408 works seamlessly with Digital Performer to create a true workstation environment. In fact, MOTU offers a special upgrade from AudioDesk, which comes with the 2408 system, to Digital Performer 2.5 for just $395. This makes our Mac system an especially good buy. On the Windows side, MOTU offers ASIO drivers written specifically for Cubase VST. The 2408 also supports Logic Audio Platinum, Opcode Vision DSP, Cakewalk Pro Audio, Sound Forge, and other popular software.

One possible fly in the ointment for Windows users should soon be resolved. Although the 2408 supports ASIO, it doesn't support Microsoft's DirectSound, which allows multiclient audio output. Consequently, you can't play back audio from Cubase while playing audio from Unity or Retro. You can save the Unity or Retro files in WAV format and import them into Cubase, but that's a hassle. (The yet-to-be-released ASIO 2.0 support should resolve this problem.) BitHeadz, however, is about to release a new ReWire software link that will enable BitHeadz audio to show up in the Cubase VST mixer channels. You'll then be able to use VST's EQ and effects on the BitHeadz instruments. That should solve the problem nicely, and it will probably be available by the time you read this.

The MIDI Timepiece AV and the 2408 make a solid combination that can handle most film/video scoring tasks. In a typical scenario, the MTP AV receives time code from the video work print and converts it to MIDI Time Code to drive the sequencer, which is operating in External Sync mode. The MTP AV also converts the SMPTE time code into word-clock output to keep the 2408 in sync. All MIDI and digital audio tracks then follow the picture with nearly instantaneous lockup.

THE LIST GOES ON

Our film scoring studio includes the basic elements for creating and editing music for film and video, but there are other components that you'll have to consider. As with the multimedia studio, you'll need a MIDI keyboard. Also, if you are recording singers and acoustic instruments, you'll need at least one pair of good mics.

Aside from a video recorder (¾-inch or VHS), you'll also need a DAT recorder for stereo masters. Many film composers also have at least one Alesis ADAT or Tascam DA-88 for mastering. With eight tracks, you can include separate but synchronized stereo mixes for dialog, sound effects, and music on the same master tape. You can also provide alternate, multichannel music mixes in case something changes at the dubbing session. (For instance, if the brass section interferes with the sound effects, you could pull down the brass without changing the woodwinds.)

Finally, if your system expands too much (especially with external sound modules and samplers), you'll have to add a mixing board to the setup. Given the nature of this studio, a digital mixer would seem to be in order, but that, my friends, is another story.

The Music CD Production Studio

by Gino Robair and Jeff Casey

Before we specify the components of our basic and advanced studios for music CD production, it's important to define what separates the two types. After some debate, we decided that what distinguishes the basic studio from the advanced is that the first equips you to work primarily on your own projects, whereas the second equips you to accept outside clients.

Because you'll be using a basic studio to work on your own projects, you can tailor it to meet your specific needs. For example, if you want to lay down mainly dance music grooves, you won't need to purchase elaborate audio recording equipment. Or if you're in a garage band and want to record a demo CD, choosing a full-featured recording environment and an easy-to-use MIDI setup should be enough.

On the other hand, advanced studios are designed to handle just about every project imaginable. Most personal "project" studios have to be able to interface with other studios, and if you can't connect, you won't attract clients. This doesn't mean that your studio must be able to accept analog 2-inch tapes, but you do need more than just a self-contained computer setup.

We've chosen flexible systems that provide a wealth of recording, processing, editing, and mixing functions; decent MIDI capabilities; and support for popular plug-in formats. In addition, we determined that the advanced systems should have hardware control surfaces, if for no other reason than that some clients get scared by computers and want to touch a mixing console.

As you'll see, we diverged from each other at several points, including our basic system choices. But we sincerely hope that our differing views will be as instructive as our common positions.

We want a basic music-production system that can do it all—record, edit, sequence, and score. Our wish list includes a digital audio sequencer, digital audio card, a software synthesizer and sampler, a couple of MIDI control surfaces for good measure, and professional scoring capabilities. Because our wish list is rather long, We'll go through it one step at a time.

THE HEART OF THE STUDIO

A number of companies have quality digital audio sequencers with notation capabilities. They're all competitively priced at well under a grand, so the choice is a tough one. But if you're going to produce it all, Emagic's Logic Audio Gold ($499) is my pick for the digital audio sequencer. It comes fully loaded with features, yet with a price tag under $500, it enables you to channel extra money toward other items on the list.

Although Logic Audio Gold is the most difficult to master of the leading digital audio sequencer programs, the payoff is great once you've conquered it. And you will always have room to grow because of the program's great depth.

Logic Audio Gold is a fully integrated software system that gives you up to 48 tracks of 16-bit audio, eight effects buses, MIDI sequencing, and a full-featured music notation editor. The program is compatible with audio interfaces from most manufacturers, so you should have no problem upgrading your audio hardware in the future. In addition, when you want to move to 24-bit audio and increase the number of digital audio tracks to 96, you can step up to Logic Audio Platinum through Emagic's upgrade program.

You can customize the program's user interface to a high degree. One way to do this is to use the Environment feature, which allows you to define the flow of audio and MIDI data. With this feature, you can configure the various elements of your physical studio by connecting their virtual representations. This allows you to create templates of the configurations used for specific projects. By delving deeper into Logic Audio Gold, you can use the Environment to do more interesting things with the flow of MIDI data by connecting virtual objects. Preset Environments will help you get started.

Logic Audio Gold comes bundled with the Sound Diver librarian program, WaveBurner for burning Red Book–compliant CD-Rs, and BIAS Peak LE for editing stereo audio files. Combined with Gold's recording, editing, mixing, sequencing, and scoring features, these tools give you the beginnings of a powerful workstation, and you're on your way to creating a professional-quality CD master. Furthermore, Logic Audio version 4.0 should be available by the time this article goes to press. Among other things, the program includes 31 new plug-ins.

AUDIO I/O

You'll need an audio card, so we're choosing Emagic's Audiowerk2 ($299), a 2-channel version of the company's Audiowerk8 that supports up to 24 tracks with Logic Audio Gold.

MicroLogic AV, WaveBurner, and ZAP (Emagic's audio-file compression program) come bundled with Audiowerk2, making the package a powerful system in itself. You won't need Micro-Logic AV, of course, because you have Logic Audio.

SOFTWARE SYNTHS

The logical choice for a Mac software synth and sample player comes from BitHeadz. The company's Retro AS-1 analog synth emulation software ($259) and Unity DS-1 sampler ($449) are good companions for Logic Audio Gold because they can work directly in the Logic Audio environment without using OMS.

Retro AS-1 gives you three oscillators and two filters per voice, as well as two insert and two global effects. It is 16-part multitimbral and 32-note polyphonic, with envelopes and LFOs limited only by the processing power of your computer. A collection of presets is included, giving you an immediate palette of vintage sounds. Retro AS-1 version 1.2 has improved effects, supports ASIO, and links easily to the Keyfax Phat.Boy MIDI controller (which we'll discuss shortly).

Unity DS-1 is a stereo software sampler that requires no additional hardware. It supports a number of common sound-file formats, including SDII, WAVE, AIFF, SampleCell, Akai 1000, and SoundFont 2.0. Unity DS-1 can also record audio and includes an editor for sculpting digitized audio into the perfect sample.

The downside to these programs is that they are CPU intensive, and you'll have difficulty running them simultaneously with the digital audio sequencer. You can circumvent that problem by recording some of the sounds into audio tracks when you meet your processing limits. This solution takes care of the other drawback to this setup: because of the nature of ASIO drivers on the Mac, you are able to run only one application at a time per audio card. A simple way to get around this limitation is to use Sound Manager as the Retro or Unity driver, plug the Mac audio outputs into the Audiowerk2 inputs, and record the sound. If Logic Audio supported the ReWire software link (as Cubase VST and Digital Performer do), this wouldn't be an issue. However, these are problems we can live with for the time being.

SEIZING CONTROL

A mouse is not the ideal hardware interface to use when you're editing on the computer. Therefore, we're going to add two MIDI control surfaces: one with knobs and one with sliders and buttons. The Keyfax Phat.Boy ($250) gives you 13 knobs to grab. As mentioned earlier, it interfaces well with Retro AS-1 but can also be mapped anywhere else a knob is appropriate in the system. (The mapping assignments in the Phat.Boy are fixed, but they can be remapped and routed within Logic Audio.)

You'll also need a simple but handy fader box, and the Peavey PC 1600x ($400) fits the bill. It enables you to mix your audio with real faders, punch tracks in and out with real buttons, and tweak a few knobs to control the software synth or MIDI-controllable effects plug-ins.

You now have a complete system that will provide many years of productivity, with potential for easy expansion and upgrading.

MAKING WELCOME ADVANCES

Everything for the basic Mac studio could be incorporated into the advanced studio; however, the advanced system is designed to do more, and better. Remember, the purpose behind an advanced studio is to be able to accept CD-production projects from a variety of clients as well as to produce your own projects.

The centerpiece of the advanced system that we've chosen is Digidesign's Pro Tools digital audio workstation. Pro Tools gives you that edge to handle any sort of project that a client may bring. There is a wide range of software products that interface beautifully with Pro Tools, from sequencers and software synths to extremely powerful plug-ins.

The current state of the art is Pro Tools/24 MIX ($7,995), which provides all of the DSP needed for 16 channels of 24-bit TDM-based recording, mixing, and editing on one PCI card. By using a little less real-time processing, you can mix up to 64 tracks of audio with one card. This is particularly good news for Mac users who have only three PCI slots.

To take full advantage of the 24-bit processing from beginning to end, we have selected Digidesign's 888/24 I/O audio interface ($3,695) for eight balanced XLR ins and outs with 24-bit A/D and D/A converters, eight channels of AES/EBU digital I/O, and two channels of S/PDIF I/O. If you need more I/O, you can connect as many as nine 888/24s together for 72 channels of discrete I/O (though you'll need more computer muscle for that).

You'll also need a digital audio sequencer. To match the depth of the Pro Tools system (as well as to take advantage of the easy upgrade from our basic Mac studio), we've picked Emagic's Logic Audio Platinum ($799), which has all the features of Logic Audio Gold but fully integrates with TDM systems.

We're not going to use a software synth or sampler with the advanced system because none of the current crop support the Digidesign Audio Engine, which is required to address the Pro Tools hardware. You could add another audio card for this purpose, but you're better off buying Digidesign's SampleCell II Plus PCI card ($1,295).

Long available on the Macintosh and recently released for Windows NT as well, SampleCell II Plus is a complete sample-playback/synthesis card that offers 32-note polyphony, eight outputs, and a powerful editing environment. All the number crunching takes place on the SampleCell card, which comes with 32MB of RAM, so your CPU only has to run the editing application. Hundreds of megabytes of samples are bundled with the system. We'll also buy the optional TDM module ($395), so that the SampleCell II's editing environment can run as a TDM plug-in and the sounds can be triggered from within Pro Tools.

PLETHORA OF PLUG-INS

Now that we're in the land of TDM, we can choose from any of the fine, real-time plug-ins from TC Electronic, Focusrite, Waves, Lexicon, Apogee, and Line 6, among others. Depending on your immediate budget and needs, you can assemble enough reverbs, compressors, EQs, and other effects to cover traditional signal-processing chores without using outboard devices.

The first set of TDM plug-ins you should get is the Waves TDM Bundle ($1,000), which is a good choice for basic mixing and mastering situations. Part of the Waves package, Q10 ParaGraphic Equalizer, handles EQ chores and provides two to ten bands of mono or stereo EQ per channel. TrueVerb is a fine-sounding reverb with plenty of parameters. You also get C1 Compressor/ Gate, a frequency-sensitive dynamics processor for compression, expansion, and gating; L1 Ultramaximizer for maximizing volume when mastering CDs; S1 Stereo Imager for adjusting the stereo image of a mix; and PAZ Psychoacoustic Analyzer for real-time audio analysis.

INTERFACE ACE

If you don't have good, reliable sync, you aren't ready to bring in clients. You'll also need a MIDI interface to hook up your Mackie Human User Interface (HUI)—which I'll discuss shortly—and any other external MIDI devices you may have. Here, I've chosen to invest in a MOTU MIDI Timepiece AV MIDI interface/synchronizer ($595), which combines an 858 MIDI interface with a synchronizer that can handle word clock, MTC, ADAT sync, Superclock, and SMPTE.

Although you might not need it yet, you would be wise to invest in a Digidesign ADAT Bridge ($1,245) sometime in the future, especially if you add an ADAT to your system. With the ADAT Bridge, you get 16 channels of Lightpipe digital I/O.

If you're willing to spend some more money on your advanced system, buying a better control surface would be a wise investment. The Mackie HUI ($3,499) is a fully automated controller tailored for use with Pro Tools. It features motorized faders, assignable V-Pot rotary controls, level meters, dedicated plug-in controls, tape transport buttons, eight assignable channel strips and buttons, two mic preamps, and a jog wheel.

Every function of Pro Tools is immediately within reach on the HUI. Because Pro Tools mixing is fully automated, you can get by with HUI's eight faders. If you need to expand, you can add another HUI, or, if you need to save money, add a Peavey PC 1600x or two.

FINAL NOTES

Constructing a studio such as this one is somewhat pricey, but by investing in top-level gear, you can draw a more select clientele. Pro Tools audio and session files are easily interchangeable between Windows and Mac platforms, so sharing work with other Pro Tools studios is no problem. With this desktop system, you should be able to handle almost any project that a client presents you.

Because you'll be producing primarily your own projects in your basic studio, you won't need a lot of gear to get in the door. Fortunately, we have some excellent choices that will give you pro quality for a relatively small amount of money.

The centerpiece of the basic Windows studio is the Yamaha SW-1000XG PCI sound card ($700). The SW-1000XG provides an XG wavetable/physical modeling synth engine (complete with a software wavetable editor), a 12-track digital audio recorder and mixer, DSP effects, basic I/O, and XGWorks digital audio sequencing software—all in all, a comprehensive working environment for MIDI-oriented production.

The PCI card houses a 64-note, 32-part multitimbral AWM2 tone generator, which is capable of generating more than 1,200 sounds derived from 20MB of wavetable ROM. You also get 46 discrete drum kits. The synth is compatible with Yamaha XG and General MIDI sounds, and Yamaha VL, VH, and DX sound generation is possible if you have the optional PLG100-series expansion boards. By choosing this card rather than focusing on a software synth, you get plenty of nice synth voices without devouring CPU time. MIDI In and Out jacks are provided on a breakout cable.

On the audio side, the SW-1000XG can record up to four tracks simultaneously and can play back up to 12 tracks. Recording can be either 16- or 32-bit (but, oddly, not 24-bit), and sampling rate can be set to 8, 11, 22, 44.1, or 48kHz. Channel EQs are available, as are seven independent, 24-bit effects processors that can be applied to the output of audio or MIDI tracks. Effects can also be applied to live inputs as they are recorded, giving you a means of conserving DSP power during mixdown.

However, assuming that you plan to do professional work, even with a basic system, the SW-1000XG's I/O configuration is inadequate. It gives you S/PDIF digital I/O on RCA connectors and only two channels of analog I/O, and the inputs accept either mic-level or line-level signals. The S/PDIF and analog ports are not independent, so this is really a 2-in/2-out card.

Therefore, the next component that we chose to add to this studio was Event Electronics' Layla ($1,099), which includes a PCI audio card and breakout I/O module. The system comes bundled with Syntrillium's Cool Edit Pro multitrack recording and editing software, which will come in handy. You can install multiple systems, and you're limited only by the number of PCI slots available on your CPU. Of course, we have already used up two slots.

Analog I/O abounds on Layla: the card has eight inputs and ten outputs, with 20-bit, 128$\times$ oversampling A/D and D/A conversion. S/PDIF digital I/O (which can handle 24-bit audio) is provided on RCA jacks. The S/PDIF ports are independent of the analog ports, so you get full-duplex recording, with 10 simultaneous record channels and 12 simultaneous playback channels. That takes care of our I/O problem nicely. The system can sync to word clock or Superclock as well as to MTC. Internal audio processing and recording is 24-bit, and all of Layla's recording functions are handled by the lightning fast Motorola 56301 chip.

Syntrillium's Cool Edit Pro gives you an abundance of real-time and offline processing tools in addition to support for Microsoft DirectX plug-ins. You get good waveform-editing tools, and more than 20 file types are supported. You can use Cool Edit Pro with a software sequencer; however, if you plan to do extensive audio/MIDI productions, you'll probably want to add an integrated digital audio sequencer to handle those chores.

SOFTWARE SAVVY

Although XGWorks comes bundled with the Yamaha SW-1000XG and provides decent integrated software for audio recording and MIDI sequencing, it's not on a par with dedicated digital audio sequencers. Fortunately, the SW-1000XG and Layla are compatible with almost any modern third-party digital audio sequencer.

I have selected Cubase VST/24 ($799) for several reasons. The program is very powerful and easy to use. It offers full GS, XG, and GM compatibility, so it works nicely with the Yamaha SW-1000XG. The sequencer gives you a wide array of editing tools, in addition to four arpeggiators, several quantize variations, and algorithmic-composition functions. MIDI Clock and MTC can be generated, and comprehensive notation and printing features are provided. Having scoring capabilities integrated with your sequencing and recording environment is an important feature if you want to copyright your compositions or provide scores for session players.

On the audio front, Cubase VST/24 can handle up to 96 channels at mixdown, although your computer hardware will ultimately determine this number. Support is offered for several sampling rates and resolutions, including 24-bit, 96kHz (useful if you upgrade to a system that supports 24/96 recording). ASIO is also supported, and, as an added bonus, Cubase VST/24 interacts directly with, and routes audio from, another Steinberg program, ReBirth (more in a moment). Each channel features dedicated EQs, insert effects, and aux sends. An 8-unit effects rack accommodates any of the growing number of VST plug-ins on the market, and VST Master-Insert effects are also available.

Audio editing is delightfully straightforward with Cubase VST/24, and an abundance of tools are provided, including VST-format plug-ins. And remember, you also have Cool Edit Pro's many tools. There are times when a dedicated 2-track waveform editor comes in handy.

Appendix E **445**

Before moving on, we'll admit that we could have started with a less expensive version of Cubase and upgraded later. However, we really want VST/24's 24-bit recording features, so we're willing to spend the extra money up front.

If you plan to produce lots of urban and dance music, think about buying a phrase-based audio editor. Our personal choice is Sonic Foundry's Acid ($399), which won *Electronic Musician's* 1999 Editors' Choice Award for "Most Innovative Product." Although Acid can't run in sync with other recording or sequencing software, you can export Acid files to Cubase VST/24, Cool Edit Pro, or XGWorks for incorporation into larger projects.

Despite the wealth of VST plug-ins, our first plug-in purchase would be a non-VST package, TC Works' TC Native Essentials ($199) for DirectX. This package includes a reverb, equalizer, and dynamics processor, each of which can accommodate multiple tracks at mixdown. Why do I like Native Essentials? It has the same high-quality processing capabilities as TC Electronics hardware devices.

SOUNDS ABOUND

If you're going to produce a lot of electronic music, you'll probably want a wider variety of sounds than the SW-1000XG provides. You might decide that you'd rather have a second synth-equipped card than have the ample audio I/O of Layla, for example. Or you might want to use a software synthesizer.

A neat arrangement exists between Steinberg's ReBirth software synth ($199) and Cubase. Steinberg's ReWire technology allows the two programs to share the same transport controls and internally streams ReBirth's outputs directly into Cubase VST's mixer channels. ReBirth offers some fantastic vintage techno sounds, and we know people who are making some killer grooves using this combination. You can extensively customize the program, and alternative versions are available on Steinberg's Web site at www.us.steinberg.net.

A KNOBBY QUESTION

Because ReBirth is now part of your basic Windows studio, you need a Keyfax Phat.Boy for controlling the program's real-time parameters. The Phat.Boy also is preprogrammed for controlling XG synths, so it's a fine match for our Yamaha sound card.

Making Music with Your Computer

It's hard to imagine a personal studio for music production that lacks a MIDI keyboard of some sort. However, which one you choose for your studio depends on personal factors that cannot be addressed in this article. For example, you might be a MIDI guitarist, percussionist, or wind player who needs only a small keyboard controller for playing pads and simple lines. Then again, you might be a professional keyboard player who needs a controller with weighted keys and piano-like action. Therefore, we're going to avoid making a recommendation here.

MOVING ON UP

Designing the advanced music studio was easier than designing the basic one. That's because the advanced studio needs to have a wealth of hardware and software available to handle practically every task, and therefore—unlike with the basic studio—we weren't forced to narrow down as many choices. Of course, this meant more fun for us spending our play money! But before we could indulge myself, we needed to settle on a core system. We found the solution in PARIS—not the city, the DAW.

HARD-CORE

We've been working with Ensoniq's PARIS in our personal studio for almost a year now, and saying that we've been pleased with the results would be an understatement. Before converting to PARIS, we were die-hard users of Pro Tools, so you understand that we have always been picky about the tools we use for producing music. We still think Pro Tools is a fine product, but once we switched, we realized that PARIS is on a par with professional DAWs that cost two or three times as much.

At the heart of PARIS is a PCI audio card that supports 16 tracks of simultaneous playback and records at either 16- or 24-bit resolution. But 16 tracks is not a lot, which is why PARIS offers intelligent submixing: each group of 16 tracks can be submixed to a stereo pair, and eight submixes are permitted— quite a flexible arrangement. In addition, PARIS offers two recording modes, Constrained and Free-Form; the latter allows you to record multiple takes (up to 999) on every track.

The mixing section provides four bands of fully parametric EQ, eight aux sends, and five inserts on every channel. The effects are all top-notch and include an array of dynamics processors, reverbs, delays, and pitch effects. Support has recently been added for the VST and DirectX formats (more in a moment).

Dynamic mixdown automation is available for level, pan, and mute, and you get a graphic automation-editing window. The system's block-style audio editing is surprisingly powerful, and PARIS comes bundled with Steinberg's WaveLab Lite for more detailed editing chores.

Unlike most other workstations, PARIS has channel EQs that are uncompromised by other engaged processing: a dedicated 4-band EQ is always available to every channel regardless of how many multi effects or dynamics processors are in use. (You never want to have to tell a client, "I can't change that EQ because I printed it on the track to conserve DSP resources.") In our studios, we can typically open a dynamics processor on every channel, in addition to four or five multi effects processors. Not bad. But even better, when you perform a submix, all DSP resources are freed up for the next group of tracks. Submixes can easily be recalled and tweaked, so you're not committed to any particular mix.

PARIS comes with a hardware control surface, the Control 16, which provides channel faders, transport and locate controls, and a jog wheel, in addition to channel EQ, aux send, and pan controls. In a project studio, it's important to have equipment that clients can see. Many analog diehards are reluctant to record digitally, let alone on a computer, and the thought of not being able to touch a mixing console might scare clients away. Overall, the combination of intuitive software and the Control 16 makes PARIS very easy to use.

PARIS is available in several configurations, each offering different I/O options. For this studio, we recommend the Modular Expansion Chassis (MEC) bundle ($3,895). The MEC ships standard with four channels of 20-bit analog I/O, as well as S/PDIF and word-clock I/O. It provides nine expansion slots for adding any combination of 8-channel cards, including 24-bit A/D, 24-bit D/A, and ADAT optical I/O ($499 each). We're going to buy an extra A/D and D/A card, and we'll add an ADAT card for compatibility with the outside world. Incidentally, E-mu–Ensoniq is planning 8-channel Tascam TDIF and AES/EBU I/O cards, so PARIS will be able to interface with practically every major format. The 24-bit converters sound great, especially when used with PARIS's 24-bit recording capabilities.

To top it off, E-mu–Ensoniq has announced compatibility with a variety of digital audio sequencers, including our program of choice, Cubase VST/24. Coupling Cubase VST/24 with PARIS is going to make one killer DAW.

TAKING UP A COLLECTION

You're going to need a wealth of supporting software over and above what our core system provides, starting with effects plug-ins. With Cubase and PARIS, you have access to VST and DirectX plug-ins, and we'd start our plug-in collection with the Waves Native Power Pack bundle ($500), which includes the L1 Ultramaximizer, C1 Compressor/Gate, Q10 Paragraphic EQ, and S1 Stereo Imager. These plug-ins are industry staples. Also, check out Arboretum's Hyperprism multi-effects plug-in ($349); it's an amazing program.

Every professional studio has a sampler, and because we're doing the job on a computer, we're going to go for a software sampler. The NemeSys GigaSampler ($795) is a great choice because it allows you to play samples directly from your hard drive, eliminating the need for a RAM buffer.

For this studio, we'd consider Sonic Foundry's Acid a mandatory purchase—you can produce entire hip-hop and dance tunes using this program alone. You should also purchase a dedicated 2-track waveform editor. Although Steinberg's WaveLab Lite ships with PARIS, for this studio, you'll want the full-blown version, WaveLab 2.0 ($499), for its support of 24- and 32-bit audio files. Really, what's the point of recording at 24-bit just to do your mastering at 16-bit? And mastering is what WaveLab is all about—in fact, the program is designed specifically for assembling and tweaking music for CDs.

WaveLab supports the VST and DirectX plug-in formats, although the onboard dynamics processors and EQs are certainly good enough to tackle the most demanding mastering tasks. Steinberg's dedicated mastering plug-ins, specifically Loudness Maximizer and Magneto ($199 each), would make nice additions to the collection; the latter provides effective analog tape-saturation emulation for warming up digital signals. You might not be able to afford them right away, but plan to add them both later.

WaveLab also offers comprehensive playlist assembly. Although most CD-R drives come with disc-authoring software, you won't need it; WaveLab supports disc-at-once burning direct from a playlist. Granted, you can't use WaveLab to burn data CDs, but the program is quite efficient for creating audio masters and one-off reference disks.

SOUND ADVICE

You'll need to offer your clients an array of sounds, so a selection of sound cards and software synths is in order. Keep in mind that there will be a physical limit to the number of sound cards you can install in your CPU, and you will be able to use only one software synth at a time (assuming your computer is of average speed). This limitation is not a major one: you can save the output of the sequenced synth part as an audio track in Cubase. At worst, you might have to patch the output of a sound card to a PARIS input, and if you have digital I/O on the card, that's no big deal. A versatile sound card and software synth should suffice.

To start, we'd pick up an E-mu Audio Production Studio ($699), which provides two 32-voice synth engines. The APS has a unique all-RAM configuration that allows you to customize literally every sound in your arsenal. (The drawback to this is that an additional 32MB of computer RAM must be allocated to the APS.) The APS provides MIDI In and Out ports, which eliminates the need for a separate MIDI interface.

Because you're using Cubase VST/24, you could go with Steinberg's ReBirth as your software synth (which allows direct audio transfer to Cubase mixer channels). However, we'd also purchase a copy of Seer Systems' Reality ($495), which offers an impressive array of synthesis techniques, including AM, FM, subtractive, and physical modeling.

HARDWARE CENTRAL

As noted, PARIS has a hardware control surface. In addition to this, you'll need a MIDI master keyboard controller; which one you choose is a matter of taste, but the Fatar keyboards are good bargains if you don't need onboard sounds. As with our basic studio, we can't resist the Keyfax Phat.Boy, which provides a great way to tweak real-time synth parameters.

Finally, for your studio to be compatible with work coming from outside, we recommend purchasing an MDM tape recorder and a DAT recorder that supports AES/EBU and S/PDIF. Alesis ADATs are by far the most popular MDM format for music production, so being able to connect to that world is a major consideration. we won't spec particular models, nor will we put a DAT and ADAT on my list of purchases, but consider them essential extras, like reference monitors and microphones.

A PENNY SAVED

Even when you keep your high-ticket items under control, it's easy to get carried away when designing a pro studio. You could certainly cut some corners in your studio—for instance, live with fewer plug-ins—and still be fine. Furthermore, you can start small and build up slowly to the next level. So don't let that big total scare you away; just plan carefully, with growth in mind, and enjoy the trip.

Index

orchestral choirs, 145

orchestration, 10, 58, 84, 112, 118, 138, 141-145, 155-156, 161, 288-292

organ, 57-58, 72-74, 76, 78, 80-81, 220, 274, 284, 291-293, 385

OS kernel, 176

ostinato, 67-69, 85, 117

Out port, 194-196, 246

pages per minute (PPM), 185

panning, 141, 209, 224, 227, 242-245, 293, 381-383, 425

parallel minor, 108

parametric equalization, 277

Pascal, Blaise, 164

Pascal language, 178

passing tones, 11, 34, 53, 71, 94

pattern practicing, 52

PCs, 171, 188, 430

PCI, 171, 441, 443-444, 447

pedal tone, 12, 72

pentatonic scale, 49, 116

percussion, 2-4, 145, 148, 155-157, 160, 219-220, 222, 237, 288-289, 383, 385, 388

performance data, 192, 198, 204-205, 215, 223, 242, 249

Performer, 17, 170, 172, 192, 199, 205, 208, 233, 240-241, 257, 433-435, 440

period structure, 97

phrygian, 37-38

physical modeling, 146, 148, 264-265, 280, 283-284, 291, 411-413, 415, 443, 450

piano picking, 68-70, 78-79, 81, 87, 89-90

piano-roll view, 227-228

pitch bend, 203-204, 206, 208, 226-227, 230-231, 242, 244-246, 263, 266, 292, 406

pitch change, 277

pitch shifting, 275-277

poignant chord, 108

poly mode, 212, 215

polychord, 22-23, 89

polyphonic aftertouch, 206-207

pop music, 1, 28, 42, 49, 87-89, 95, 291, 387

power chord, 76-78

power supply, 168-169, 403

PPM, 185

preemptive multitasking, 174

primary chord factor, 60

primary chord qualities, 64

printers, 170, 185

Pro Tools, 172, 405-406, 434-435, 441-443, 447

program change messages, 207-208, 213

pulse notes, 241

quantization, 9, 232-236, 247-248, 270-271, 273, 293

QuickTime, 185, 281, 405, 421-427, 432-433

RAM, 166-167, 170, 176, 181, 186-187, 222, 275, 393, 402, 415-416, 441, 449-450

random access memory, 166-167

real sequence, 99

real-time, 69, 142-143, 161, 168, 170, 195, 205, 215, 217, 219, 223, 228-229, 245-249, 256, 267, 281, 284, 293, 392, 402, 407-408, 412, 441-442, 445-446, 450

real-time MIDI, 246, 249

real-time modifiers, 267

recapitulation, 114-115

recordable CD, 187

refrain, 114, 288

refresh rate, 186

relative minor, 49, 104, 110

resonance, 244-245, 256, 266, 268, 284-285

resonant filter, 256

retransition, 113-114

retrograde, 117, 240

reverb, 264, 380-381, 383, 387, 408, 424, 442, 446

rhythm and blues, 49, 54, 72-73, 281, 292

rhythmic shift, 98

ride cymbal, 2, 4, 222, 293

riff tones, 45, 47

riffs, 9, 247, 291, 293

ring modulator, 262

rock music, 76, 125

rockabilly, 12

ROM, 166, 175-176, 443

Roman numerals, 26

rondo, 114-117

root, 10-12, 18, 21-22, 24, 27, 38, 42-44, 48, 51, 60-61, 63, 75, 121-122, 124, 127-129, 135-136

rootless voicing, 127-128

sample and hold, 261

sample dump, 280

sampling, 156, 261, 264-265, 269-278, 280-281, 283, 285, 414-416, 444-445

sawtooth waveform, 253, 284